"In giving us *The Shooters* [Metz] has performed the very difficult feat of debunking many stories of the *High Noon* and Matt Dillon–type of eye-to-eye, quick draw shoot-out, without lessening the drama and excitement. He has proven that truth can be just as interesting—if sometimes uglier—than fiction."

—*EL PASO TIMES*

THE
SHOOTERS

L E O N   C L A I R E   M E T Z

BERKLEY BOOKS, NEW YORK

THE SHOOTERS

A Berkley Book / published by arrangement with
Mangan Books

PRINTING HISTORY
Mangan Books edition published 1976
Berkley trade paperback edition / September 1996

The Penguin Putnam Inc. World Wide Web site address is
http://www.penguinputnam.com

ISBN: 0-425-15450-5

BERKLEY®
Berkley Books are published by The Berkley Publishing Group,
a division of Penguin Putnam Inc.,
375 Hudson Street, New York, New York 10014.
BERKLEY and the "B" design
are trademarks belonging to Penguin Putnam Inc.

PRINTED IN THE UNITED STATES OF AMERICA

15   14   13   12   11   10   9

TO CHERYL

who read and approved it first

CONTENTS

THE
SHOOTERS

Composite of a Shooter by Michael Schreck

1

SHOOTERS

THE GUNFIGHTER as portrayed in the movies, the television screen, the dime novel and popular folklore is a myth. The drama of two gunslingers meeting in the street at high noon, the lightning fast draw, the roar of exploding powder, the impact of bullets, the crumpling of a body; these situations were, and are, illusions. They had little if anything to do with reality.

Of course there were shootouts. Many card games erupted into violence. Guns flashed and people died, especially innocent bystanders. These opponents were not gunmen in the accepted sense of the word nor were they dexterous with a revolver. A bonafide gunfighter rarely let himself be drawn into this type of trouble. Instead he sought the percentages and drew his weapon when the odds were on his side. Most shootings took place between cowhands, farmers, businessmen, drifters; men usually under the influence of liquor and not professional gunmen.

The term "gunfighter" did not even exist one hundred years ago. Newspapers usually referred to such characters as "gunmen" or "shooters." "Gunfighter" and "gunslinger" are modern terms cranked out by Hollywood wordsmiths and popular fiction writers.

The fast draw is a modern innovation. It did not exist in the so-called Wild West. In the period between the late 1860's and the early 1890's (heyday of the gunfighters), few towns had been terrorized by roving outlaw gangs and almost none had ever seen a gunfighter.

Practically all towns west of the Mississippi had laws against carrying weapons. People ignored these ordinances but, nevertheless, kept their six-shooters out of sight. Guns were either tucked inside a belt, slung from a shoulder holster or shoved in a pocket. Gunmen dressed about like everybody else; they wore city clothes. They never worried about blinding speed but sought to gain the advantage, drawing and shooting when the opponent least expected it. Those who did wear belt holsters invariably rode them high on the hip where it was more comfortable. The now familiar Hollywood "hoglegs" would have popped the eyes of a western citizen.

Revolvers in the Old West were not too reliable but they were fairly accurate and reasonably durable when maintained properly. The most popular weapon was the Colt Single Action .44 or .45 with the four and three-quarter-inch barrel and black rubber grips. A popular name for the Colt .45 was the "Peacemaker," although many rueful men dubbed it, as well as all other single action models, the "Thumbbuster." These weapons had to be cocked by pulling the hammer back before firing. This was done by using the second joint of the thumb (and not the ball of the thumb). A careless handler often received a busted thumb for his efforts or shot himself in the leg or the foot.

Cartridges ranged in quality from fair to very poor. There are several instances of baffled citizens vainly snapping pistols at each other, neither revolver functioning at all. Hammer notches, firing pins, springs; all could break at the most embarrassing moments. While the average gunman was not a good shot, he did not have to be. Most shootings took place within a range of from six to ten yards. A gunman did not aim, he simply pointed and fired. For longer distances, the gunman preferred a rifle or shotgun.

Law officers and even outlaws supplemented their incomes with gambling and often had a financial interest in brothels as well as other nefarious occupations. For instance, Wyatt Earp was a well-known confidence man, and once, the sheriff of Wheeler County, Texas ran him out of Mobeetie for selling gold bricks. Billy the Kid described himself as "one who works with cattle." Pat Garrett pioneered a remarkably complex irrigation plan for the Pecos Valley. Doc Holliday was a dentist; John Wesley Hardin, an attorney; Clay Allison, a cattleman. Holdup men such as the James and Dalton brothers were gunmen only incidentally; their business was robbery, not killing people.

Although many communities had some notable bloodlettings, killings were not everyday affairs and, in fact, they were quite rare. Where Matt Dillon of TV's *Gunsmoke* shot outlaws weekly for two decades, that was pure entertainment and strayed far from the truth. During the bloodiest year in Dodge City (1878), only five men were slain in gunfights. At the time of the great trail drives when Dodge was experiencing its worst violence (1876-1885), only fifteen men are recorded as having been killed by gunfire.

El Paso had enough violence to make Dodge City look like a Girl Scout encampment, and yet the statistics do not bear out that El Paso was a dangerous place to live. In 1881, El Paso's most violent year, eight persons died in shootouts, five in one particular week. Otherwise, during its first quarter century of incorporation (1873-1896), fewer than thirty people were transferred to Concordia Cemetery because of gunshot wounds.

An examination of arrest records throughout the West during the heyday of the gunman furnishes some surprising statistics. Murder placed far down the list in crime. The most persistent offenses were drunkenness, assault, larceny, thievery, vagrancy, gambling, burglary and carrying concealed weapons. Adultery, fornication, bigamy and seduction cases sometimes jammed the court dockets. Prostitutes usually paid a fine of $10 a month which amounted to virtual licensing. These fees were often the largest source of municipal income.

Such terms as "misguided individuals" or "coddled prisoners" would have blown the sensibilities of most police officers and judges. Justice, however, was not severe. Murderers often went free. Nearly half of all adults arrested were never arraigned. Practically all citizens believed that widespread inefficiency and corruption subverted the ends of justice.

For a while small towns like El Paso did not even have a jail, so that prisoners were chained to a tree or locked in a vacant room. It became a big event to watch the shackled lawbreakers shuffle in lockstep toward the train for transportation to the state penitentiary (in

Texas at Huntsville.) In 1881, El Paso's city fathers purchased two cages from Chicago at a cost of $900 each. These cells were eight feet long, seven feet wide and seven feet high. The top, bottom, sides and rear were of solid quarter-inch steel. A small barred area in the front door provided the only light, and tiny holes were drilled in the roof so that "foul odors could escape." Inside were two skimpy canvas cots "made of the very best materials." Into the cells were thrown drunks, prostitutes, vagrants, murderers and often the insane.

True, the western gunfighter is a myth, but he is an indelible part of our folklore. Today, because of new interpretations, he stands at the crossroads. Many years ago he began as the defender of the oppressed, a man who had the strength of ten because his heart was pure. As he largely appears in books or on the silver screen, he still has the strength of ten, but his heart is no longer pure. He is often brutal. He lusts.

Only time can tell whether or not he will ever revert back to the lonely, courageous, psychological figure willing to sacrifice himself for the common good. However the story turns out, the gunfighter is here to stay. He will be riding into the sunset for a very long time to come.

In this total scheme of crime and violence, the gunfighter, as we know him now or the shooter as folks knew him then, was simply a small spoke in a huge wheel of events, but he influenced literature and the way men still think of themselves. Small though his numbers were, he became the western romantic figure. He and the cowboy have become legends. To most of us the Billy the Kids, the John Wesley Hardins, the Wild Bill Hickoks, embody the concepts that Americans treasure — freedom, independence, democracy, the triumph of good over evil, the belief that one good man acting against overwhelming odds can still prevail. The biographies in this book are not meant to reestablish the gunfighter as a hero or to debunk him, but to set the record straight. Few were all good or all bad. They were true to themselves, acting according to the light as they saw and understood it. That is sufficient to be remembered. The rest of us should do as well.

2

BILLY

THE ENDURING LEGEND

BILLY THE KID is the most enduring legend of the American West. More movies, books and magazine articles have featured him than any other frontier figure.

No one is certain where the Kid was born. For many years it was thought that New York City had the honors, but historians now discount that. Generally it is believed that he came from Illinois, Indiana or Kansas. He told an 1880 Fort Sumner, New Mexico census taker that he was born in Missouri, and there is no valid reason to dispute it.

The Kid's real name was not William Bonney, although no one has yet figured out where he acquired the Bonney name. Possibly it came from a relative. At any rate, he was born Henry McCarty.

Legend tells us that the Kid killed twenty-one men, that he shot his first man at the age of twelve while defending his mother's honor, and that he died at the age of twenty-one. Not so. While a positive total of his victims cannot be exactly tallied, an educated guess places the figure at somewhere between four and eight. The Kid must have been about seventeen when he killed his first man, and his mother had already been dead for three years. Finally, if the census taker is to be believed, the Kid would have been twenty-six years old when he died.

The youth stood about five-foot-nine, weighed less than 160

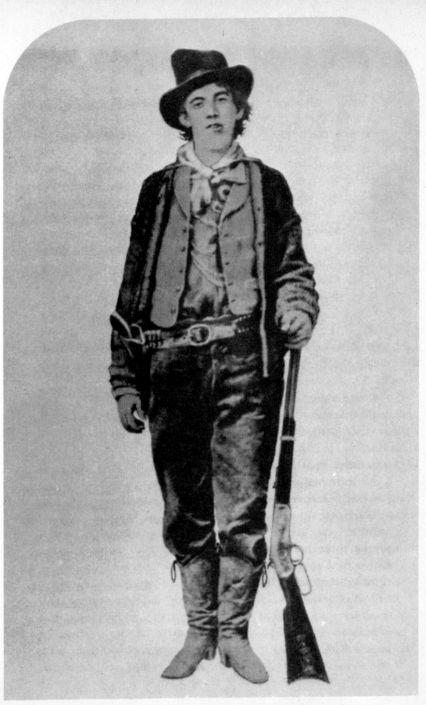

Billy the Kid . . . except for when he was in jail it could be said that he had a cheerful disposition.

pounds, had small hands and feet, blue eyes and scruffy blond hair. Two oversized front teeth protruded slightly. He was right-handed and wore a high-crown sombrero with a green hatband. Over the years he habitually whistled "Silver Threads Among the Gold," and except for when he was in jail it could be said that he had a cheerful disposition.

Billy spoke fluent Spanish, was popular with the girls, and though he never married there are some strong rumors that he fathered two daughters and one son. He was not a hoodlum, a homicidal maniac, a moron, or simply a nice boy who never did anybody any wrong. The facts show that he had above average intelligence and excellent leadership capabilities. While he did not love to kill his enemies, he had no objections to it, and neither did anyone else. No one ever doubted his personal courage.

At the close of the Civil War the widow Catherine McCarty and her two sons, Joe and Henry, were in Marion County, Indiana. The father's name was Michael and he may have died in the war, or he may simply have disappeared. The term "widow" was sometimes an expedient explanation for unattached status.

Mrs. McCarty became acquainted with William H. Antrim, a discharged private from the Indiana Volunteer Infantry. By 1870 both were in Wichita, Kansas where Catherine purchased a lot, filed on a quarter section, and operated a hand laundry. Antrim seems to have been a farmer, carpenter and part-time bartender.

On March 1, 1873, after an obviously procrastinating courtship, the two were married in Santa Fe in the First Presbyterian Church. While some writers have described Antrim as a ne'er-do-well and a drifter, the man deserves a better press than he has received. He seems to have done his best to provide for the McCarty family, and absorbed in the process some heartbreaking disappointments.

Mrs. Antrim suffered terribly from tuberculosis, and after the marriage they all moved to Silver City, New Mexico. While life in a mining camp could hardly be described as one of life's beautiful experiences, the Kid's boyhood was not too unpleasant. Reportedly he did quite well in school, and his letters to Governor Wallace a few years later reveal a solid ability to express himself. His former teacher described him as "quite willing to help with the chores around the

17

school house." He also had a bent for singing and dancing, and performed as "end man" for the town minstrel show.

His mother died on September 16, 1874, and the shattering of the family began. Antrim could not exert much influence. The older brother Joe drifted around the West before dying in Denver, Colorado on November 25, 1930 at the age of seventy-six. No one claimed the body and it went to the Colorado Medical School. As for Henry Antrim (Billy the Kid), within a year of his mother's death the law had him in jail.

According to the Grant County *Herald* of September 26, 1875, "Henry McCarty [Billy the Kid] was arrested and committed to jail to await the action of the grand jury on the charges of stealing clothes from Charley Sun and Sam Chung. It is believed that Henry was simply the tool of Sombrero Jack who did the actual stealing while Henry did the hiding. Jack has skipped out."

Young Antrim decided to skip out too. After two days of confinement, he squeezed his slender frame up the chimney and headed for Arizona where he stayed the next two years and became known as "Kid Antrim," or simply "The Kid."

Near Camp Grant the Kid worked as a civilian teamster for the post sawmill. On August 17, 1877, he killed his first man.

The shooting took place in the tiny community of Bonito. The Kid had been playing cards with Frank P. "Windy" Cahill, a husky blacksmith. The two men began to argue, and Cahill called the Kid a pimp. Antrim snapped back a stronger reply, and the two men wrestled. The Kid was quickly thrown to the ground where he rammed a six-shooter into Cahill's stomach and pulled the trigger.

A coroner's jury declared the killing to be "criminal and unjustifiable," and Antrim was escorted to the post guardhouse, the only reliable jail in the area.

It is not clear exactly how the Kid escaped. One of the most reliable stories is that a soldier opened the door, fired a few shots in the air, and Antrim scampered away. The fugitive "borrowed" a fast horse in leaving.

In early fall of 1877, the Kid showed up at the Jones Ranch at Seven Rivers, New Mexico, on the far east side of Lincoln County. Here he dropped the name of Antrim, and became William Bonney, or simply Billy the Kid. Before long he found employment at the John

Tunstall ranch, and became involved almost by accident in the most notable range fighting of the West, the Lincoln County War.

War in Lincoln County

The Lincoln County War was the bloodiest range conflict in the West. It was not a war in the sense of soldiers, or tanks, or mobilization, but an entire county, seventeen million acres, writhing in conflict. Everybody chose up sides against one another. Each faction sought total victory, but before this victory could be obtained, many lives would be lost.

The cast of the Lincoln County War reads like a "Who's Who" of western titans. There was Billy the Kid, eventually to become the drama's best known participant although he did not start the war, end it, or even play one of the leading roles. There was John Chisum who owned more steers than he could count and grazed them on land that it took days to ride across; Alexander McSween, a lawyer who talked piously about God and the goodness of man but dreamed of riches; Susan McSween, the lawyer's red-headed wife who dominated her husband and would have won the war all by herself if she had been a man. There was Major Lawrence G. Murphy, a former military man who loved liquor almost as much as he did power, and who died before the war he helped start ever ended; and John Tunstall, the Englishman who has been touted as the "good guy'" but in reality was a scheming, conniving individual who overmatched himself. Finally there was Lew Wallace, the mediocre former Civil War general who wrote *Ben Hur* while living in the Santa Fe Governor's Palace and never quite understood the drama going on practically beneath his windows.

Writers have dramatized this conflict, penning some interesting tales that missed the fundamental truths. The war was basically an economic conflict in which both sides suffered injustices and were the victims of atrocities. Neither faction had a monopoly on goodness or evil any more than on courage.

In Lincoln flourished the "House of Murphy", a saloon and store controlling the business interests in the county. In alliance with

Thomas B. Catron of the notorious and powerful "Santa Fe Ring", the House planned to destroy John Chisum and take over his beef contracts at Fort Stanton. In the meantime, John Tunstall and Alexander McSween planned to open a mercantile store and bank in Lincoln, thus forcing the House of Murphy toward the wall.

In spite of many hard feelings, the House of Murphy hired McSween to collect a life insurance policy of $10,000 on Emil Fritz, a Murphy partner who had died in Germany. The lawyer collected, but for reasons still not completely understood, he refused to turn over the money. The House screamed foul and charged embezzlement.

When Sheriff William Brady, who was bought and paid for by the House, tried to pick up McSween's cattle as part payment, the wily lawyer turned his stock over to Tunstall. The Englishman immediately headed for Lincoln where he planned to argue that the cows belonged to him all the time. With him were Billy the Kid, as ragged and as nondescript as he looked, and several ranchers and farmers who doubled as hired guns. However, while these "protectors" were chasing turkeys through the underbrush near present-day Ruidoso, a band of sheriff deputies (who were also hired guns) came upon Tunstall and shot him to death on February 18, 1878.

In early March the Kid and a few others flushed Frank Baker and William "Buck" Morton, two members of the sheriff's posse, from a cow camp near the Pecos River. The two men were promised a fair trial, but were killed while allegedly "trying to escape."

A month later on April 1, Sheriff Brady and deputies George Hindman and three others were strolling down the main street of Lincoln. As they walked past the deserted Tunstall building, the fence and corral gate vanished in a cloud of gray smoke. At least six rifles crashed as Billy the Kid and his companions took vengeance. Brady died instantly. Hindman lay in the dust for a few minutes moaning for water, then died. The other deputies escaped, as did the assassins.

Three days later on April 4, the Kid and his gang, led by Dick Brewer, tangled with Andrew "Buckshot" Roberts at Blazer's Mill southwest of Ruidoso in one of the classic shootouts of the Old West. It ended in a stalemate with Brewer dead and Roberts dying of his wounds.

On April 9, the Lincoln County Commissioners appointed John Copeland as sheriff, but on June 1 Governor Samuel B. Axtell removed

Copeland and substituted George "Dad" Peppin. Peppin had been one of Brady's deputies.

McSween swept into Lincoln for a showdown on July 14 with fifty or sixty men, including the Kid. Although the attorney outgunned the sheriff almost three to one, he did not try to take over the town even though he had warrants from a justice of the peace for the arrest of Peppin's men. McSween sealed off three downtown buildings and barricaded them. However, before he could make up his mind to fight, reinforcements for the sheriff arrived and the odds shifted back in Peppin's favor.

On the first two days of fighting only a horse and a mule were hit. On the third day a deputy who had been firing from high on a mountainside was himself shot. He died a month later. Meanwhile, Colonel N. A. M. Dudley of Fort Stanton, on the pretense that "one of his men had been fired on by the McSween faction," led his forces into town with a Gatling gun and a mountain howitzer. He took no part in the fighting; he just camped his soldiers in a position whereby the McSween people would have a hard time shooting without doing it over the heads of the military. The lawyer's forces realized it was all over, and that night about two-thirds of them deserted across the Rio Bonito. This left only McSween, his wife, and about fourteen men bottled up in the family house.

The sheriff's deputies set the home afire on July 19, five days after the initial siege. The flames spread through the building, feeding on flooring, rafters and door frames. Slowly the roasting, panting men retreated from one room to the other, determined to hang on until dark. Mrs. McSween ran outside and asked Colonel Dudley to protect everyone inside the house. He laughed.

Billy the Kid took complete charge, as Alexander McSween lay on the verge of mental and physical collapse. The Kid diagrammed a plan of escape, telling the others that if they could survive until nightfall, a run-for-it would be tried.

About 9 p.m. Harvey Morris, who read law in McSween's office, dashed from the burning building. He was shot dead within a few feet of the door. Following after him in rapid succession came the Kid and several companions. They escaped into the darkness.

Left behind were McSween and a few others who feared the flaming guns as much as the burning embers. "Will you accept our surrender?" McSween called to Peppin. A deputy named Robert Beckwith answered that he would.

Beckwith stepped forward to accept the enemy guns just as fresh gunfire broke out again. No one knows who started it. When it finished seconds later, Beckwith, McSween and two others lay dead. The Lincoln County War had ended with dramatic suddenness.

Though the House won, it was too weakened by the conflict to ever again exert political or economic power in Lincoln County. Many original leaders on both sides were dead. All that remained was to round up the fugitives.

The chase

Billy the Kid's legend really begins from the moment of his escape from the burning McSween home. Until then he had been simply another gunman, an obscure fugitive on a wanted list. Now he would come into his own with exploits and feats destined to make his name a household word for generations.

President Rutherford B. Hayes had been getting regular reports on the Lincoln County difficulties, and he liked none of it. He dismissed New Mexico Governor Samuel Axtell and replaced him with Lew Wallace. Since Wallace could not make up his mind about who of the Lincoln County belligerents were the most guilty, and since he was anxious to bring peace to the region, he issued an amnesty proclamation for all except nonresidents. That left the Kid's status very uncertain.

The warring factions in Lincoln County tried to get together. The Kid met with Jesse Evans, a dangerous gunman employed by the House of Murphy. After reaching an agreement, they stepped into the streets to celebrate the peace talks and chanced upon Houston Chapman, a one-armed attorney employed by Mrs. McSween to prosecute Colonel Dudley and Sheriff Peppin for arson and murder. Angry words crackled and someone (not the Kid) shot Chapman dead, drenched the body with whiskey and set it afire. It lay in the road for over twenty-four hours.

A few days later the Kid wrote Governor Wallace and denied any involvement with the killing. He offered to testify against those who were. The governor asked for a midnight meeting in a Lincoln Justice of the Peace office. On March 17, 1879, the two men met. The Kid agreed to tell in open court all that he knew and the governor agreed to exempt him from prosecution and to give him an executive pardon for all past crimes.

Unfortunately, District Attorney William R. Rynerson (sympathetic to the House of Murphy) ignored the governor's wishes and made plans for prosecuting the Kid instead of punishing the murderers of Chapman. When Billy heard no reassuring words from Wallace, he did what any sensible person probably would have done. He walked out of jail and never voluntarily returned. On January 10, 1880, he shot and killed Joe Grant in a Fort Sumner saloon brawl.

Meanwhile, the star of Pat Garrett had begun to rise. Originally from Alabama, Garrett had been in Lincoln County only three or four years. Taciturn, introspective, sarcastic, he would become the West's most noted sheriff, and eventually one of its most tragic figures. Some authorities claim that he rustled cattle with the Kid. Undoubtedly he knew the Kid, perhaps very well, but their temperaments were so different that a close friendship is thought unlikely. The Kid referred to Garrett as "the old woman," and Garrett spoke of Billy as "a brave man." Each credited the other with plenty of courage and determination; and each realized that in this most dangerous of all games, one or the other would soon die.

In November of 1880 Garrett became sheriff on a "law and order" platform. He immediately left Roswell, New Mexico with a posse and headed for Fort Sumner, known hangout of Billy the Kid.

The Kid happened to be in White Oaks (now a ghost town near Carrizozo) occasionally taking pot-shots at residents. A posse chased Billy and his friends to the Greathouse Ranch where a siege began. When it became a standoff, Deputy James Carlyle went inside to parley. The outlaws took him prisoner, and the posse sent in word that if he were not promptly released, a hostage would be shot. When a gunshot roared outside, Carlyle thought the posse was keeping its word, so he jumped through a window. Gunfire knocked him down, and he crumpled dead in the snow. The gunmen escaped, and the question of who actually shot Carlyle has never been satisfactorily resolved.

Within a short time Billy the Kid wrote Governor Lew Wallace and said the posse members thought Carlyle was an outlaw trying to escape and mistakenly shot him themselves. The Kid took his opportunity also to deny leadership of a gang of badmen, and he criticized Garrett for unjustly harrassing him. The governor responded by placing a $500 reward on the head of Billy the Kid. It did not read "dead or alive," nor was it ever placed on wanted posters. A New Mexico newspaper carried it as a one-sentence paragraph.

As the Kid's panicked followers fled the Greathouse Ranch toward what they believed to be the safety of Fort Sumner, Pat Garrett and a large posse were quietly closing in on the town. On the night of December 19, Garrett set his trap.

He took over the abandoned Fort Sumner hospital. The wife of Charles Bowdre, one of the Kid's trusted friends and lieutenants, lived nearby, and the sheriff knew the outlaws would soon come into town to visit her. So the posse dealt themselves a few hands of poker and settled down to wait.

Early that evening the snow stopped falling. Moonlight lit up the frozen crust, creating a brilliant contrast of brightness and heavy shadows. About 8 p.m., Garrett heard riders approaching. He stepped out onto the porch, obscured by the darkness and a dangling harness, and cocked his rifle.

Pacing slowly, strung out in single file, hunched against the cold, rode Billy the Kid and his band. Now we get some insight into the Kid's canny nature. Suspicious, he turned and rode to the end of the line and asked Billie Wilson for a chew of tobacco. That plug saved his life.

This change of position left Tom O'Folliard in the lead. He rode up to the hospital building without even lifting his eyes, and his horse stuck its head under the porch roof practically right beside the poised sheriff.

Garrett yelled for them to surrender, and the outlaws quickly scattered. O'Folliard made a grab for his pistol just as Garrett fired. During the wild shooting everyone escaped except O'Folliard. His horse bucked and plunged for several yards down the road before Tom finally brought it under control. Slowly he turned and rode back toward the lawman, pleading, "Don't shoot, Garrett, I'm killed."

The sheriff took the young fellow off his horse, carried him inside and laid him on a cot. Everyone examined the wound and agreed that it was fatal. "Oh my God. Is it possible that I must die," O'Folliard gasped. "Tom, your time is short," Garrett replied softly.

"The sooner the better," muttered the gunman. "At least then I will be out of pain."

When O'Folliard died about an hour later, Garrett walked outside and told the townspeople to return to their homes. Looking in the general direction of the dark New Mexico hills, he knew that somewhere up there the Kid would be waiting. The chase would continue.

A sentence of death

Striking east from Fort Sumner, the Kid's gang galloped toward an abandoned rock house at Stinking Springs, twenty-five miles away. Behind them, coming relentlessly through the snow and threatening weather, rode Garrett. About three o'clock in the morning he and his men trailed the fugitives to the one-roomed structure and surrounded it.

Garrett called a council of war, and everyone agreed that if the Kid were killed first, the others would probably surrender. As the only person familiar with the Kid, Garrett ordered the others to hold their fire until after he had signaled. Billy wore a high-crowned sombrero with a green hatband. Pat would shoot the instant he identified it.

In the pre-dawn light a heavily bundled figure stepped through the open doorway carrying an oat bag for the horses. Garrett whispered "that's him," and raised his rifle. Mistakenly he shot Charles Bowdre, the heavy slug knocking the outlaw back inside the house where Billy took a close look at his friend and said, "They've killed you Charlie, but you can get a few of them before you die." He placed a revolver in Bowdre's hand and shoved him back out the door.

Bowdre staggered across the frozen snow, blood gushing from his wounds. "I wish—I wish—I wish," he said. Then he collapsed in Garrett's arms and died.

All day long some casual firing and good natured bantering went on between the two sides. Garrett asked the Kid to come out and get a bite to eat; the Kid said he couldn't spare the time. However, by late that afternoon, with the aroma of food drifting from the campfires into the house, the Kid decided that he had more time than originally thought. A dirty handkerchief waved from a window. After Garrett promised everyone safety and fair treatment, he accepted their surrender. Within a short time he had securely tied his prisoners to their horses or onto buckboards, and on Christmas Day the bone-weary group rode back into Fort Sumner. Garrett carried the body of Charlie Bowdre to his wife and told the weeping woman to purchase her husband a suit of burying clothes and send the statement to him.

Garrett and his prisoners arrived in Las Vegas, New Mexico, on the 26th, preparatory to traveling by train to Santa Fe. They came into town through a surly crowd which demanded the person of Dave Rudabaugh for the murder of a Las Vegas jailer during a prison break. As a recent arrival in the Kid's gang, Rudabaugh had a reputation for viciousness unmatched anywhere in the western states. Some folks suspected also that he had not bathed in years, and a newspaper reporter remarked that Rudabaugh had obviously not been raiding any clothing stores.

A mob took possession of the train during the next morning, vowing that it would not leave until Rudabaugh had been handed over for quick justice. Garrett did manage to get his prisoners on board, then turned and advised the other passengers that they might wish to leave since "we are liable to have a hell of a fight in a very few minutes."

Pat Garrett warned the mob that if necessary he would turn the prisoners loose and give them guns for defense. Billy the Kid began to revile the citizens, shouting threats of what he would do if he obtained a weapon. Outside Garrett stormed back and forth, cursing and pushing unauthorized people off the train. He threatened to shoot a local deputy sheriff. The crowd seemed enough awed by Garrett to not press its luck, but not frightened enough and intimidated to back completely off from its actions. Finally a United States deputy marshal offered his services. He climbed into the locomotive, shoved everyone aside and began pulling levers until the wheels started running. Away the train went without a shot being fired. (Rudabaugh soon escaped from jail and allegedly went to Parral, Mexico, where he terrorized the community. The peons shot him, cut off his head and impaled it on a stake.)

Shortly after being jailed in Santa Fe, the Kid tried to tunnel his way out, but was caught and placed in solitary confinement. With escape now closed, he wrote Governor Lew Wallace a short note on

January 1, 1881. "I would like to see you if you can spare the time," it said. Apparently the governor had no time to spare, for he never went to see the prisoner.

Two months later the Kid wrote again, telling Wallace that he had letters dating back two years which certain parties were anxious to see. (These letters, if they ever really existed, have never been identified.) "I shall not dispose of them until I see you, if you will come immediately," the Kid wrote. Once again the governor ignored him.

On March 4 the Kid wrote again: "I expect that you have forgotten what you promised me two years ago this month, but I have not. I have done everything that I promised I would, and you have done nothing that you promised me. I am not entirely without friends. I shall expect to see you sometime today!"

Finally he desperately wrote on the 27th: "For the last time I ask. Will you keep your promise? I start below tomorrow."

The promise repeatedly mentioned concerned the offer of executive clemency for testimony during the Chapman murder inquest. As for the matter of "starting below tomorrow," this referred to a change of venue to Mesilla, New Mexico, forty miles north of El Paso, where he would be tried for the murder of Sheriff William Brady. It is ironic that the territory chose to punish him for that particular crime since it had been committed by a body of men, all of whom had been pardoned by the governor's amnesty. The Kid was not the leader of those particular assassins, nor is there any proof that his bullet took Brady's life.

Counsel for the defense was Colonel Albert J. Fountain, one of the most controversial West Texas and southern New Mexico politicians who ever lived. His eventual death in the New Mexico White Sands would become one of the state's greatest murder mysteries. For years Fountain had been the scourge of New Mexico bandits, several of whom were shot to death while under arrest for "trying to escape." On April 8 he announced himself and his client ready for trial.

The trial lasted two days and was devoid of the usual protections nowadays given defendants. No known record of testimony is extant, and the newspapers were mute. Judge Warren Bristol (a House of Murphy advocate) gave the all-Mexican jury a choice of two verdicts: acquittal or murder in the first degree. Bristol warned them that "there is no evidence before you showing that the killing of Brady is murder in any other degree than the first." Naturally, the twelve men came in with the proper judgment.

Bristol granted no appeal, and the Kid remained silent when sentence was passed. The judge ordered Sheriff Garrett to take the prisoner to Lincoln and on Friday, May 13, 1881, "hang him by the neck until his body be dead." The stage was now set for the most dramatic escape in western history.

End of the trail

Under heavy guard Billy the Kid left Mesilla for Lincoln and his quick date with the hangman. Deputies locked him in the upstairs room of the courthouse which served as a jail. No bars were on the doors or windows, but large chains on his ankles and wrists kept him fastened securely to the wooden floor.

Assigned to guard him were J. W. Bell, a quiet individual whom everybody liked, and Bob Olinger, sometimes called "Pecos Bob." Olinger has been accused of tormenting the Kid, taunting him about the forthcoming hanging. This may or may not be correct, but a strong suspicion exists that these stories may have been circulated in order to make Olinger's forthcoming murder seem not only justified, but commendable.

On April 28, while Garrett was in White Oaks collecting taxes, Olinger parked his shotgun in the sheriff's office about noon and went across the street to Wortley's restaurant. During his absence Billy asked Bell for permission to visit the toilet, and the two men went downstairs and out back. The story is that someone hid a revolver in the privy and the Kid slipped it under his shirt. Regardless of how he armed himself, on the way back Billy turned at the head of the stairs, brandished a gun on Bell, and ordered him to put up his hands. The deputy spun around and started running as two shots rang out. Both bullets missed, but one ricocheted off the wall and passed through Bell's body. He staggered outside and died in the yard.

From across the street, Olinger heard the shots and thought Bell had killed the Kid. He came running across the road just as Billy reached the second story window with the deputy's shotgun. "Hello

Bob," he said as Olinger paused below. Then a trigger was pulled and the deputy died instantly. The Kid walked outside to the porch and fired the other barrel into Olinger before breaking the weapon across the railing. Next he called for a tool to remove his chains, and someone tossed him a pickax which removed only one leg iron. In disgust he "borrowed a horse," and rode away.

For weeks the Kid remained out of sight and everyone thought he had fled to Mexico. Garrett seemed depressed, and practically refused to even look for the outlaw. Then in early July his deputy John Poe told Garrett an incredible tale of how Pete Maxwell, a resident of Fort Sumner, had sent word that Billy the Kid was in town. Maxwell wanted the Kid eliminated because of affairs the Kid was having with local girls.

Garrett and Poe went to Roswell for another deputy, Thomas "Kip" McKinney. The three men headed at a rapid pace for Fort Sumner, arriving on the evening of July 14.

The Kid was in town enjoying himself at a dance while these events were unfolding. About eleven o'clock he returned to a nearby sheep ranch, but thereupon decided to return to Lincoln and visit a girlfriend. Once there he removed his vest and shoes, relaxed in an old chair, and spoke of being hungry. Picking up a knife he walked barefoot toward the quarters of Pete Maxwell where a fresh quarter of beef hung on the north porch.

Near midnight as he strolled toward the building, he stumbled upon deputies Poe and McKinney, neither of whom recognized him. Both of these lawmen spotted the Kid about fifty yards away, but assumed the slight figure to be a friend of Maxwell's.

The Kid's reaction startled each man, for he did not know them either. He jerked his .41 caliber pistol and called out, *"Quien es?"* (who is it?). McKinney, who had been squatting, hurriedly jumped up when that pistol poked out at him, and in doing so caught his right spur in a loose board and nearly toppled off the porch. As the deputy struggled to right himself, Billy noticed that he carried sidearms, something few Mexicans were inclined to do.

Inside the dark bedroom Pat Garrett had been sitting on the edge of the bed and questioning Maxwell when their conversation froze in mid sentence. They recognized the Kid's startled voice outside.

As they paused, the Kid leaped across the porch and backed into the bedroom. "Pete, who are those fellows outside?" he asked.

He then noticed Maxwell's visitor for the first time, but he did not recognize Garrett because of the darkness and the sheriff's sitting position on the bed. Stepping closer, he laid his hands on the covers and asked the stranger, "Who is it?" As Garrett moved while reaching for his gun, the Kid jumped backwards into the center of the room—hesitating—revolver at full cock and leveled, but not wanting to mistakenly kill a friend. Twice more he asked, *"Quien es? Quien es?"*

Garrett's pistol swung free and he fired twice. The first bullet struck the Kid almost squarely in the heart, and the second thundered into the wall. Pat jumped up and raced outside, almost knocking Poe down in his haste. "That was the Kid in there, and I think I got him," he panted. At this moment Pete Maxwell came charging outside dragging his bedclothes. Poe started to shoot him, but Garrett knocked the gun aside, crying, "Don't shoot Maxwell."

No one would reenter the room to determine if the Kid were dead. A local resident finally held a candle to a window. Through the open doorway the Kid's body lay on the floor, a butcher knife in one hand, a six-shooter in the other.

Over the years many stories have sprung up which throw doubt upon the Kid's death. According to these rumors Garrett shot and killed someone else, and the body was palmed off as Billy the Kid. There are many tales that the outlaw lived out a long life in Mexico. Just a few years ago C. L. Sonnichsen and William V. Morrison collaborated on a very well researched book entitled *Alias Billy the Kid*. The authors pointed out several strange inconsistencies in the records, and they presented an old-timer named Brushy Bill Roberts who claimed to be the Kid. The largely uneducated fellow knew more about the Lincoln County War than most experts.

All things considered, Garrett did indeed kill the Kid. The sheriff had nothing to gain by fraud. To have claimed the Kid dead and then have him turn up a few months later would have ruined Pat Garrett. There is no evidence in the Kid's background that he could have been counted on to remain out of sight indefinitely. Also, some of the townspeople would have stayed silent, but certainly not all of them.

Following the Kid's death, he was laid out in an oversized white shirt. Burial took place in the Fort Sumner graveyard between his two friends Charlie Bowdre and Tom O'Folliard.

The grave site is now covered with a concrete slab and surrounded by a chain link fence. The question is, does the Kid really lie there? Many years ago that cemetery was abandoned, headboards and stone markers were either blown down or knocked over, the Pecos River flooded the site and changed the scenery as well as washing away some of the bodies, and the army transferred practically everyone they could find to the national cemetery at Santa Fe. So under that concrete may be a soldier, an unknown civilian, Billy the Kid, or nobody. No one is absolutely certain, and it is a good bet that no one is ever going to find out. So even in death the Kid remains an enigma, as well as one of the most remarkable personalities in history.

*Sam Bass . . . people thought (he) was giving
"them high and mighties" a strong dose of what
they had coming.*

3

SAM BASS

A SQUARE SHOOTER

"*Sam bass was born in Indiana, it was his native home;*
And at the age of seventeen, young Sam began to roam.
Sam first came out to Texas, a cowboy for to be—
A Kinder-hearted feller you seldom ever see."

Show me an East Texas lad of a generation or so ago who didn't know the words to that stanza and I'll show you someone who thought the Alamo was a grocery store.

Sam Bass, a likable young highwayman was an honest-to-goodness legend in his time. There was hardly a dry eye in Texas when the Rangers finally ended his career with a fusillade of bullets.

No one is certain what Bass looked like although there are several photographs purporting to be him. We know that he was born in Mitchell, Indiana, on July 21, 1851, that his parents died young, and that he left the state about 1869. He stood about five-foot-eight, weighed about 140, had black hair, dark eyes and a sallow complexion. He walked with a slight stoop and even spoke with a nasal twang. Such is the stuff of which legends are made.

Things looked up for Sam in Denton, Texas. It started when he acquired a sorrel mare named "Jenny," but better known as the "Denton Mare." She was not the fastest horse in Texas, but she could run with the best. She won enough races to change Sam into a fellow with a deep attachment for the sporting life and lots of money. Soon he sold the mare and teamed up with Joel Collins, a ne'er-do-well saloon keeper and gambler.

They headed for Deadwood, South Dakota, where rumor had it the miners did not know how to gamble. This was apparently false. Bass and Collins lost their cash at the tables almost overnight. Since neither cared for honest work, robbing stages seemed like the next easiest way to earn a living. They teamed up with Jim Berry, a freckled Missourian who had a wife and four children back home, Bill Heffridge, a Pennsylvanian with two wives (neither of whom were in Dakota), Tom Nixon, a Canadian, and a gent known only as Reddy.

They stole several saddle horses and left to meet the Cheyenne stage. As it came churning around a bend, the gunmen stepped into the middle of the road and convinced John Slaughter, the driver, to rein in. The holdup might have gone well except that the stage team shied into Reddy who angrily blew Slaughter off the driver's seat with a shotgun blast. The noise caused the horses to bolt, and the stage raced into Deadwood without being robbed. Company officials nailed the dead Slaughter's bloodstained vest to the stage-line door as an incentive to vigilantes.

As for Reddy, his partners thought seriously about killing him. He had cost them whatever money the stage held and had put their necks in danger of a noose. The outlaws conferred and then drummed Reddy out of the gang. He drifted to Fort Griffin, Texas, where vigilantes caught him rustling horses and promptly lynched him.

Bass and his bungling buddies laid low for a few weeks, and then robbed a series of stage lines in succession. From one stage they got $11, from another a dozen peaches. Altogether they picked up barely enough money to feed themselves between jobs.

Since stagecoach robbing obviously was not profitable, the bandits turned to trains. At Big Spring, Nebraska, on the night of September 18, 1875, they struck the Union Pacific, and this time were much luckier. Following the usual threats and warning shots, the train crew and passengers surrendered their valuables.

The passengers kicked in $13,000, four gold watches and a ticket to Chicago. None of the women were searched. As Bass went down the line turning pockets inside out, he returned $20 to a one-armed man and told him to sit down and be still.

In the baggage car, the robbers found several hundred dollars in paper money but did not really strike it rich until someone carelessly kicked a wooden box. Out spilled $60,000 in bright, newly minted, double eagle $20 gold pieces.

The boys packed their booty into sacks and pockets and boxes and whatever they could find, and left the state practically unmolested, later dividing the cash and going separate ways. Nixon dropped out of sight. Collins and Heffridge were caught by the sheriff and a squad of soldiers, who happened to be out looking for Indians. The two bandits tried to make a fight of it, and came out second best when the cavalry shot them to pieces.

Berry went to Mexico, Missouri where he lived it up until a bank became suspicious of those $20 gold pieces he was spending so freely. A posse ambushed the outlaw and damaged his left leg so seriously with shotgun pellets that Berry died from shock.

Sam Bass went back to Denton and the good life, but could not stay out of trouble. He formed a small outlaw gang, started robbing stages again, and as before failed to make any real money. So, in 1878, Bass' new gang shifted to train robbery hoping for a more lucrative source of income. At Allen, Texas they tapped the Houston and Texas Central for $20,000.

During the next few weeks the outlaws struck across central Texas, particularly the Dallas-Fort Worth area. They robbed the Hutchins train and held up the Texas Central at Eagle Ford and Mesquite. Surprisingly no one was killed though many shots were exchanged and a few people were wounded. On one occasion, an express agent refused to slide open the heavy train doors. Bass unhooked the wooden railroad car, rolled it to a siding, piled wood under it, then saturated the wood with oil. When he threatened to set the whole contraption afire, the doors banged open in a hurry.

Sam Bass became the most talked about as well as the most popular person in the state. At this time, Texas had a mostly rural population, small farmers existing in the most primitive conditions. Correctly or not, they blamed big business, the banks and the railroads for exploiting them. People thought Bass was giving "them high and mighties" a strong dose of what they had coming to them and the average citizen cheered old Sam on as Pinkerton detectives, Texas Rangers, confused bounty hunters and large posses swarmed across central Texas. Newspapers referred to the gang as "Sam Bass and Company" and named the struggle the "Bass War." The Dallas region became the center of headhunting activities, and yet Bass remained near Denton and lawmen couldn't find him. Only once did the hunters and the hunted actually clash, and that was by accident. During a short, but fierce exchange of gunfire, Arkansas Johnson, an outlaw, dropped out of the game and retired to the cemetery. The other outlaws escaped.

With lawmen now tightly guarding the trains, Sam Bass and company planned to rob the Round Rock bank. It might have been a successful effort except that someone betrayed them to the Texas Rangers.

As the robbery time arrived, Sam expressed suspicion of the many strangers in town. They might be rangers, but they looked like ordinary cowboys. He shrugged off his thoughts. He and his two companions, Seaborn Barnes and Frank Jackson, had already spent several days around town resting horses for what was expected to be a fast ride out. Nobody recognized them.

But Round Rock was full of law officers, especially rangers. There were Dick Ware, later to become a U.S. deputy marshal in El Paso, and George Herold who would become a popular and long-time El Paso police officer, a man still remembered by many old-timers. Herold would shoot Bass, but Ware would take the official credit.

As the three outlaws strolled down the street toward the bank, saddlebags slung over their arms as if prepared for a big withdrawal, Deputy Sheriff A.W. Grimes noticed a suspicious bulge under one man's coat. Sauntering over to Bass and not realizing who these men were, he placed his hand on Sam's side and said, "Say Mister, are you carrying a gun?" Those were his last words on earth.

As it was now too late and too dangerous to transact any bank business, the outlaws raced for their horses, with the rangers and half the town in pursuit. Dick Ware shot Barnes in the head, killing him instantly. A storekeeper mangled Bass' hand with a wild bullet, and as Sam and Jackson reached their animals, Herold shot Bass in the back. Sam struggled into the saddle, and wouldn't have made it without Jackson's help.

Jackson then did a brave thing. Turning in the saddle he continued firing his revolver with such close effectiveness that the pursuers ducked while Bass rode away. Then the two outlaws disappeared.

Both Bass and Jackson hid out in a cedar brake, and that night Jackson did what he could to bind Sam's wounds before escaping. Early the next morning Sam staggered out of his hiding place to seek help. Several hours later the rangers found him lying under a tree.

To the very end Sam refused to talk. When the rangers asked for a confession and information he replied, "It's against my profession. If a man knows anything, he ought to die with it in him."

As the days passed, he began to feel better and thought he might recover. Then his condition deteriorated. When told the worst, he said, "Let me go." A few minutes later he cried out, "The world is bobbing around." Those were his last words, and he died on July 21, 1878, his birthday. The epitaph reads:
"A brave man reposes in death here. Why was he not true?"

"Sam met his fate at Round Rock, July the twenty-first;
They pierced poor Sam with rifle balls and emptied out his purse.
Poor Sam he is a corpse now and six feet under clay;
And Jackson's in the brushes, trying to get away."

Black Jack Ketchum . . . he fully expected to go straight to hell after his death . . . remorse and repentance were not part of his nature.

4

BLACK JACK KETCHUM

A TRUE LOSER

"BLACK JACK" TOM KETCHUM was not a man to admire. He was smart in a cunning, crafty sort of way, physically strong, and deadly in the sense of callousness and brutality. That he had nerve, nobody questioned.

Somehow he never quite had the stuff of which legends are made. It could be that his exploits as a highway and train robber came at a wrong time in history—a period when citizens were tiring of blood and thunder, when they were beginning to see these holdup artists not as Robin Hoods, but simply as hoods. Another factor to the detriment of a Ketchum legend was that he lacked style. For if there were a common thread running through the lives of all legendary heroes, it would have been style.

In the final analysis, Black Jack Ketchum could not even die right. Yet, it is the incredible and gruesome nature of his death that makes folks remember him today.

Those who knew Ketchum described him as a tall man, powerfully built, with dark skin, piercing dark eyes, and the usual handlebar mustache. He was hardly an intellectual.

He grew up around San Saba, Texas, where he was born on or about October 31, 1863. Like many boys of his time, he took to wild ways. In December of 1895, after a short career of petty crime, he and a few friends shot and killed John N. "Jap" Powers, a rancher living near Knickerbocker, Texas. Mrs. Powers assisted with the murder, and she went to jail. Tom and his friends fled to New Mexico.

A bandit named Will Christian, better known as "Black Jack" Christian, operated along the Arizona-New Mexico border. In a twist of fate, Christian and Ketchum became confused by law officers. For a long time most of Ketchum's crimes were blamed on Christian. When lawmen shot and killed Christian in Graham County, Arizona, the authorities identified him as Tom Ketchum. From then on the real Tom Ketchum became Black Jack Ketchum, an alias he never really asked for, but accepted as one of those inscrutable ironies of history.

In 1896, near Liberty, New Mexico, the Black Jack Ketchum gang tapped the United States post office for a withdrawal of $44.69, hardly an outstanding sum even in those pre-inflation days. Postmaster Levi Herzstein took his loss seriously and organized a small posse to ride in pursuit. A few miles away they approached their prey, no doubt a surprise to both parties. The outlaws shot and killed Herzstein and another man, and sent the posse scurrying back to Liberty.

All of the bandits rode unharmed across the state line into Texas and on the night of May 4, held up a train in Terrell County. The train crew couldn't or wouldn't open the express safe so the gang blew it apart with dynamite and escaped with several thousand dollars. Capt. John R. Hughes and a force of Texas Rangers chased the outlaws back into New Mexico where they hid in Colfax County.

A few months later the boys were getting restless again. They stopped the Texas Flyer and hit it for another cash withdrawal. After lining the crew up at gunpoint, and with the passengers cowering inside the coaches (with an occasional bullet fired through the windows to make sure everybody kept his head down), the gang tried twice to dynamite the heavy safe.

In frustration they shoved fourteen sticks under the box and laid a quarter beef across it to muffle the explosion. The resultant bang practically blew the baggage car off the tracks, but it did open the safe. Ketchum and his gang emerged with a total of $3,000, much of it torn to bits and pieces.

Laying low until December of 1896, the gang struck the Southern Pacific at Stein's Pass near the New Mexico-Arizona line. Unknown to the outlaws, the railroad anticipated a robbery and had the express car packed with Wells Fargo agents. No sooner had Ketchum stopped the train than the express doors slid open and shotguns boomed.

For half an hour the battle raged with neither side doing much damage. Then outlaw Ed Cullen carelessly leaned over to pick up a cartridge and in so doing exposed his head. "Boys, I'm dead," he screamed, as the shotgun slugs tore into him. At that, the Ketchum gang lost their nerve and fled. The posse removed Cullen's body to Lordsburg, New Mexico.

The Stein's Pass fiasco spelled the end of Black Jack Ketchum even though only one man lost his life. Other outlaws expressed displeasure at Ketchum's inept leadership and, supported by Sam Ketchum (a brother), the gang decided they could do without Black Jack. He rode off in one direction and they in another.

Sam Ketchum, Will Carver and Elza Lay drifted back to Turkey Creek Canyon in Colfax County. In July of 1899 they held up the Colorado and Southern Railroad and escaped with several thousand dollars plus some boxes of peaches and sacks of clothes. A few days later, law officers caught the gang inside the canyon. In the inept battle, one of the law officers was killed and two of the outlaws wounded. Lay was soon captured near Carlsbad, New Mexico, and sentenced to a long prison term. Sam, barely able to ride because of a shoulder wound, surrendered meekly and was sentenced to the territorial prison in Santa Fe. His injured arm continued to cause trouble and he died on July 24 of blood poisoning.

Meanwhile, Tom (Black Jack) Ketchum became a prime suspect in the so-called Yavapai County, Arizona massacre. Senselessly, two men were killed and another wounded. Ketchum denied involvement but circumstantial evidence indicated otherwise.

On the night of August 16, Ketchum held up the Folsom, New Mexico train. Acting alone, he forced the train crew back toward the baggage car and called for the doors to open. A mail clerk, a coach away, uncertain of what was happening, poked his head outside and was shot through the jaw.

Conductor Frank Harrington, armed with a shotgun, crept as close to Black Jack as he dared. Stepping into the open, he and Ketchum fired almost simultaneously. Black Jack's rifle slug grazed Harrington, and Harrington's shotgun blast peppered Ketchum's right arm with pellets. Ketchum reeled off into the darkness and the train moved on.

Too weak to ride, Tom settled down beside the track and awaited arrest. At about seven the next morning, a freight train lumbered slowly toward him and Ketchum placed his hat on the end of a rifle and waved it feebly to attract their attention. He surrendered to the train crew which sent him to the closest town, Trinidad, Colorado. From there he was transferred again to the territorial prison at Santa Fe, New Mexico. At the prison, surgeons amputated his mangled right arm.

In September of 1901, the law pronounced Black Jack fit for trial in Clayton, New Mexico. The Territory charged him with felonious assault upon a railroad but would not accept his plea of guilty since conviction carried an automatic death sentence. Judge Mills appointed an attorney to defend him.

The trial had its high and low points, its periods of humor and boredom. Ketchum did not deny his guilt, and, in fact, testified rather candidly, accepting blame for most of the robberies. At its conclusion, the judge had no alternative except to pronounce the death sentence, intoning, "between now and the day of your said execution, you prepare yourself by repentance for your past evil deeds to meet your God, and may God have mercy on your soul."

Ketchum returned to Santa Fe and awaited the results of his appeal to the United States Supreme Court, a plea calling the death sentence "cruel and unusual punishment" since no one had ever been executed for the robbing of a train (nor would anyone ever be again). The appeal was denied.

Back went Ketchum to Clayton for execution. As the Territory's best known prisoner, he gave numerous interviews, most of them on the subject of death and the hereafter. He fully expected to go straight to hell after his death, and remorse and repentance were not part of his nature.

According to him, he had killed no one, ever. He bitterly believed that the people whose lives he spared had testified unsympathetically against him and had thus encouraged his death. His philosophy of life could be summed up in a short paragraph he wrote on April 26, 1901, the date of his hanging.

"My advice to the boys of the country is not to steal horses or sheep, but either to rob a train or a bank when you have got to be an outlaw, and every man who comes in your way, kill him; spare him no mercy, for he will show you none. This is the way I feel, and I think I feel right about it."

With his hair cut, his mustache trimmed, wearing a new suit of black clothes, Black Jack Ketchum mounted the thirteen steps leading up to the gallows. Before him stood a large crowd of curious Territorial witnesses, editors and photographers. He stepped into the middle of the trap door, the rope was adjusted around his neck, a hood draped over his head and attached to his coat with safety pins. Manacles held the left arm tightly against his side.

In order to spring the trap door, Sheriff Garcia had to cut a rope with an axe, but Garcia was drunk. He missed the first swing, the blade biting deep into the wood, requiring some effort and a minute or two to extract it. On the second swing, he severed the rope, and Black Jack Ketchum hurtled into eternity.

In the process, however, the force of the fall caused the rope to sever Ketchum's head from his body.

*Tom Smith . . . a law officer . . . as handy with his
fists as his six-shooters.*

5

TOM SMITH

HE BROUGHT THEM IN ALIVE

In spite of hundreds of western movies and TV scripts, there are very few accounts of gunmen in the Old West using their fists. It wasn't a fear of breaking a delicate hand bone that bothered them. It was as if the ordinary gunman, as separate from the run-of-the-mill bully, put himself above such mundane practices as fist-fighting. The gunman was a specialist in killing. He was not interested in breaking someone's nose. Nor was he interested in getting his own broken in return.

Tom Smith was an exception. He was as handy with his fists as his six-shooters. As a law officer, he won fame for disarming and bringing wanted men in alive. While some of those corralled toughs awoke the next morning with sore heads, they were at least still among the living.

No one knows where Tom Smith called home. Most accounts say he was born in New York City sometime between 1830 and 1840. He was described as about five-foot-eleven, 170 pounds, and handsome in a rugged, appealing sort of way. He had intelligence and was quiet spoken. No one ever saw him gamble, and he quit drinking at an early age.

Those were the days of Manifest Destiny, when the railroad construction crews were sweating their way across the mountainous West,

45

spinning steel at an incredible pace. Management provided tents and ramshackle shanties for its workers, and fifty steps away would be saloons with gamblers, prostitutes and the usual riffraff eager to take the laborer's dollar.

These camps were mobile, capable of being torn down or set up practically at a moment's notice, they usually lasted until track had been laid fifty or sixty miles ahead. Then everything was torn down, loaded on flatcars and sent racing ahead to the next location, a practice known as "Hell on Wheels." The expression stuck like a spike in a new crosstie.

Only a few camps became semi-permanent and one was Bear River, Wyoming. It incorporated, passed laws, and even organized police who cracked down on the working-man's sins of drunkenness and disorderly conduct. Considering that the railroad hands were terribly exploited, that drinking and fighting and gambling were practically their only recreation, they resented rigid law enforcement.

The laborers stormed into Bear River, destroyed the newspaper, tore down the jail, released the prisoners and bottled up the lawmen in a storeroom.

Tom Smith took the side of the laborers. He charged the barricades and emptied his revolvers into the solid walls. It was a brave but foolish act which came before he quit drinking. The police shot him and almost took his life. When the battle ended, fourteen dead men lay scattered on the ground. Troops from Fort Bridger restored order.

Following his recovery, Smith became known as Bear River Tom Smith and the construction workers chose him to police their camps. With him in charge there were no more riots, no more killings.

In 1870 Abilene, Kansas advertised for a marshal to keep the half-wild Texas cowpunchers in line. Bear River Tom Smith applied, but when the mayor looked into those quiet eyes, he simply did not believe that Smith could control the trail hands.

Smith went to Colorado while Abilene had the unhappy experience of going through one marshal after another, none of whom could stand up to the tough cowboys. In desperation the mayor telegraphed Smith to come as soon as possible.

Smith told the town council that Abilene would never be tamed until the cowboys surrendered their weapons before entering town. So when the city fathers passed the necessary ordinance, Smith enforced it first against a bully named "Big Hank." When Hank went for his gun, Smith knocked him unconscious with one punch. A week later the marshal took another man's weapon away from him and beat the surprised individual savagely about the head and body, punctuating the fight with an order to leave town in five minutes. It turned out to be three minutes longer than needed.

Thus with two demonstrations of nerve and ferocity, the marshal had convinced the Texas cowboys and the town that law had come to Abilene. Trail hands began checking their weapons at the hotels and saloons. Smith even invaded the red light district of Abilene and confiscated a wheelbarrow of derringers from the ladies.

The community raised his salary to $150 a month and $2 for every arrest. A pair of pearl-handled revolvers were presented him, weapons never fired in anger, but used to good advantage from horseback. His position in the saddle gave him tremendous leverage for cracking a law-breaker across the head with those long-barreled six-shooters.

Toward the end of the year 1870, as the cold weather set in and herds from Texas slowed, Smith resigned to become a United States deputy marshal with headquarters in Abilene. One afternoon the sheriff hurried into Smith's office and asked for assistance in arresting a farmer named Andrew McConnell, a murderer who had taken refuge in a sod hut right outside of town. Since the affair was clearly outside of Smith's jurisdiction, he did not want to become involved. Nevertheless, he offered to do what he could.

When the two officers reached the dugout, McConnell was inside. A friend named Miles guarded the door. Smith glanced over at the sheriff, asked for the warrant, and said he would make the arrest if the sheriff would watch Miles.

As Smith disappeared inside, Miles sensed that the sheriff lacked his partner's courage. He reached down, picked up an ancient carbine, pointed it at the lawman and snapped it. The cartridges were so faulty and the firing pin so rusted, that the gun malfunctioned. The sheriff scampered away and did not stop until reaching town.

Inside the dugout Smith grabbed McConnell around the neck and dragged him outside. As they struggled in the dirt, Miles slipped up behind and clubbed the marshal unconscious with the faulty carbine.

The two men threw the marshal down, picked up an ax and chopped off his head. Thus died Bear River Tom Smith who had never killed another human.

Jesse James

Frank James

*The James Boys . . .
the Civil War created
conditions whereby
the greatest outlaw
gang and band of
marauders America
has ever known
could operate.*

6

THE JAMES BOYS

ONE CANNOT DISCUSS the James boys without discussing the Younger brothers. One cannot discuss the Younger brothers without discussing William Clarke Quantrill. And one cannot discuss all three without discussing the Civil War, for there is where it all began.

The war created conditions whereby the greatest outlaw gang and band of marauders America has ever known could operate. These men were not products of city slums, they were born and raised on the farm where they might have been poor, but never destitute.

These outlaws were the "free spirits" of their time, men who tasted blood during a period of conflict, and liked it. They took advantage of chaotic conditions. It is true that they had excuses and justifications for the victims they killed, the banks and railroads that they robbed, the terror that they brought. Such people have always found vindications for their acts, no matter how grotesque or bloody.

Yet, these men are all legends today, folk heroes with songs written about their exploits. Historians still argue over whether "The Dirty Little Coward that Shot Mr. Howard" actually laid Jesse James in his grave.

Jesse James became one of the first Western heroes, a man as famous in his own time as Buffalo Bill.

Most people lived on farms with little to look forward to except rising before the sun came up, working all day in the fields, and retiring to a shack and a bed when it became too dark to see. When sick or injured, they toughed it out, or died. Many Americans, therefore, took heart when someone broke the chains of monotony, even though that particular person usually paid for his freedom with his life, or a long jail term.

One of the worst, certainly the meanest, of these early outlaws was William Clark Quantrill who was born at Canal Dover, Ohio, July 31, 1837, the son of a schoolmaster. Over the years he became well-read and learned to write with a legible hand. His restless feet called him to bloody Kansas; Kansas with its proslavery and abolitionist sentiments, where terror and death were the order of the day, where men fought out their blind grievances in much the same brutal manner as northern Ireland does today.

By 1860, Quantrill became a Kansas Jayhawker, a nightrider obligated to free the slaves and, incidentally, free any slave holders of cash they might have on hand. As killings and counter-killings rose in intensity, the Union declared him an outlaw, and ordered the military to shoot him down wherever he might be found. Quantrill promptly went to Richmond, Virginia, and tried to talk the Confederacy into giving him an officer's commission. With that in hand, he could safely shoot civilians who opposed him, but if captured he himself would be treated as a prisoner of war, and not as a guerrilla. (Soldiers were simply imprisoned or paroled; whereas guerrillas were executed on the spot.)

The South refused their blessing for his plan of operation, and turned down the commission. Quantrill took one anyway, returning to Missouri and Kansas and calling himself a colonel. It sounded impressive.

Meanwhile, the James boys and the Youngers had ridden into camp. Alexander Franklin James, better known as "Frank" James, was born about 1843, in Missouri, and grew up to be a tall, lanky youngster, taciturn and serious, a man who never, or at least rarely, laughed.

Jesse Woodson James came along in 1847, and like Frank, he was the son of Robert James, a preacher-farmer who joined the gold rush to California and died there. The mother married again, but divorced

50

her second husband for nonsupport, and then married Dr. Reuben Samuel, a physician.

Jesse was a born leader, full of devilishness, with an oval face, the cheeks smoother than a shaved bowling ball. Except for a constant habit of blinking his eyes, he could be considered handsome.

When only sixteen, Frank enlisted in the Confederate army and fought in the bloody battle of Wilson's Creek. Afterwards he came home on furlough, and was arrested by Union officers who released him on parole. He immediately joined Quantrill.

The Union militia questioned Dr. Samuel about his relationship with Southern partisans and when the answers were not satisfactory, the cavalrymen left Samuel dangling from a tree limb. His wife witnessed it and when the soldiers left, she cut her husband down before he had choked to death and gone to wherever it is that physicians go when they die.

The same soldiers paused in a field where they found Jesse plowing. They did not hang him, but they did administer a sound flogging. After recovering, he too joined Quantrill.

In camp were Cole and Jim Younger, second cousins by marriage to the James Boys. The Youngers were persons of some consequence in Jackson County, Missouri. Their father, Colonel Henry Washington Younger, was a wealthy man by some standards, and he twice served in the state assembly.

His family sympathized with the South, and suffered the consequences. Thugs murdered and robbed the Colonel; nightriders burned the Younger home. As one biographer stated it, "Incidents such as these might embitter even long-suffering people. The Youngers were not long-suffering."

Instead these two Younger brothers, Cole and Jim, joined Frank James (Jesse was not there at the time) at the Quantrill headquarters. They were readying to wipe Lawrence, Kansas from the face of the earth, if possible.

To be fair, Lawrence was hardly a peaceful, God-fearing settlement. It headquartered the Jayhawkers, who gave no mercy to Quantrill partisans. The guerrillas hated the town, and all that it represented.

Quantrill and his fierce, bearded raiders debated the issue, and decided the plunder and revenge would be worth the risk. Therefore, a column of 450 lean riders snaked out of camp, all expertly mounted and heavily armed. For two days they rode, approaching Lawrence on the morning of August 20, 1863. As they neared town they took a prisoner, questioned him, then beat his brains out and left him dead along the trail.

The guerrillas hit Lawrence like a cannon ball through Kleenex. To the partisan credit, there were no cases of rape or injury among the women. Otherwise the sacking and murder was complete.

Husbands were shot in front of screaming wives and children. After an orgy of blood-lust that went on for hours, Quantrill's weary raiders rode into sanctuary in Missouri, leaving behind a smoking town, two million dollars in damages, and 142 dead men, the bodies scattered in the street or thrown into the burning buildings. Only one guerrilla was slain.

The South recoiled with horror at the massacre and repudiated it. The North adopted a scorched earth policy of its own, and issued the infamous "Order No. 11" whereby the Missouri counties of Cass, Bates, Jackson and part of Vernon were depopulated. Everyone had two weeks to clear out. After they departed, their homes were looted and burned, the grain crops destroyed. Left behind was a charred scene of unparalleled destruction, waste and misery. For decades this part of Missouri would be known as the "Burnt District," and so deep would be the bitterness that outlaws such as Jesse James could operate there almost with impunity. Many of the residents might have disliked Jesse, but they despised the authorities.

As for Quantrill, with his food and shelter cut off, he went south to Texas where his men began killing southern citizens. On Christmas Day, 1863, the guerrillas terrorized Sherman, Texas. This time the authorities arrested Quantrill, but allowed him to escape. He took his gang up around the Red River, where they fought among themselves and split up. Perhaps only half-a-dozen followed Quantrill back to Missouri. With a price still on his head, Quantrill moved his base of operations to Kentucky where, thirty miles southeast of Louisville, his remarkable luck ran out.

On May 10, 1865, Union soldiers ambushed what was left of his command, and Quantrill himself pitched forward into the mud, his backbone shot out, rain pelting down on his face. He was 27.

As for the James boys, the end of the war left them unprepared for

52

civilian pursuits. On April 15, 1865, Jesse and six guerrillas were attacked by a column of Kansas and Wisconsin cavalrymen as the Confederate partisans were heading into Lexington, Missouri to surrender. A bullet tore a hole through Jesse's right lung, but he hid in the brush and escaped.

When found, the authorities figured he would die, so they issued him a pass into the Nebraska Territory where his mother and stepfather lived. Somehow his parents pulled him through, and during that period of convalescence he met his future bride—his own cousin Zerelda Mimms.

During those days he also rounded up many of his old comrades, especially his brother Frank and the Younger brothers. Together they plotted some of the most sensational robberies in history.

The James gang rides

With the close of the Civil War, and the recovery of Jesse James from a critical lung wound, he and a band of bearded, unemployed former guerrillas, would swagger into a saloon, gamble, drink heavily, and then thunder out of town while firing their pistols in the air. Naturally, the more respectable citizens stayed inside their homes and did not so much as peek through their boarded-up windows.

Some historians believe that Jesse, in his own way, was improving upon the Quantrill tactics, using terror to cow a town while its bank was being robbed. Whatever his motives, the facts were that on the morning of February 14, 1866, he and a small band of raiders roared into Liberty, Missouri driving the terrified residents off the street. While half-a-dozen men waited in the street, pot-shooting at windows, four others dismounted and with grain sacks held tightly in their grimy hands, entered the local bank. They removed $15,000 in gold coins and $45,000 in bonds, the latter being of no use and thrown away.

As the outlaws rode out of town they paused long enough to shoot a nineteen-year-old college student four times. So the gang had robbed its first bank and committed its first murder.

A posse followed the outlaws, but the lawmen showed little enthusiasm for the task. After a few hours they returned to Liberty saying that the trail had been lost in a fresh snow.

And so Liberty, Missouri achieved a certain amount of dubious fame. It was the site of the first bank robbery ever committed in the United States. Such an offense in those days thoroughly shocked the country and led in part to the James legend. Such a deed had not only been unheard of, it could not even be imagined. Who would have thought of robbing a bank to get money.

This first robbery by the James gang was an unqualified success. All they needed to do now was figure out a way to spend those gold coins without attracting attention. They solved the problem by heading south to San Antonio, Texas where a "fence" exchanged the gold for greenbacks and silver, all at a forty percent discount. This gave each gang member about $1,000 apiece, which wasn't bad money for a half-hour's work.

On their way out of Texas, the outlaws paused at the John Shirley farm, the owner being a former Quantrill guerrilla who was now married and had an eighteen-year-old daughter named Myra Belle. Myra would come down through history to us as the notorious Belle Starr. She wasn't a raving beauty by any means, but she would do in a pinch.

She and Cole Younger became a little chummy, and eight months after the outlaws went back to Missouri, she gave birth to a daughter whom she named Pearl Younger.

Meanwhile, the James gang hit the bank at Lexington, Missouri for $2,000, and six months later stopped long enough in Richmond, Missouri to tap the till for $4,000. During the second robbery, angry citizens put up a stiff fight. None of the outlaws were hurt, but a banker was wounded and three others, including the mayor, were killed.

No warrants were issued for Frank and Jesse James because the lads always carried "alibi cards," identification papers placing them in church, or engaged in other pious pursuits during the robberies and killings.

Some gang members were not so fortunate. Dick Burns, Andy McGuire and Tom Little, each captured separately, were strung up without benefit of trial. The citizenry believed that even if the lynched were not guilty of the Richmond holdup, they richly deserved hanging anyway. So it wasn't as if the posses might have made mistakes.

Now the Pinkerton Detective Agency entered the chase. The Pinks, as they came to be called, realized the James boys were not the ordinary slack-jawed criminals. These outlaws were canny, tough, desperate and merciless. While headquartered in Missouri, they ranged widely across the nation. On May 20, 1868, Cole Younger and Jesse James held up the Russellville, Kentucky bank and left with the usual grain sack filled with coin and greenbacks.

During the next few years the gang hit the bank at Gallatin, Missouri and killed a man. They also struck Columbia, Kentucky and Kansas City, Missouri.

Then came a switch in technique as the outlaws held up their first train, the second such attempt in history. (The first had been an inept robbery in Indiana some years earlier.) On the night of July 23, 1873, they derailed the Rock Island Express fifty miles east of Council Bluffs, Iowa, by removing part of the track. The engine rolled over, burst the steam boiler, and scalded to death the engineer. Although the bandits picked up about $7,000, it was a small amount compared to what had been expected. The James boys had hit the wrong train.

To work out their frustrations, the gang held up a stagecoach near Malvern, Arkansas, and two weeks later robbed the Iron Mountain Express as it rolled into Gads Hill, Missouri. This time they did not derail the train, but forced the entire population of Gads Hill into the depot and held them prisoner until the holdup had been completed.

By now the James boys had enough money to marry, and each did so in 1874. It is said that both men were faithful to their wives.

The Pinks began closing in, or at least tried to. Considering the clumsiness of the detectives, it is surprising that the Pinkerton Agency developed any reputation at all for destroying outlaw gangs.

Louis J. Lull and James Wright, two Pinkerton agents posing as stock buyers, nosed around the Ozark Mountain country in Missouri. Apparently they knew little about cattle, for they aroused the suspicions of John and Jim Younger. The brothers cornered the two detectives and began asking hard questions. Lull fired a hidden gun which almost instantly killed John Younger. More by reflex than anything else, John squeezed a shotgun trigger and severely wounded Lull. Jim Younger then killed both detectives and buried his brother in an orchard.

Another Pinkerton, John W. Whicher, tried to play the part of a poor man looking for work in the backwoods of Missouri. Jesse and

Frank took him prisoner, tried to question him, and when they received no answers, they shot him full of holes. By the time the body was found, hogs had eaten away part of the face.

For those who keep score, the outlaws now led three to one, and the Pinkertons were furious. They smuggled other detectives into Missouri, and in January, 1875, one of them sent back word that the James brothers were visiting their mother at the Samuel farm.

One night a posse of armed Pinkertons and several deputies surrounded the log farmhouse. Inside were Dr. and Mrs. Samuel (the mother and step-father of Jesse and Frank James), their two youngest children, and an old Negro woman servant. At 10 p.m. the Pinkertons closed in, and threw a lighted hand grenade through a window. The Pinkertons swore it was an iron flare, filled with flammable fluid, but weighted at the bottom so that it would sit upright after striking the floor.

Whatever it contained, it exploded. The blast tore the right arm off at the elbow of Jesse's mother. Archie Samuel, her eight-year-old son, was disemboweled and died. Dr. Samuel and the Negro woman received serious cuts and burns.

To make matters worse, neither Jesse nor Frank James were within miles of the place.

The blast ended the Pinkerton usefulness in the case. The savagery of that "night of blood" horrified half the nation, and newspapers across the country denounced it. So deep did feelings run about the matter, that the Missouri legislature introduced and nearly passed an act giving amnesty to the desperados.

The James gang laid low for a few months, hiding with relatives near Nashville, Tennessee. Jesse used the alias J. B. Howard, while Frank went under the name of Frank Woods. Reportedly the boys attended church regularly, and Jesse even preached a few sermons.

Nevertheless, they were soon active again in their old pursuits. On September 1, 1875, they hit the Huntington National Bank in West Virginia. One outlaw died in the holdup which otherwise was successful.

Three months later the gang cracked the Kansas Pacific Railroad at Muncie, Kansas and got away with $60,000, the richest haul of their careers. This included not only the express car cash, but passenger contributions as well. Jesse and the boys felt so good about it all, that

56

they celebrated by holding up the Missouri Pacific. This time they simply found a sharp curve in the line, stacked cross-ties on the track and waited until the panicked engineer brought the train to a grinding halt. An estimated $8,000 left with the outlaws.

Jesse and Frank now thought in terms of one more strike, a robbery that would make them rich and enable them to retire. Looking north they considered the stuffed banks in Northfield, Minnesota. Reportedly a bunch of Swedes and Norwegians lived around there, foreigners who could be trampled upon by a rough tough gang which took no nonsense from people who spoke "silly" English.

The desperados therefore made preparations for the greatest holdup of their professional careers. Little did they realize that the Northfield raid would be a disaster, the beginning of the end.

The Northfield raid

Jesse James picked his men carefully for the Northfield, Minnesota raid. Besides himself and brother Frank, he included the three Youngers, Cole, Jim and Bob, Clell Miller, Charlie Pitts and Bill Chadwell.

Chadwell, a daring, reckless desperado already wanted in Minnesota, had for weeks argued that the gang was wasting its time on small western and Midwestern banks. The small, swarthy outlaw kept insisting that big hauls were awaiting them in Minnesota, and Jesse finally concluded that he must be right.

So the eight-man gang rode out of Missouri, traveling in pairs, planning to rendezvous in St. Paul. There they turned southwest to check out the Mankato bank since it promised the most money. However, the building was undergoing reconstruction work and the sidewalk superintendents hanging around in droves made a robbery too risky.

Therefore, the outlaws agreed on the bank at Northfield, a town of 4000 prosperous and God-fearing people. Posing as cattle buyers, the men rode into the village from different directions, carefully reconnoitering its law officers, the escape routes and the First National Bank.

Jesse, thoroughly in command, picked himself, Bob Younger and

Charlie Pitts to enter the bank. They would saunter into town first, have lunch, and then casually lounge at the bank street corner until Bill Chadwell, Jim Younger and Frank James came charging in from the south, and Clell Miller and Cole Younger from the opposite direction.

At one o'clock, September 7, 1876, it all happened. The old swoop and hurrah tactics, so familiar during the days of Quantrill, lost much of their effectiveness because the robbers were recognized before the shooting actually began. The James gang, screaming rebel yells and firing pistols reached the center of town at a fast gallop. Cole Younger paused in the street fronting the bank, dismounted and swaggered around with a six-shooter in each hand. He yelled and fired at anything that moved or looked like it might move.

Pitts and the two James boys dashed into the bank to confront the cashier and two tellers. No customers were there. Since the vault outer door stood ajar, Jesse stepped inside to open the inner door, and as he did so, the cashier jumped forward to slam the door and lock him inside. Charlie Pitts stopped it by bashing him across the head with a gun barrel, and knocking him half senseless to the floor.

At the same instant a teller bolted for the back door. Pitts fired and missed, but the bullet whistled by close enough to give the teller certain strengths he did not know he had. Instead of opening the door in the usual manner, he went right through it.

Outside, Pitts pursued and shot at the fleeing man and hit him in the shoulder. The fellow faltered momentarily, then picked up speed again and vanished. He survived.

During all this time, none of the bank robbers had tried opening the inner vault door, which was unlocked. No doubt they were getting rattled by the outside racket, now beginning to sound like a real battle. Apparently those Northfield folks were no ordinary sod-busters. They had guts, they had guns, and they were shooting to kill.

Gone was the James element of surprise and terror. When the shooting began, Cole Younger yelled at a seventeen-year-old boy to get off the street, but the Swedish immigrant couldn't understand English. He stammered in confusion, and Younger killed him.

Northfield was beginning to organize. Two hardware stores passed out guns as fast as they could be taken from the cases. A medical student bored a hole right through Clell Miller and killed him on the spot. (Years later, that same student, then a doctor, had Miller's skeleton on display in his office.)

Cole Younger, nursing a shoulder wound, lurched into the bank and yelled, "Let's get out of here! They're killing us!"

The James boys grabbed up the till money, ignoring the safe which they still did not realize was unlocked, and backed toward the door. As they reached it, a teller stuck his hand in a drawer, and paid for it with Jesse's bullet in his brain.

The West's finest and most successful holdup men were being decimated. Bob Younger jumped on a horse only to have it struck by a rifle bullet and crash land beneath him. He jumped free as a ricochet shattered his right elbow. Miller and Chadwell lay dead in the street. Jim Younger had been shot through both shoulders and part of his jaw had been blown away. Blood covered Cole from head to foot. Even Jesse and Frank were hit by shotgun pellets. Only Pitts remained unscratched.

As the desperados climbed on horses — theirs, each other's or someone else's, this was no time to be particular — and headed out of town, Bob Younger screamed from beneath an iron stairway, "Don't leave me! I'm shot!"

Cole heard the yell, realized his brother was missing, and careened back through the street of death. He picked Bob up, and they rode out together.

The fugitives might have been overtaken as easily as a herd of milk cows at feeding time, but an effective pursuit couldn't immediately be organized. When a posse did strike the trail, the gunmen had vanished with only an occasional splash of blood to mark their passage.

A thousand men fanned out across the bleak countryside as the James gang stumbled south and west, desperately trying to flee the state. Their horses gave out, the wounds festered, and the men were weak and starving. The skies clouded over and rain poured in torrents. Roads and trails became quagmires as horses and men sank to their knees in the mud.

All suffered from a lack of food and rest and shelter, but Jim and Bob Younger seemed to be in particularly bad shape. James was obviously the more critical, yet Bob's splintered elbow had almost incapacitated him with pain. Neither man could scarcely ride, slowing down the others so that, according to the most prevalent story, Jesse wanted to shoot Jim so that he would be out of his misery "and the rest of us can get going." However, Cole Younger (who was there) stated in his autobiographical *Story of Cole Younger* that Jesse wanted to kill Bob.

Whatever the facts, the dispute caused a rift between Jesse and the Youngers, and the gang split up. The James boys went in one direction; the Youngers in another. Pitts, the only healthy member in camp, wavered and then struck out with the Youngers. He would pay dearly for his loyalty.

Riding one horse together, Jesse and Frank shot their way through a posse picket line near Lake Crystal. In the darkness, a lucky bullet from the lawmen found a mark. It went completely through the horse, through the right leg of Frank and did not stop until it thudded deep inside Jesse's thigh. The two men, now on foot, fled into a cornfield where the deputies hesitated to follow until daylight. On the next morning the James brothers robbed a farmer of two gray plowhorses. On these they crossed Minnesota into Dakota Territory and dropped from sight.

The Youngers and Pitts were not so lucky. They shot their way across the Blue Earth River Bridge at two o'clock in the morning, and then began robbing chicken houses to eat. As progress was slow, a posse closed in and trapped them in a thicket. Pitts died when a fusillade of rifle bullets cut him down. The Youngers made a short fight of it, but after being further shot up, surrendered. So two weeks after robbing the Northfield Bank, it was all over for two-thirds of the James gang.

Cole Younger had eleven wounds. Bob could stand, although he had several minor wounds and a shattered right elbow which hung from his shoulder like a broken tree branch. Jim had a body full of eight buckshot and one rifle bullet. His broken jaw gave him a macabre appearance.

Yet, the Youngers all survived. They lived by a code, and they refused to break it and answer questions. When able to stand trial, all pleaded guilty to charges of murder, robbery and assault. By doing so they escaped hanging, and were sentenced to life imprisonment in the Minnesota State Penitentiary.

Bob died there of tuberculosis on September 16, 1889. Cole and Jim served twenty-five years each and were released. Shortly afterwards Jim committed suicide in a St. Paul hotel room, despondent because of his inability to find a job and because of a soured love affair. Cole became religious, preached many a sermon, and died in Missouri on March 21, 1916.

The James boys were still loose and running. However, their time, too, was almost up.

The dirty little coward that shot Mr. Howard

Frank and Jesse James may have fled all the way to Mexico following the aborted Northfield bank robbery. At any rate, they were back in Missouri by 1879, Jesse using the name J. B. Howard, and Frank becoming B. J. Woodson. By now they were in need of money, so they set out to raise funds in the usual and accustomed manner.

On the night of October 7, a recreated James gang entered the village of Glendale, Missouri, crowded the entire population into the depot, and waited for the Chicago and Alton to come chugging through. After the station agent flagged the train to a stop, the bandits extracted expense money of $35,000, which included the usual passenger contributions.

In addition to the James boys, the outlaws consisted of Dick Liddil, Billy Ryan, Tucker Basham (a not too bright farmer), Ed Miller (the young brother of Clell Miller who was slain at Northfield) and Wood Hite.

Dick Liddil was more of a lover than a fighter, and the widow Martha Bolton attracted him. She invited the gang to hide out in her Richmond, Missouri home, and introduced them to her brothers, Charles and Bob Ford.

Two years later on July 15, 1881, the James Gang hit the Rock Island train. Jesse and Frank James, plus an unidentified bandit, all sporting heavy beards, boarded the train as casual passengers at Cameron, Missouri. Sixty miles further, four other men boarded, walked to the locomotive tender, and when the train arrived in Winston, they ordered the engineer to stop.

As the train halted, conductor William Westfall recognized the James boys. Westfall had taken the Pinkertons to their rendezvous at the Samuel farm on the night those detectives tossed a bomb into the house. Although Westfall was not responsible for what happened, the James boys hated him. He ran for the door, and Frank shot him in the arm. Jesse shoved his brother aside, and sank a slug where the conductor's hatbrim touched his head.

The panicked passengers scrambled for the exits, but a few shots fired overhead returned them to their seats. Only a stone mason insisted on leaving, and Frank killed him.

Missouri weather had been hot and humid, and as a result the baggage and express car doors were ajar in hopes of catching the slightest breeze. The desperados jumped inside before the doors could be slammed shut, beat the guards senseless and escaped with nearly $10,000.

Whereas a few short years before, Missouri had expressed outrage at the senseless bombing of the James home, now the same state roared over the murder of Westfall and the stone mason. Governor Thomas Crittendon offered a $5,000 reward for any member of the James gang, plus $10,000 apiece for Jesse and Frank.

Tucker Basham and Bill Ryan were soon arrested, more for being drunk than anything else, and William H. Wallace, prosecuting attorney for Jackson County, Missouri, vowed to imprison them. Meanwhile, the James brothers bragged that no gang member would ever be convicted in Jackson County, the home base of operations.

After a noisy trial, the jury voted guilty, a resounding verdict literally driving the first nail in the coffin of Jesse and Frank. Not only did the brothers see the end coming, but so did much of Missouri.

Jesse began cracking under the strain. He imagined Ed Miller plotted to turn him in, and Ed's body turned up shot to pieces beside a remote road.

Hite and Liddil fell out over the affections of Mrs. Bolton, and Liddil, in connivance with Bob Ford, shot Hite to death and buried him in a dirty horse blanket.

Since Hite and Jesse were first cousins, Liddil began to fear for his life. He sent Mrs. Bolton to Governor Crittenden and the governor promised clemency if Liddil surrendered and turned state's evidence. On this basis the outlaw turned himself in and confessed to twenty-two robberies he and the James boys had carried out. Crittenden gave Liddil a conditional pardon.

All roads now led toward the capital and an audience with the governor, and traveling it were Bob and Charles Ford. Since no outstanding crimes were charged to them, they sought exact figures on the heads of Jesse and Frank James, plus some assurances that the money would be paid dead or alive. Crittenden said it didn't make any difference.

During all this time Jesse James, better known around St. Joseph as Mr. Howard, lived respectfully with his wife and two children, a boy and a girl. In late March, 1882, Jesse and Bob Ford rode over to Jackson County and visited the Samuel farm. After returning they made plans for robbing the Platte City, Missouri bank.

On April 3, as Jesse, Bob and Charlie sat chatting in the James home, Jesse rose to straighten a picture. To do so he removed his coat and guns, and climbed upon a straight-backed chair shoved against the wall. Bob and Charles glanced at each other, Charlie winked, and Bob drew a pistol. Holding it within four feet of Jesse's head, he pulled the trigger. The resultant gunshot ended an era. The West's best known and most famous outlaw tumbled off the chair and hit the floor on his face, dead.

After Jesse died, his mother visited the governor and requested a pardon for Frank. Crittenden promised the surviving desperado protection, but said he would have to take his chances with a judge and jury.

Frank accepted those terms, and went on trial for the stone mason killed during the last robbery. It was a sensational trial, with emotion and public opinion riding solidly on Frank's side. He went free and never again faced charges.

As the years passed, a bony, thin, tight-lipped Frank James spent his time on the Samuel farm, living with his mother and his family. He worked as a special policeman at the Tivoli Theatre in St. Louis, but people were more interested in seeing him than the show girls. A Chicago brewer financed a Frank James-Cole Younger Wild West Show complete with cowboys and Indians. The show was a modest success until Frank's health forced him to drop out. The old, ex-outlaw died quietly on February 18, 1915, at the age of seventy-two.

As for his long deceased brother, Jesse, Missouri and the entire nation were stunned at the callous manner of his death. Bob and Charles Ford had expected to become heroes, and instead saw themselves branded as the most infamous of traitors. Overnight a popular national ballad sprang up.

"Twas a dirty little coward,
That shot Mr. Howard,
And laid Jesse James in his grave."

Neither Bob nor Charlie had the mentality to cope successfully with these events, and they, too, became tragic figures of a sort, worthy of compassion and understanding. Four years later Charlie Ford, puzzled, bitter, filled with remorse, plagued by bad health, shot himself to death in a weed patch in Richmond, Missouri.

Bob took his blood money and went to Colorado where ten years later he opened a tent saloon in Creede, a mining camp he had been run out of twice and then allowed back in on the promise of good behavior.

On June 8, 1892, Edward O. Kelly (or O'Kelly), who wanted to be known as the man who killed the killer of Jesse James, walked up to the bar and laid a shotgun across it. Bob Ford died almost instantly. (Kelly met his death in 1904 while resisting arrest in Oklahoma City.)

And so ends the Jesse James story. The still-young outlaw was taken to his mother's farm and buried with the following gravestone inscription:

"Jesse W. James
Died April 3, 1882
Aged 34 years, 6 months, 28 days
Murdered by a traitor and coward whose
name is not worthy to appear here."

7

THE DALTONS

BROTHERS ON THE PROWL

THE DALTONS were brothers, a rough, vicious outlaw gang that ranged from the Ozarks in Missouri to Silver City in New Mexico. They were first lawmen, and performed credibly in a dangerous profession. Then, for no other reason except greed, they set themselves against society and began stealing horses and holding up trains. As bank robbers they were crashing failures; and yet their one single exploit in this field, with its crazy madness and courageous recklessness lifts them above the ordinary run of bandits and gives them a permanent niche in the Western Pantheon of fame.

There were fifteen of the Dalton children, and the West can be thankful that only four of them went bad. As a father Lewis Dalton wasn't much. He had been a fifer during the Mexican War, and afterwards operated a saloon until his wife badgered him into seeking more respectable employment, a decision she lived to regret since he rarely did anything afterwards except bet on slow horses. Hard work gave him the chills.

Adeline, his wife, bore the children and her hard-drinking Irish husband with the proper fortitude. She was distantly related to the Youngers. Most accounts describe her as a tiny, waspish woman who despised the Youngers who became outlaws, believing them a disgrace

Emmett Dalton
Bob Dalton and sweetheart

Grat Dalton
Frank Dalton

to the family. Accordingly she tried to pass on her strong, fundamentalist religious beliefs to her children. She did not smile much, but then life handed her very little to be cheerful about. Just managing to exist was terribly difficult for this family. Over the years she and her wandering, ne'er-do-well husband practically stopped talking, and became about as compatible as Custer and Sitting Bull.

As for the children, there was Grat, the oldest of the outlaw boys, born in 1861. He was heavy fisted and could count to ten if he had enough time. There was Bob, the actual gang leader. He had a weakness for money and women, and somehow always came up short on both. There was Frank, perhaps the only law-abiding one of the entire bunch, and Bill, who dreamed of becoming Governor of California. Finally there was Emmett, the youngest. He was the only survivor of the Dalton's last ride, and in fact wrote a book about it, or at least allowed his name to be placed on one. Naturally, his version of events placed the Daltons in romantic, sinned-against circumstance. Subsequent movies made the Daltons look pretty good too.

In 1882 the Daltons rode to Indian Territory (Oklahoma), where they raced horses and fought occasional brawls. As their reputation spread, Frank, Bob and Grat went to work as "Cherokee Policemen."

Frank soon caught the attention of Isaac Parker, the famous Fort Smith, Arkansas hanging judge. He commissioned the Dalton boy as a United States deputy marshal, a laudable addition to those brave and largely unsung marshals who picked up two dollars for every prisoner delivered, and six cents a mile for travel expenses. The work was so dangerous that almost one-third of Parker's men—sixty-five out of 225 —died in the line of duty.

Frank might have become well known had it not been for his outlaw brothers. As it was he met his end in 1887 while chasing whiskey runners. In a fierce shootout, three bootleggers were killed, but so was he. Frank became the first Dalton to die with his boots on, and the only Dalton to die honorably.

Grat and Bob, unlike their brother whom they apparently did not mourn at all, remained policemen and spent much of their time shaking down travelers for various sums of money. When they caught a Sooner sneaking into the Territory, they gave him a choice of paying a bribe or going to jail.

Incredibly, Bob still became police chief in the Osage nation. However, his dishonest operation fell apart when his cousin Minnie began courting another man. While Bob himself had a friendly relationship with several women, he did not want Minnie getting "involved" with anyone else. He solved the problem by arranging for her boyfriend to turn up dead with a bullet in the neck and then listed him as a criminal who had "resisted arrest."

Some Oklahomans were a little suspicious of that shooting, but withheld their comments until a storekeeper accused an Indian youth of being a wanted man. The brothers promptly shot the boy to pieces. Though he lived, public opinion forced the Dalton resignations.

The citizens finally realized that the Daltons had been using their official status as a cover for horse stealing. The Daltons fled into the western Ozarks for refuge and became, in effect, an organized outlaw gang for the first time. Since Kansas and Oklahoma were at least temporarily closed to them, they headed for Silver City, New Mexico.

Texans, especially those tough border men from El Paso, dominated the action in Silver City. Gambling tables, though crooked, were in full swing with plenty of armed men nearby to see that no one used a gun to recover losses. In disgust, the Daltons held up a gambling establishment near Santa Rita. Except for Emmett who was shot in the arm, no one was injured.

After the gang rode triumphantly back into Oklahoma, the Daltons split up. Emmett took refuge in the home of a friend while Bob and Grat visited their brother Bill in California. Bill would have been wise to refuse his brother's refuge, since he was married, had two children, and was politically rising in the state. Already he had put himself on the side of the common man by denouncing the Southern Pacific. Under the influence of his brothers, he would soon do more than just upbraid the railroad.

Train robbers had recently been entering the state in record numbers, so the officials looked at any tough-looking strangers with suspicion. As the Daltons were about as suspicious as anyone could get, it was not surprising that warrants went out for their arrest when three men held up the Southern Pacific during its regular run between San Francisco and Los Angeles. One employee was killed, and the bandits escaped.

A grand jury indicted the Dalton brothers. Bob quickly fled back to Oklahoma whereas Grat and Bill were taken into custody. In two interesting but separate trials, a jury found Grat guilty, but Bill innocent.

However, Bill had no sooner left the courtroom than he was arrested and jailed in connection with another train robbery.

As these California events took place, Bob and Emmett Dalton, accompanied by Bitter Creek Newcomb and Blackface Charlie Bryant were robbing trains in Oklahoma. Bob had given careful instructions that no grangers (farmers) would be molested, and that no one was to be killed unless absolutely necessary.

Their first robbery went smoothly. During their second holdup Bryant callously murdered a young depot agent. To make matters worse, the sacks they had assumed to be bulging with greenbacks turned out to have nothing but old telegrams and cancelled waybills. Dalton swearing could be heard all the way to the Mexican border.

War against the railroads

Following that first Southern Pacific holdup, the Daltons fought off several posses before going into hiding. They killed a lawman in the battle of Twin Mounds, Oklahoma.

Blackface Charlie Bryant ignored all advice to stay out of sight. He had been feeling ill, so he checked in at the Rock Island Hotel in Hennessy and called a doctor. Before long Marshal Ed Short came to his side too, and placed him under arrest. Since the town had no jail, the lawman placed him on a train and, out of pity for the sick man, loosened his handcuffs. From somewhere Bryant snatched a pistol, and in a face-to-face duel he and the marshal shot each other to death.

The Dalton brothers showed no concern about Bryant, but looked forward to the biggest haul of their career. This time they would assault the MK&T Railroad which rumbled through eastern Oklahoma heading for the Texas banks to deposit cotton money.

Bob gathered an assortment of seven men around him, and as the train ground to a stop, the outlaws jumped aboard and took the engineer prisoner. Next they threatened to dynamite the express car unless the doors were quickly opened, which they were. As the bandits dug valuables from the safe, several passengers stepped outside from the coaches and made threatening motions to attack. Bill Doolin, a well-known outlaw in his own right, sneered that he would handle these interruptions, and in a fury he rode toward the milling people and wildly fired his pistol into the air. Everyone scrambled back inside and gave no more trouble.

When the gang met later to divide the loot, the Daltons did away with the equal-risk, equal-share policy. On the pretense that he and Emmett were retiring from the outlaw business, Bob picked up about $9,000 for the two of them, and handed less than $300 apiece to the others. That the Daltons could make such an arrangement stick is incredible considering the dangerous caliber of their assistants.

In the meantime Bill and Grat Dalton rode in from California. Bill had been acquitted of the second train robbery charge, and Grat had simply escaped from jail. With their reappearance, Bob and Emmett called for a celebration. What could be better than robbing another train.

On the cloudy night of June 1, 1892, as lightning zig-zagged across the brooding skies, the Dalton gang rode into the town of Red Rock on the Otoe Indian Reservation. Only Bill did not tag along. He agreed to play the part of a straight man, keeping out of trouble, but reporting to his brothers the presence of any large money shipments being transported across the territory.

Gradually the Red Rock train rolled down the tracks and into the station. Somehow it looked ominous. A strange darkness pervaded the passenger coach behind the express car. The question became: should the gunmen attack or not? As they argued among themselves, the train pulled away into the night and left behind several frustrated Daltons who were not certain if they had just made the smartest or stupidest move of their lives.

As the boys turned to leave, one of them noticed that the train tracks were vibrating again, an unexpected occurrence since no additional trains were expected. The first train had simply been a decoy designed to lure unsuspecting highwaymen into a trap. Now the express car and coaches were pausing right beside the Daltons, and there was not a law officer in sight.

Of course the holdup was not without difficulty. The Daltons threatened to dynamite the express car unless the doors were opened, and not only did they steal the money, but they took ladies finery from the merchandise boxes, and the lunches belonging to the trainmen.

Hundreds of lawmen now combed the Indian Territory looking for the Daltons, but all in vain. By June 17 the Stillwater *Gazette* reported that "the pursuing parties have returned, and the chase of the bandits has been entirely abandoned."

On July 15 the Daltons were back at their familiar line of work, this time in Adair, Oklahoma. At 9 o'clock that night they walked into the station and relieved the ticket agent of all his cash. Then while waiting for the train, they made themselves comfortable on the rough wooden benches.

As the train came in, Bitter Creek Newcomb kept the loungers bunched together at the end of the station platform. Grat and Emmett took the engineer prisoner and Bob Dalton, Dick Broadwell and Bill Powers went through the usual motions of talking the express car messenger into opening the doors.

Suddenly three riflemen opened fire from a coal shed. United States Deputy Marshal Sid Johnson, Captain J. J. Kinney of the railroad police, and Captain Charles Le Flore, head of the Cherokee National Police banged away, but soon quit. Johnson took a serious wound, and the others lesser injuries. The Daltons escaped unscathed, but the same could not be said for innocent bystanders. Two doctors were shot and one of them killed as they watched the fight from a drugstore window.

The Daltons escaped in spite of several more bloody brushes with searching lawmen. Afterwards they grumbled about the increasingly small returns that railroad holdups were bringing. Consequently, they geared themselves to do something that no outlaw gang had ever accomplished. They would rob two banks at one time.

Last ride of the Dalton brothers

For awhile the Daltons debated whether to rob the one bank in Van Buren, Arkansas, or the two banks in their old hometown of Coffeyville, Kansas. They decided upon Coffeyville for many reasons, one being that it had two banks. No one had ever robbed two banks before at one time.

There was no unanimous agreement. Bob Dalton favored it, and he was the leader. Grat favored it, but he wasn't very bright. Emmett favored it, but he was still young and kept wanting to outperform his hero, Jesse James: Bill Dalton thought they were all crazy, and should stick with an occupation they understood: robbing trains. Bill Doolin supported Bill Dalton. He spat a stream of tobacco juice, and said he would not commit suicide. Bill Powers and Dick Broadwell agreed to go along with Bob.

Coffeyville had less than 4000 souls, saved and otherwise. Its streets were unpaved, and it had the look of a frontier settlement. Yet it was a thriving, prosperous town with doctors, lawyers and businesses. The First National and the Condon banks were the city's pride, and were practically right across the street from each other.

During early October, 1892, the Daltons rode toward Coffeyville while Bob explained the plan. He and Emmett would rob the First National, the largest and most heavily guarded. Grat, Powers and Broadwell would take care of the Condon. Only Emmett argued with this arrangement, insisting that he and Grat change places, and that he, not Grat, should boss the Condon robbery. However, Bob refused to consider it. He needed someone dependable backing him up. If there was an expendable Dalton brother, it had to be Grat. Emmett was too good a man.

On October 5, with a stick in the dirt Bob diagrammed the town and the banks. Escape lanes were carefully plotted. The entire task should take a maximum of fifteen minutes. The Daltons would wear false whiskers, Powers and Broadwell bandanas. Everyone wore fancy new clothes and carried new Winchesters. The Daltons did not want to look like a bunch of saddle tramps in their greatest robbery.

They hit town right at bank opening time before too many withdrawals could be made. On their way in they passed several former friends but were unrecognized in spite of those ridiculous whiskers. As a matter of fact, no one paid any attention until the Daltons reached the public square, dismounted and began dogtrotting toward the banks, Winchesters at the ready. Suddenly someone screamed, "There go the Daltons."

Coffeyville suspected the Daltons were coming. Rumors were all over, and well-known law officer Chris Madsen had warned community officials. Immediately hardware stores began distributing rifles and shotguns. The outlaws had virtually ridden into an armed and waiting camp.

Bob and Emmett Dalton barged into the First National and ordered everyone to raise their hands. Grain sacks were thrown on the floor and the teller ordered to fill them up. The bankers protested that the vaults could not be opened until later, but Bob growled that it was time now . . . . and sure enough, it was. Shooting had already started outside, as men took up positions all around the building. Bob checked the vault to make sure it was empty, and came out seconds later with $5,000. Bankers and patrons were shoved out into the street first. The Daltons came behind, determined to fight their way out of town.

Heavy gunfire forced them back inside the bank, and they raced to the back door and into the alley while clutching $21,000 in a sack. Charles Baldwin, a store clerk, stood there with a rifle in his hands. Bob shot him down as the two brothers dashed through the alley and out into the street where they also killed George Cubine and Charles Brown. From down the block, Tom Ayres, the bank cashier, raised himself to the window to see what was happening. Bob glanced a bullet off his head.

The two Daltons had miraculously accomplished the impossible. They had invaded an armed and forewarned town, robbed its biggest bank, shot down several of its finest citizens, and made it to their horses. All they needed do now was ride out. But where were the others? At that instant a loud roar of gunfire echoed from the Condon. "We'll have to go back and help Grat," Bob said.

The other outlaws were having their problems due to the slow thinking of Grat Dalton. When told that the vault would not open for ten minutes, he believed it and settled down to wait. As time ticked by, people from outside began shooting. Already Broadwell and Powers were swapping fire with several citizens, and Broadwell had taken a bullet in the shoulder. Grat decided to wait no longer, and asked where the back door was. A banker said there wasn't any, and once again Grat let himself be fooled.

Altogether he had about $4,000 in silver dollars, a heavy bundle. Bankers carried two bushels of coin toward the waiting outlaw horses, but lost their nerve in the face of all the gunfire. Dalton grabbed up $1,000 in greenbacks, hardly a large enough sum to die for, but it was a little late to think of that now.

The three outlaws dashed outside and Powers was hit almost immediately. He made it to his horse, but was shot down when he tried to mount. Dick Broadwell took another wound. Staggering from one bit of cover to another, he mounted his horse and rode a half-mile out of town before bleeding to death.

Grat was hit at least twice. Dropping the money he staggered into an alley where the world was just a blur to him. Nevertheless, he swung the Winchester and kept it banging. Down went Charlie Connelly, the town marshal. By this time Bob and Emmett raced up, and they too were pinned down in what is today known as "Death Alley."

Gradually the fighting slowed as everyone picked his target. Bob stepped into the middle of the alley to check a nearby roof, and a sniper shot him squarely in the chest. He reeled backwards and sat down heavily. John Kloehr, a stable proprietor, moved in and shot him again. Kloehr could also see Grat blindly wandering around. Taking careful aim, he shot the wounded Dalton in the throat, the bullet breaking his neck.

Only Emmett had an opportunity to escape, though wounded in the arm and the thigh. He might have gotten away with money, for he still clutched a sack tightly as he swung his leg over the horse. But then he did an incredibly brave act, earning for himself the respect and admiration of many men.

Turning his horse, he raced back into the gunfire, heading for his wounded brother Bob. Pausing, he stretched down his hand, but Bob was too weak to take it and pull himself up. At that instant a double-barreled shotgun roared, and Emmett pitched off his mount. The battle was now over. Four bandits, four citizens and several horses had been killed. Many had been wounded, including Emmett, who would survive.

For hours the dead outlaws lay in the street. The body of Powers was brought in from outside of town, and photographs were taken of the dead. Souvenir hunters tore at the Dalton clothes for whatever pieces they could carry away. The banks recovered all but $22 of their money.

Emmett survived to get a life term in the Kansas State Prison, but was released after serving fourteen-and-a-half years. He never again rode the Owl Hoot Trail, but instead married his childhood sweetheart who had been faithful to him, after a fashion, for all those years. On July 13, 1937, at the age of sixty-six, he died in Hollywood, California. To the end he had one saying which he habitually mumbled over and over, "Crime doesn't pay."

8

ELFEGO BACA

LAST OF THE OLD-TIME SHOOTERS

MEXICAN OR MEXICAN-AMERICAN gunslingers never achieved the notoriety of their Anglo counterparts for various reasons.

An Anglo might hang around town and make a nuisance of himself by shooting people for years before public patience finally tired and some of the more aggressive citizens dangled him from the crosstie of a telephone pole. Mexican pistoleros received much less consideration.

Mexicans had a natural reluctance about notching dead men on their pistols. They made superb, even ruthless bandits and revolutionaries, always formidable opponents when aroused, but that's about as far as it went. Except for individuals such as Joaquin Murieta, a California bandit so obscure and legendary that many historians doubt he even existed, the trade of gunfighting did not interest the average Mexican.

But exceptions existed, and Elfego Baca is the best known example. While possessing his personal eccentricities and color, he had the usual characteristics common to most gunmen. He was, and is, controversial. He drank too much; he talked too much (the stereotype of the silent Westerner is a myth, as most of them would talk off an arm and a leg, given the opportunity); he had a weakness for wild women; he was

*Elfego Baca . . . the last of the old-time gunfighters
died quietly at the age of eighty.*

often arrogant and, of course, he showed no compunction about killing people.

His mother liked to play baseball, and so it came as no surprise to anybody when she interrupted the game one evening in 1865 and gave birth on the ballfield to Elfego at Socorro, New Mexico.

His father Francisco, with the reputation of a hard-case, moved the family to Topeka, Kansas when Elfego was still a toddler. The lad attended school, and had ample opportunities for fighting with gringo kids who, whatever their faults, were not too familiar with Mexicans and therefore lacked the racial prejudice usually found in New Mexico and Texas.

At fifteen Baca returned to Socorro, a young man now speaking better English than Spanish. His father sold the family business in Topeka and also returned to New Mexico, becoming city marshal of Belen, a small village upriver from Socorro. One afternoon the older Baca shot and killed two cowboys for hurrahing the town. A court decreed he went too far in the performance of his duties, and put him in jail at Los Lunas.

Elfego cut a hole in the roof and pulled his father to safety, after which Francisco fled to one of the settlements near El Paso (apparently Ysleta, Socorro or San Elizario).

Young Baca continued living in the New Mexico community of Socorro until 1884 when at the age of nineteen he had already built himself a solid reputation as a gunhand. He even purchased a mail-order badge, and pretended he had some kind of legal authority. An opportunity to show his stuff came when a deputy sheriff from Frisco, New Mexico (now Reserve) told some tales of how the cowpunchers were terrorizing the village.

Baca pinned on his badge, declared himself a lawman, and conducted a private investigation. It revealed the nearby Slaughter outfit as the chief troublemakers. In particular, a cowboy named McCarty habitually rode up and down the main street shooting at signs and whatever else attracted his fancy. So Elfego looked up the alcalde (justice of the peace in this case), and asked him to swear out a warrant for McCarty's arrest. The JP said something profane, indicating that Baca should go back to Socorro.

Undeterred, Baca headed uptown to harness the lawbreakers. He found McCarty and some friends gathered in the street, all minding

77

their own business, but doing it in a loud tone of voice. Baca grabbed McCarty by the collar, stuck the business end of a pistol barrel in his ear, and ordered him to step lively toward the jailhouse. Tomorrow the prisoner would be taken to Socorro for trial.

Late that afternoon, a group of cowboys led by the Slaughter foreman, confronted Baca near the jail and demanded McCarty's release. Elfego refused to negotiate or discuss the matter. Instead he warned the cowboys that he would count to three. If within that length of time the men had not moved on, everyone could consider the last number as a signal to start shooting.

Baca immediately and calmly began to count, not hesitating between numbers. "One, two, three," he said, and then he pulled his pistol and started shooting. A bullet nipped the leg of a rider, and the other shots went wild. Instead of the cowboys firing back, their rearing animals put them in a state of confusion. The foreman's horse flipped all the way over, fatally crushing the trail boss. The cowboys carried him off, and the town stayed quiet for the rest of that day and all night.

The next morning another justice of the peace agreed to try McCarty. Baca took his prisoner to court, and the judge fined the cowhand $5 for disturbing the peace.

When it was all over, angry cowboys began milling in the street. Baca knew he was in deep trouble, and when someone fired a shot, he took off by sprinting down an alley. A tiny *jacal* (shack) provided the only cover, but a woman and two children occupied it. Elfego chased the residents out, and settled down to defend himself.

Rancher Jim Herne rushed the building while brandishing a rifle, but not firing. Baca pumped two bullets into him, and Herne staggered off to die.

On the face of it, a more unlikely spot to withstand a siege could not be imagined. The building was constructed of upright posts chinked with mud. Some of the cracks were very large. Fortunately the floor had been dug out to about eighteen inches below ground level, and that's what saved Baca.

For the next thirty-six hours the cowboys kept him pinned down in what has to be one of the most incredible one-man-stands in history. Over eighty cowboys surrounded the building, and they poured hundreds, perhaps thousands, of slugs into the shack. The door alone had nearly 400 bullet holes. A broom handle was hit eight times. Through it all Baca lay flat on the dirt, occasionally rising to fire through the cracks in the wall. Some stories say he killed several attackers, but other than Herne he does not seem to have hit anyone.

The cowboys tossed torches on the roof, but the dirt prevented a fire from starting. They hurled dynamite, and it went off with a shattering roar, collapsing part of the roof. No one knew whether Baca still survived.

The next morning they got their answer. Smoke curled up from the chimney remains, and the aroma of food reached the beseigers. Baca was fixing breakfast.

The second day dragged on with only sporadic firing as many of the cowboys returned to the ranch. Late that afternoon a deputy sheriff named Ross, whom Baca knew and trusted, offered Baca assurances that if he came out and stood trial, no one would harm him. Baca agreed on the condition he could keep his guns. And that's how it all ended.

Baca went by buckboard to Socorro where he stayed in jail for four months. Finally he went on trial in Albuquerque, and was acquitted twice on charges of murder.

Jail time gave Baca an opportunity to think about life in general, and he made up his mind to be a criminal lawyer and peace officer. He also made up his mind to get married, and at the age of twenty he tied the knot. A son and five daughters were eventually born of the union.

Over the years Baca became a peace officer, acquiring the customary knife and ice pick wounds common to that hazardous occupation. He arrested the noted outlaw Jose Chavez y Chavez, and was instrumental in putting Jose Garcia behind bars too. Garcia had cut his mistress into quarters, and hung the meat out to cure.

In 1894 the New Mexico Bar Association admitted him to practice. Since then as now, many lawyers thought of themselves as politicians, he decided to run for office. As time went by he was elected mayor, county clerk, school superintendent, assistant district attorney and district attorney.

Baca became an articulate spokesman, usually for Baca, but sometimes for other causes as well. The Mexican Revolution interested him, and General Huerta named Baca as his American representative. When General Jose Salazar jumped across the international border in order to live and fight another day, the American officials arrested him for violation of the neutrality laws. Baca rose to his defense. However, he did not rise very far because military authorities kept Salazar incommunicado. Finally, Baca did get his client transferred to the jurisdiction of a civilian court, and placed in the Albuquerque jail. Not long after that he broke out, and escaped to Mexico.

In order to keep his contacts, Baca spent a lot of time in El Paso and Juarez. One afternoon, Celestino Otero, who supported a different faction of the Mexican revolution, agreed to meet Baca at an El Paso cafe. Baca arrived, stepped out of his car, and Otero fired. The bullet struck Elfego in the groin, but the old gunman wasn't napping. He fired twice in return, and Otero died with two bullets through the heart. Baca survived easily, and an El Paso jury acquitted him.

In his fifties now, mustachioed, plump, full of bouncing energy and long-winded stories, he ran for sheriff of Socorro County. Most reports say he was the best peace officer Socorro ever had.

And when the famous Tivoli in Juarez hit the height of its gambling fame during prohibition, who did the management hire as its chief bouncer? Elfego Baca, of course. As one biographer worded it, "His duties were light. But he was not paid for them. He was being paid simply for being there."

During that period, with gambling establishments being held up all over Juarez on a regular basis, no one ever tried to rob the Tivoli. Baca might have stayed on indefinitely, except that he once bounced the son of the Juarez police chief. Early the next morning Baca was out of work.

Baca returned to the practice of law in New Mexico, unwilling to retire to the rocking chair. For years he was a local fixture of controversial pride, an anachronism of another time, a colorful individual whose fires of life still flamed in his droll and witty stories. In the summer of 1945 New Mexico shook as a mushroom cloud ushered in the world's atomic age. A couple of months later the last of the old-time gunfighters died quietly at the age of eighty.

9

PRINT OLIVE

JUST PLAIN MEAN AS HELL

Isom PRENTICE OLIVE, better known as "Print" had ridden with the Texas Volunteers during the Civil War. When the fighting ended he returned to Williamson County, Texas, and the ranch of his father.

Thousands of Longhorn cattle prowled the back country, all of them wild and dangerous mavericks. Until an animal was branded it belonged to anyone who could throw a lariat over its horns and had the guts (and strength) to drag it out of the thickets.

Everything was open range, but in point of fact whoever owned or dominated the waterholes had an effective control of the surrounding land. Any stranger caught branding in that area could be considered a rustler, and the Olives hated rustlers.

Rod Murray turned out to be Print Olive's first rustler. The rancher shot Murray off his horse, then took him home and patched him up. Murray survived to go to work for Print.

Not so fortunate was rustler Dave Fream. He and Print shot it out from horseback and Fream lost. Even though Olive was wounded in the fracas, he went on trial for murder. A jury scoffed at the charge and set him free.

As Print Olive recovered from his wounds he took a trail herd toward Kansas. Homesteaders saw a potential source of income when

Print Olive . . . posted his land: All cattle and horse thieves PAY ATTENTION. Anyone caught riding an Olive horse or driving an Olive cow will be SHOT ON SIGHT.

these drives crossed their land, and they charged a suitable fee which sometimes amounted to robbery. Most of the cattle bosses paid up. Others claimed the fees amounted to graft, and tried to bluff or bully their way through. Print in particular had a black cowboy named James Kelly, better known as "Nigger Jim," or "Print's Bad Nigger." As a gunhand he had a few peers, and might have been as well-known as Billy the Kid or John Ringo if his skin had been white.

Olive would send Kelly out to bargain with the settlers, and as one cowboy recorded it:

"That big black boy with his gun would sure tell them punkin' rollers where to head in at. He'd roll up his eyes like a duck in a thunderstorm and grit his teeth — Lord, he could play a tune with his teeth. Most of the settlers were poor northern folks that never seen any colored people and was scared of them anyway. When they saw Kelly they would come down quick enough from $25 to $5 as the price for watering the herd."

In Ellsworth, Kansas, Kelly saved Print Olive's life when the rancher argued with a card sharp named Jim Kennedy. Before Olive could move from the table, Kennedy shot him through the hand, the groin and the thigh. Nigger Jim intervened by blowing sufficient holes in Kennedy to temporarily put him out of action.

As Olive had previously moved out on the cattle trail to facilitate the healing of his first wounds, he returned to Texas for recuperation. However, cowboys and farmers were still roping mavericks that the Olives had a prior claim to. "All cattle and horse thieves pay attention," one sign read. "Anyone caught riding an Olive horse or driving an Olive cow will be shot on sight."

Williamson County now entered a period of open warfare. Atrocity begot atrocity as the Olives and their neighbors hamstrung each others' horses and cut the tongues from prized cows. The Olives caught James H. Crow and Turk Turner butchering two mavericks, shot them dead and wrapped the bodies in green cowhide. To the Olives the overcoats were a fitting shroud.

This and other murders brought so much hostility to the Olive doorstep that the family took its Mexican *vaqueros* and black cowboys to Nebraska in April of 1877. Everyone would make a new start.

But in Texas, times were changing. With the nation just a year past the Battle of Little Big Horn, military posts were scattered everywhere across the plains and giving as much protection as possible to the numerous settlements. There arose a universal demand for beef, and many a disgruntled individual saw quicker profits in stealing cattle rather than breeding them. Once again the Olives posted their land: rustlers would be shot on sight.

All of the Olive brothers took their turn at guard duty, and one afternoon Bob topped a rise and discovered a herd of seventy-five cattle being penned and ready for slaughter. The young rancher asked for proof of ownership, and Ami Ketchum, who bossed the men taking the livestock, showed Bob a bill of sale bearing what appeared to be a forged Print Olive signature. Bob went to the sheriff, and the sheriff deputized him to make an arrest.

On November 26, 1878, Bob Olive and a three-man posse surrounded the Ketchum home and called for those inside to come out and surrender. Instant shooting started, and Luther Mitchell, a friend of Ketchum's, shot Olive through the lungs. The wounded man lived two days before drowning in his own blood.

One of Nebraska's biggest manhunts began, and Ketchum and Mitchell were soon caught in Loup City. A judge ordered them transferred to Custer town, but somewhere along the way the sheriff succumbed to threats or cash or both, and turned the prisoners over to Print Olive.

Seating the two men in a wagon, the Olive cowboys drove into the back country and paused under an elm tree with low-hanging branches. Rope went over the limbs, and nooses were roughly knotted around the trembling necks of Ketchum and Mitchell. Mitchell began to beg, and Print shot him with a rifle, the slug knocking him backwards. His boots kept him in the wagon, the rope prevented him from falling to the ground.

Olive turned to the driver and said "move it," and the wagon lurched forward. Except for the head and neck the bodies hit the ground, but *vaqueros* rectified this shortcoming by pulling the two men high into the air and snubbing the ropes off on the tree.

The two dead men hung there for awhile, then the bodies were burned, carried to a steep embankment and the side caved in. This might have been a permanent burial except an arm protruded up through the dirt. When discovered, the corpses were removed, taken to town, photographed and reburied.

Such callous killings split Nebraska down the middle. Some men said that Ketchum and Mitchell got what they deserved; other residents recoiled in horror at the grisly slayings.

Print Olive denied setting the bodies afire with coal oil (evidence suggests that a couple of drunken employees did it), but he nevertheless went on trial in Hastings, Nebraska. In a court scene filled with passion and threats, the governor feared a mob might take control. He requested federal help, and General George Crook sent 100 of Uncle Sam's finest to keep order.

So in an atmosphere of near hysteria, the jury found Print Olive guilty of second degree murder, and on April 17, 1879, sentenced him to life at hard labor in the Nebraska State Penitentiary. However, powerful friends worked in his behalf, and after twenty months of confinement he won a new trial and acquittal.

Print Olive returned but not as the same man. Legal expenses had nearly broken him. His father died. Half his livestock froze to death during a bitter winter. Nigger Jim drifted away, spending his declining years in Ansley, Nebraska, where he died in February, 1912.

Olive moved his family and holdings to Dodge City, Kansas where he established the Sawlog and Smokey Hill ranch operations. The Western Kansas Stockman's Association elected him a director. Gradually old Print was becoming respectable.

Only his oldest son Billy caused any trouble. The boy was a fiery offshoot of his old man in temperament and good looks. After killing a man in a drunken brawl, Billy fled to Indian Territory and became a bully and a rustler. One afternoon in Beaver City a couple of men ambushed him, and that ended his short career.

Meanwhile, Print Olive had co-signed a note for Joe Sparrow, a ne'er-do-well cowboy, businessman, braggart, part-time desperado whose life ended in Mexico in 1924. Joe paid the money back except for $10, and the bank forced Print to make good.

Olive threatened Sparrow and received several promises to pay, but never any money. Instead the young dead-beat brooded about the matter, then slipped into Trail City, Colorado, where he waited for Print to make one of his periodic trips to town.

Print Olive died on Monday, August 16, 1886. He stepped off the train in Trail City while discussing with enthusiasm some of his future plans. With a big smile he headed for his favorite saloon, and stepped through the swinging doors into the blazing gun of Joe Sparrow.

Aultman Collection

Dallas Stoudenmire . . . within three days of his arrival, El Paso would explode in a spasm of violence that would leave four men dead in practically as many seconds.

10

STOUDENMIRE

EL PASO MARSHAL

Few western towns rivaled the blood and fury of El Paso in its early days. It reached a peak of greatest violence in the 1880's and 1890's. Strangely enough its best known blood-letters, Dallas Stoudenmire, John Selman and John Wesley Hardin came to El Paso after it had supposedly become civilized.

El Paso was just another sleepy adobe village named for its neighbor, Paso del Norte (now Juarez), across the Rio Grande. In the early 1850's, only a scattering of ranches dotted the north bank of the river. Hart's Mill and rambling hacienda existed where the Hacienda Cafe is now. Benjamin Franklin Coons owned what is now downtown El Paso, an area called Coonsville, Franklin and El Paso among other things. Another settlement, Magoffinsville, was owned by James Wiley Magoffin. It squatted near the present vicinity of Piedras and Alameda streets. Hugh Stephenson owned a ranch where Concordia Cemetery is now.

Miles of sagebrush and mesquite separated these locations and Apache Indians stuck many an arrow in travelers going from one to the other. Between fifteen and twenty miles southeast were the big towns of Ysleta, Socorro and San Elizario, settlements separated by vast distances of frequently hostile environment. People traveled in groups, the men heavily armed.

Possibly the largest single identifying factor of early-day El Paso was the bosque, a thicket of jungle-like growth extending for miles up and down the river. The Rio Grande cut through a gorge near the site of the present smelter, splashed over a waterfall, bumped into a rather porous dam and meandered lazily in a series of widely looping bends beginning about where the Santa Fe Street bridge is today and continuing past Fabens.

It became a dense five-mile-wide thicket in some places, complete with cottonwoods, tall grasses, wild animals and narrow trails that led everywhere and nowhere. As a natural flyway, the Rio Grande attracted millions of duck and geese in annual migration. Often, the skies were so dense with fowl that trains in later years would stop to allow the passengers and crew to shoot game. It was a magnificent spectacle, the likes of which will never be seen again.

The bosque was considered cruel and treacherous. This region by the river, though it was the mother of life, took as well as it gave. Quicksand was always a terror. Even worse than the elements were the dregs of humanity hiding out in the swamps and thickets, outcasts of three cultures; Indian, Mexican and Anglo.

During the 1850's and 1860's, what is now known as El Paso began to exert itself. The town ended, or began if you will, a block or two south of present Paisano Drive and extended to about where the Plaza Theater is today, the latter area then known as the Plaza. The present San Jacinto Plaza was then the public square and ofttimes used as a dump for corral manure.

El Paso Street was the main thoroughfare, named not for being the center of town but because it led to Paso del Norte, now Juarez. Many called this street The Alameda, which in Spanish is a tree-lined boulevard. To get to Mexico, you left the end of the street, walked a quarter-mile through the thickets and waded the Rio Grande. If the water happened to be high, travelers jumped into a rowboat and pulled themselves across the river by means of a rope tied between cottonwood trees on opposite banks.

The village extended about two blocks on either side of El Paso Street, and communications with the outside world were by stage or wagon train. The houses were of mud (adobe), flat-roofed and one story. By the late 1870's a row of tents extended for several blocks east on San Antonio Street.

The Las Vegas, New Mexico *Optic* called El Paso the "jumping off place of creation, a country equal to the orthodox church belief in Hell." Any view closer than fifty or sixty miles away revealed "nothing but sand hills, the most barren waste imaginable with but a few mud houses and a scant supply of cottonwoods trying to relieve the oppressive monotony."

Basically the community had no law and except for a few instances did not need any. Only after progress arrived did the town get violent. There were occasional arrests and executions in Juarez. There was that one eye-popping incident at Socorro in 1851 when Boundary Commissioner John R. Bartlett's men tried, and then hanged several American teamsters from trees in front of the Socorro mission. Texas Ranger units in Ysleta, usually the county seat when San Elizario did not have the honor, did their best to keep Mexican bandits, outlaws and desperados across the river and out of El Paso County.

In 1881, El Paso, with its population of three or four hundred, awakened to a new sound: a train whistle. The railroad chugged in, not from the east as one might expect but, from the west, from San Francisco.

Overnight the little adobe crossroads astraddle the gateway to Mexico became a subject of interest to half the nation as railroads raced one another to be the first to arrive. Land speculators, businessmen, preachers, outlaws, fiddlefoots of every description and degree or lack of integrity headed for El Paso like maggots toward an open wound. In their wake came prosperity, an appalling degree of lawlessness, as the newcomers sought excitement.

Since Juarez had approximately 5000 citizens, ten times the population of El Paso, it was there that most of the established saloons and palaces of entertainment could be found.

One of the strangest episodes ever to happen on the border began on January 28, 1881. Several Americans identified as Frank Thompson, Frank O'Neal, J. C. Cain, Les Davis, Patrick Ryan, Frank Allen, Hugh Cox and Joe King, and two fellows nick-named Nibsy and the Lafayette Kid, headed across the river for some song, gambling and female companionship.

Before long the group met a thoroughly intoxicated Mexican with a lot of money on him. They took him for a little walk, helped themselves to some of his cash and went carousing. An hour later, they stumbled across their same rich amigo again who was still on a spending spree. Everybody went for another walk.

Incredible as it seems, the same incident happened a third time. The chagrined Americans grabbed the Mexican under the arms, dragged him a half-mile out into the desert, stripped him and made certain he had no more money. This time they pushed their luck too far.

Their victim returned to the center of town, sober and shivering and headed straight for the military commander (soldiers policed Juarez at the time) and told his story. A dragnet quickly went out. Every American, guilty or innocent, was hauled into custody.

Meanwhile, over in El Paso, a rumble of outrage arose. The Mexican authorities assured Charles C. Richardson, the American Consul in Juarez, that speedy trials would begin within the week. Nothing happened. The Americans began planning a jailbreak.

They were aware of the Mexican practice of allowing wives and sweethearts to visit loved ones in jail. On February 18, a visiting day, several Mexican lady-friends of the captives walked through the prison gates with loaded revolvers hidden inside their colorful blouses and voluminous skirts. The guards had not bothered to search the women who simply handed over the guns to the Americans.

As the girls departed, Frank Thompson made his move, following them to the prison gates. Before the gates swung shut, he pushed his way through and started shooting. Down went the captain and one guard. He clubbed another guard unconscious. The other Americans hesitated.

Pat Ryan cautiously stepped outside and ran a few doors down the street into a bar. Soldiers rearrested him as he downed a drink. The Lafayette Kid charged out of the prison, promptly stumbled over an obstruction and rolled into a ditch. He lost his nerve and just remained there until the soldiers came to get him.

Frank O'Neal and J. C. Cain joined Thompson in a flight for freedom. They headed for the river less than a mile and a half away. They didn't make it. A Mexican cowboy, eating lunch when the break occurred, jumped on his horse and caught up with the escapees as they struggled across the *acequia* (irrigation ditch). Slipping and falling in the cold, murky water, the fleeing men snapped shots at their relentless pursuer. They didn't stand a chance against the vaquero's rifle and all three fugitives sank beneath the surface and drowned.

Their bodies were recovered and dragged by burros through downtown Juarez in a victory parade. Then, instead of sending the bodies back to El Paso, the Mexicans demanded $75 for each corpse. When the money could not be raised, the cadavers were rolled into a ditch and covered with dirt.

Three months later, in a sequel to the event, Ryan, Davis and Allen broke out of the Mexican jail again. This time, they made it to the United States side without incident. In September, Hugh Cox obtained a medical certificate and was released. However, all of this did not end the story.

A very tough crowd in El Paso growled angrily about the shootings. They identified the Mexican vaquero and marked him for death. The story continued to unfold like a tragic opera, setting the stage for one of the most complex gunslingers in western history. Dallas Stoudenmire had arrived in El Paso.

Law and order in El Paso

Law and order did not come easy to El Paso. For awhile it really wasn't needed, and neither were politicians. El Paso existed from its literal beginning in 1827 as a solitary goat herder's shack, through the early 1870's with practically no form of civil government except for a few state and federal employees.

In 1873 the community incorporated. The people elected themselves a mayor and aldermen, who in turn appointed a town marshal. Unfortunately, almost no civil and criminal records have survived that period. Either that, or no records to speak of were produced. The lackadaisical officials rarely even attended council meetings, and by 1876 the city government had finally slumbered its way out of business.

When the railroads rumbled toward El Paso in the 1880's, the town suddenly realized it was going to be a "big time" community, and if it wanted the rest of the world to recognize that fact, it had better show a little more responsibility, to say nothing of energy.

So on July 3, 1880, new elections took place. Solomon Schutz took office as mayor, and with him were six aldermen. As its first official act the town council appointed a city marshal, a position eventually to be known as the chief of police.

John B. Tays accepted the job, but regrettably Mr. Tays had some stigmas on his record. He had been the only Texas Ranger commander in history to surrender his forces, that unhappy incident occurring during the El Paso Salt War of two years earlier.

In those days one of the marshal's duties was to keep the streets in good repair. Tays and John Woods, deputy marshal and former blacksmith, would chain the jail prisoners and put them to work. Much of the time there was little to do, but when it rained, and the boulders tumbled down from the mountains and the waters washed huge potholes in the sand and caliche streets, then there was plenty of work.

Sometimes when jail labor was scarce, or when the lawmen had other chores for them to do, street maintenance tended to suffer. One particular hole on San Francisco Street caused part of a stage to disappear when it rocketed by, and the marshal tried to patch the hole with trash. The city was unimpressed by this bit of engineering, and the council ordered the police officers to clean the mess up at their own expense. Tays and Woods were dismissed in early September.

A. I. Stevens, a middle-aged wagon and carriage maker, became city marshal next. To assist him the council hired Bill Johnson, the town drunk.

Stevens also accepted the job of city tax assessor and collector, a mistake on everyone's part. On November 26 the council dismissed him too, the surviving records giving only a laconic "neglect and dereliction of duty" as an excuse. No one published details.

Kentuckian George Campbell now pinned on the badge. No one knew much about George. Allegedly he had served as a deputy sheriff in Young County, Texas. Around town most folks considered him a friendly fellow, although he hung out with a pretty tough bunch. He did retain Bill Johnson.

In those days a lot of city marshals around the West worked on a commission basis. The marshal drew a percentage of the fine levied against drunks and others who disturbed the peace. Usually the mayor presided over the Recorder's Court and most of the judgments handed down were the three dollar garden variety fines. The judge kept a dollar as his share, the marshal kept a dollar, and the city took a dollar. As might be expected, not many people were found innocent.

Of course when the marshal tangled with a really tough customer, that was something else again. Murderers and robbers couldn't be fined and turned loose. Therefore, the really dangerous tasks did not pay any money at all to the marshal.

Campbell grumbled against the system and asked repeatedly for a regular salary. As things were, he had to arrest his friends in order to make a living.

The council flatly refused to pay any salary at all, claiming they did not have a tax base for such expenditures. In this respect they were right. However, they did have cash in the treasury, and they collected it through an ingenious system of fees: fights between bears and dogs, mountain lions and dogs (of which there were no small number performed in the El Paso saloons) cost the producers $250 for each performance. Fortune tellers paid $100; occultists $25. Traveling physicians who used magnets and electrical, battery operated coils to "cure" arthritis paid from $25 to $50. The list went on and on.

Frankly, the fees were piddling amounts trickling into the city treasury. The prostitutes actually kept the city in business and enabled it to pay its own way. The girls were fined (actually licensed) $10 a month, and forbidden to appear outside of the "Tenderloin District," which took up about half the town (Oregon Street, South El Paso, San Antonio and Mesa).

Simeon Newman, the eloquent, fire-eating editor of the El Paso *Lone Star* newspaper, constantly railed at the girls. "A few days ago we saw a carriage loaded down with three or four of them, plus men, all drunk. A day or so later we saw another on the platform of a streetcar smoking a cigar and talking with the driver in foul language. The law ought to be rigidly enforced against such people until they are cured of flaunting their sin in the respectable portion of the community."

For thunder against sin, it was simply hard to beat the virtuous pen of Simeon Newman. His *Lone Star* fought vice so continuously and so relentlessly that the criminal element finally warned local merchants to either quit advertising in the newspaper or face a boycott. The *Lone Star* couldn't survive, and it folded, saying, "Every gambler, pimp and prostitute will celebrate our closing."

Nevertheless, in spite of these monies Campbell did not get his monthly salary, and he vowed angrily to make the city council reconsider its actions. He got his friends together and on January 1, 1881, they literally shot up El Paso at about 2 o'clock in the morning. The mob blew holes in alderman Joseph Magoffin's home, the door of alderman Krakauer's house was knocked sagging with numerous bullet punctures. The home of Mayor Schutz took punishment.

Campbell anticipated that the mayor and council would come to him and promise anything, even a monthly salary, for his influence to stop the riot. Instead the mayor and council huddled in a darkened building, and after a hurried consultation sent a rider to Ysleta for the Texas Rangers.

The next day Sergeant James Gillett, Corporal Lloyd and a detail of four men rode into the town. In less than an hour they restored order. Alderman Joseph Magoffin swore out a warrant against Marshal Campbell and charged him with assault to commit murder. The marshal fled to the ranch of John Hale, located in the thickets about where Canutillo is today.

With the situation under control, Gillett, Lloyd and two men from the detail returned to Ysleta. Left behind were two rangers to patrol the town, men who were friends of and sympathetic to George Campbell. The marshal returned to El Paso, shook hands with the rangers, and drunkenly rode up and down El Paso Street while firing his revolver in the air.

Next, the rangers snickered and showed Campbell the warrant for his arrest. George laughed, spat on the paper, scribbled some obscenities across it, and then rode around Magoffin's house screaming for the alderman to come out and fight like a man. The door never opened.

When Captain George R. Baylor, commander of the Texas Ranger detachment at Ysleta, heard what happened, he was furious. He stormed into El Paso and fired both rangers on the spot. That calmed things down again, and gave everyone an opportunity to rethink his position. Campbell came into the town and resigned his office while the mayor and aldermen dropped charges. The council did not want to make him mad.

On January 16 Ed Copeland was sworn in as city marshal. As proprietor of the Occidental Saloon, he had lots of experience with

94

law breakers. He also kept Bill Johnson as deputy.

A $50 monthly salary now went with the job ($40 for the deputy), and both officers could continue collecting a share of the court fines. However, the council also wrote into the ordinance for appointing the marshal a stipulation that he furnish a performance bond of $500. Ed had never even seen $500, so he was out of a job before he even got started.

While bleary-eyed Bill Johnson took over the temporary position as city marshal, the council began looking around for a hired-gun to keep the town under control. They wanted a stranger, someone with no ties to the community, a man who would kill with less emotion than it took to bite off the end of a cigar.

Over in East Texas, Dallas Stoudenmire heard the news, and he came on the run.

Dallas Stoudenmire stood about six-foot-four, had dark brown hair and green eyes. He was born in Macon County, Alabama, in 1845, and after enlisting three times in the Confederate Army (the military kept discharging him because of his age), he came West at war's end. In the vicinity of Columbus, Texas, he built a reputation as a gunman.

The city hired Stoudenmire almost as soon as he jumped off the stage. Meanwhile Campbell almost pouted at the Hale Ranch, making ugly threats against the council and whoever might replace him as marshal. Then there was the matter of that jail break in Juarez with its disastrous results. Various El Paso factions were already positioning themselves for revenge. Nobody knew it yet but within three days El Paso would explode in a spasm of violence that would leave four men dead in practically as many seconds.

But as of now, Stoudenmire had a job. He found Bill Johnson at the corner of El Paso and San Antonio Streets, told him he was fired, and asked for the keys to the jail. When Johnson took his time about extracting them from his pocket, Stoudenmire shook him, practically turned him upside down, and walked away with the keys.

From that moment on the friends of Bill Johnson did not let him forget what the new marshal had done to his pride. They plied Johnson with whiskey, and never let him draw another sober breath for as long as he lived — which was to be one more week. Then he would try to assassinate Stoudenmire, and would himself be shot dead on the city streets.

95

Blood in El Paso

Many elements made up the tough factions around the small but bustling village of El Paso in early 1881.

In addition to Dallas Stoudenmire, there was his brother-in-law Doc Cummings. According to the newspapers he was a big man, but whether that meant tall, heavy, or both, nobody knows. His birthplace and age are unknown, and the nickname of Doc seems to be a misnomer. No known evidence exists that he ever practiced medicine, dentistry or veterinary medicine.

Doc married Stoudenmire's sister in Columbus, Texas, farmed in the Panhandle, and then caught the stage to El Paso with George Washington Carrico, co-founder and first editor of the El Paso *Times*. Carrico had never been to El Paso either. Cummings and Carrico arrived on Christmas Eve, 1880, and there was no room at the inn (the Central Hotel where the Plaza Theatre stands today). Carrico raged that he spent his first night in El Paso sleeping on the hotel gambling table. His only cover was a copy of the *Police Gazette* and the management charged fifty cents for that.

Cummings opened the best restaurant in El Paso and called it the Globe since the food was imported from all over the world. The establishment opened its doors practically across El Paso Street from the present-day Paso del Norte Hotel, and the advertisements boasted "no dust, no noise, no flies." In old El Paso that was quite an accomplishment.

The Manning brothers, Doc, Frank and James were another strong and controversial element in El Paso. Doc practiced medicine, played the violin and was generally well thought of by the community. Folks described him as a small man, lean and lithe, possessing a temper as sharp as his scalpel.

With the Southern Pacific blasting its way in from the west, moving each day a few miles closer to town, Frank Manning opened a "floating saloon" at the railhead, it being little more than a ragged tent and a portable bar, both easily transported to other locations. Each day the train would steam to the end of the tracks, unload its passengers, and then retreat. The new residents would get soused at Frank's bar as they waited on the coaches, lumber wagons, and other odds and ends of vehicles to come out from El Paso and take them into town.

After the railroad arrived, Frank opened the Manning Saloon at the site of the present-day Paso del Norte Hotel.

James Manning, who contributed money to help start the El Paso *Times,* and who also once ran for mayor and was defeated, opened the Coliseum Saloon and Variety Theatre on the west side of El Paso Street at the intersection of First. According to publicity the enterprise had a "seating capacity of 1,500, a stage thirty by forty feet, and carpeted private boxes with elegant lace curtains."

It would be nice to separate everybody; Stoudenmire, the Mannings, the politicians, the Texas Rangers, the businessmen, into white and black hat types, but in truth they were all various shades of gray. They drank heavily, they caroused, they hated each other with bitter passions; and each believed in the utter righteousness of his cause. In the game of life they wrote their own rule books, but when it came time to check out, none of them ever whimpered.

Meanwhile, the vaquero who shot the three escapees from the Juarez prison, visited Colonel Baylor in Ysleta and asked the Texas Rangers to help him find stolen cattle believed hidden in the bosques near present-day Canutillo and Anthony.

Several rangers searched the area, found nothing, and returned to Ysleta. However, the Mexican still wasn't satisfied, so he and a companion continued to look around. As they paused under a tree to eat and smoke, Chris Peveler, an ex-ranger, and Frank Stephenson, a hog rustler, ambushed and killed them.

The news quickly circulated that two bodies lay in the upper valley bosque, and on the morning of April 14, 1881 seventy-five armed Mexicans rode into El Paso, all muttering threats of vengeance. They asked Gus Krempkau, former Texas Ranger and now city constable, to assist in finding and recovering the corpses.

At 11 o'clock that morning the murder victims were found and loaded into buckboards for the jolting ride into town. As the angry and threatening procession rumbled down El Paso Street, it stopped in front of Judge Buckler's office. The judge took a quick look at the bullet-riddled bodies and agreed to an inquest.

Everyone knew the two slayers' identities, but neither Peveler nor Stevenson could be found. John Hale came in from his ranch to defend them, claiming that he had witnessed the whole affair and Peveler and Stevenson shot in self-defense. Ex-city marshal George Campbell backed up Hale's story.

Everyone went inside Buckler's office for the inquest. Gus Krempkau did the translating, and most Anglos thought he favored the Mexicans. Only the judge's foresight prevented a bloodbath. He wisely insisted that all parties check their guns next door in Paul Keating's Saloon.

The whole discussion became a standoff, and the meeting broke up, the inquest dismissed. Both dead bodies were taken back to Mexico, and their armed comrades went with them. The crowds on El Paso Street dispersed or broke into small groups. Stoudenmire, on the job for three days, strolled over to the Globe Restaurant for a bite to eat.

Behind him Gus Krempkau took his licks. With his rifle under his arm and six-shooter in its holster, he left Keating's Saloon and started to mount up. George Campbell, very drunk, snarled, "Any American that is a friend of Mexicans ought to be hanged."

Krempkau, half astraddle his mule, reddened and stepped down. "George, I hope you don't mean me," he said.

"If the shoe fits, wear it," Campbell hooted. The two men exchanged harsh words about the quality of Krempkau's interpretations, then Campbell turned and stomped away, reaching for a tree limb and the reins of his own mule.

At the same instant, John Hale, who had also been drinking heavily, jumped up from a window seat and screamed, "I got him, George."

He fired, and the bullet hit Krempkau under the heart and knocked him down.

From up the street Dallas Stoudenmire heard the shot and came running. In his hip pockets (he did not wear holsters) were two guns. One he called his "belly gun," used for ramming into an opponent's belly and pulling the trigger; the other was a "long distance" weapon, accurate across a wide street.

Stoudenmire saw Hale with a smoking pistol in his hand, paused and aimed his long-barreled gun, squeezed the trigger like any practiced and experienced professional and killed an innocent bystander.

Undaunted, because things like that could happen to anyone, he aimed at Hale again, now taking cover behind a roof pillar. This time he lived up to his own accuracy expectations. When Hale peeked his head out to see where everybody was, a bullet hit him in the forehead.

With the initial excitement and killing over, an incredible sequel took place. Campbell backed into the street, pulled his pistol and, swinging it from side to side, yelled, "This is not my fight!"

As he did so, Gus Krempkau, only seconds away from death and thinking Campbell shot him, pulled his own weapon and shot Campbell in the foot and gun hand. The ex-marshal screamed and dropped his weapon, then scooped it up with his left hand. When he got it off the ground, Stoudenmire shot him in the stomach. And so in less than half a minute's time, four men lay sprawled in death on El Paso Street.

With the exception of Hale, the other bodies were undoubtedly buried either where the downtown Popular Dry Goods store is now, or where the El Paso Public Library is located, as both sites were former cemeteries.

Hale was taken back to his Canutillo ranch, but nobody could find a casket large enough to hold him. (Caskets were very scarce commodities to come by in the early days.) Since he was as tall as Stoudenmire, the task was especially difficult. Finally the undertaker simply stuffed him in an available box, propped his knees up with pillows, and buried him near where the smelter is located. His remains were later transferred to Concordia, and no doubt a house in that vicinity is presently holding him down. (In the 1880's bodies were buried all over the area in what is now the Concordia Cemetery site.)

John's ranch passed to his wife and the property became known as the Rancho Angelita. After her death the land was sold, parcelled out in bits and pieces. Today the Hale descendants live in respectable but modest circumstances in the same area. The land they once prized is a part of the El Paso Country Club district.

Since Campbell and Hale were friends of the Mannings, the brothers hated Stoudenmire for the killings. Even the rangers were upset about the death of Campbell, and several of them openly said that the marshal had no just reason for shooting him.

At any rate, back at the saloon—any saloon—former assistant marshal Bill Johnson brooded about losing his job to Stoudenmire. The Mannings inflamed his resentment, and gave him lots of free liquor.

Three days later on Sunday, April 17, as Marshal Stoudenmire and his brother-in-law Doc Cummings began their rounds (Cummings merely tagged along), they approached the intersection of El Paso and San Antonio streets. On the northeast corner lay a pile of bricks, construction material for the State National Bank. After dark Johnson stationed himself on the bricks, in one hand a double-barreled shotgun and in the other a bottle of whiskey.

Soon Stoudenmire and Cummings came up the street. Johnson heard them talking, saw their shadowy forms. He waited until they were close, stood up, aimed the shotgun, pulled both triggers at once, and missed. Stoudenmire and Cummings instantly shot him to pieces.

Across El Paso Street other potential assassins awaited. They began shooting, and a ricocheting bullet hit Stoudenmire in the heel. Nevertheless, he charged directly into the ambushers and put them to flight.

Cummings promptly organized a vigilante committee, the only one known to ever operate in El Paso. It held together for ten or twelve days, met numerous times, but disbanded without killing anyone.

Bill Johnson made his last trip to the graveyard north of the tracks. Years later when the area was being cleared for development, his old drinking buddies wanted to see how he was doing. They pried off the casket lid, and there lay Bill, looking in many respects better than those staring down at him. Then the body crumbled into dust.

Stoudenmire took refuge in the Texas Ranger camp at Ysleta to recover from his wounded heel. (Cursing did not seem to help the healing process.) When he returned a week or so later, the town split down the middle in his support. About half hated him, and the rest feared him. Everyone expected another round of violence, and it wasn't long in coming.

The death of Doc Cummings

El Paso's continuing penchant for violence could not be denied, for the Mannings and Doc Cummings seemed determined to shed each other's blood.

After the Civil War, George, James and Frank Manning came out of the Mobile, Alabama area and settled somewhere around Belton, Texas. George, a physician, married there, Frank never married anyone at all, and James found an attractive belle over in Paso del Norte in 1880. Together the Mannings raised many fine children, and their descendants are still scattered throughout the Southwest and Mexico.

The Mannings were an intriguing family group, leaders of much that was good and fine in El Paso; and at the same time dominating the gambling and liquor interests.

Samuel M. "Doc" Cummings was born in the Carolinas or Alabama, but the place as well as his date of birth is obscure. In 1874 Doc married Dallas Stoudenmire's sister, and moved to the Panhandle, where he farmed and engaged in politics, and then drifted to San Marcial, New Mexico, where he ran a hotel. By 1881 he, his wife and a small daughter had opened the Globe Restaurant on El Paso Street, two doors south of the San Antonio intersection.

Stoudenmire and Cummings were similar men. Both were heavy drinkers, quick to fight, explosive and quarrelsome in temperament, and possessing deep feelings of right and wrong. They were slow to forgive, and each was fiercely, intensely loyal to the other.

Doc fed the jail prisoners, which for the first few months of Stoudenmire's administration meant taking food to a vacant adobe room, an enclosure the El Paso *Times* editorialized could be escaped from in less than two hours if the prisoners had a jackknife.

Therefore the city ordered two iron cells from a Chicago firm at a cost of $900 each. Specifications for the cells definitely indicated the city had no interest in coddling its prisoners. The "cages", as the newspapers called them, were a harsh place to live.

Inside these cages, shouting, cursing, threatening and just lying in a stupor were murderers, drunks, common criminals and the insane. It sounds cruel, and it unquestionably was, but prison enlightenment in those days was an unheard of idea.

Cummings enjoyed his association with the jail and with his brother-in-law, the town marshal. As an unofficial arm of the law, he made occasional arrests and liked to think of himself as the town's police force during Stoudenmire's absences. In early February, 1882, a Kansas sheriff rode into El Paso on the trail of a rapist fleeing south into Chihuahua. Stoudenmire deputized Cummings to assist the sheriff.

The two men crossed the Rio Grande into Mexico, their exact destination and the eventual outcome of their quest unknown. A week or ten days later they were back in El Paso. The sheriff headed home.

Cummings returned to a town with practically no law enforcement. Stoudenmire and his chief deputy James Gillett had taken ill with influenza. Dallas recovered first, and went to Columbus, Texas, to marry. With Gillett still in bed, Cummings became El Paso's top lawman. He would do Stoudenmire a favor and clean out those damn Mannings before the marshal returned.

At about six o'clock on the evening of February 14, Cummings had his customary snoot-full. He walked down El Paso Street from the Globe Restaurant to the Coliseum Saloon and Variety Theatre. The events from then on, as noted at a coroner's inquest, went like this: Cummings asked Jim Manning to drink with him, and Manning refused, saying that as a reformed alcoholic he had been off the bottle for a year. He offered to sip some cider.

Doc sat silent for a few minutes, then brought up the subject of last year's shootout when four men were killed. He accused Manning of sicking George Campbell and John Hale onto Dallas Stoudenmire, and he charged the Manning brothers with inciting drunken Bill Johnson's shotgun attack upon the marshal. Jim denied any complicity, and Cummings cursed him as a liar.

"I can't forget all that," Doc said. "Are you fixed?"

Manning removed his coat and hat, draping them across a soda case near the bar. "Doc, what is the use of your forcing me to fight? Why can't we settle this in a peaceful manner?"

"Turn yourself loose, I am ready," growled Cummings.

"I will get on my knees," Jim pleaded. "I will do anything to settle this in a quiet way."

Cummings cursed Manning as a coward, and told him that if he couldn't fight like a man, to put his coat back on. He turned to bartender David King, and with a string of profanities ordered him to keep his hands above the bar.

"You don't have to involve him," Jim said. "He has no gun behind the bar, and besides, I do not hire men to do my fighting."

"If a man worked in the Globe, and he would not fight for me, I would kick his goddamn ass," Doc replied. "Let's go outside."

The two men stepped out onto El Paso Street where they resumed their quarreling. A bystander, hearing angry voices in the evening dusk, came over to see what was going on. He had been drinking, and when he inserted his red nose where it did not belong, Doc pushed on it with a six-shooter and threatened to kill him. After resolving that brief interruption, Cummings turned once again to James Manning, and saw that Jim had disappeared back inside.

A tight-lipped Cummings angrily came back through the bat-wing doors, sat down once more at the bar, and again demanded that Manning drink with him. Manning still refused, and King tried to verbally support him.

Doc had all the recent interruptions he could stand. In a voice breaking with fury he told King to shut up and to keep his hands in plain sight. The bartender protested he had no hidden weapon, and offered to bet $50 that no gun could be found under the bar.

As Doc and David King quibbled about the possibility of a concealed weapon, Manning ordered the barkeep to leave the room as the quarrel was not his. King refused to go, saying he would not be frightened off by threats.

Manning slid off his bar stool and stepped back into the hallway where he removed his coat and checked his revolver. Seconds later he reappeared. "All right, Doc. We will have this out," he snapped.

Cummings, in the act of taking a drink went for his gun a little late. Pistols cracked inside the room, and the acrid smoke blinded everyone, witnesses and participants.

Two bullets struck Cummings. He reeled across the room, stumbled through the doors, and fell on El Paso Street. Rolling over on his back, in death he emitted a piercing, anguished groan, and the street was silent except for running footsteps.

Frank Manning heard the shooting and came quickly. He found Doc lying in the street, removed his weapon, and went inside the saloon. A couple of part-time deputies were asking questions. Jim surrendered his six-shooter to them, saying in a dazed voice, "I stood this thing as long as I could. I could stand it no longer."

Witnesses testified that Doc fired twice. However, his revolver, as submitted by Frank Manning, had empty chambers on opposite sides of the cylinder, a strange discrepancy not investigated by the inquest jury.

As for James Manning, he admitted shooting Doc Cummings two times. Yet his pistol had but one fired cartridge, another equally strange discrepancy no one bothered to investigate.

An autopsy revealed that either bullet would have been fatal, but the medical findings also turned up the fact of a fractured skull. Dr. J. A. McKinney stated under oath that the fracture came about by being struck over the head with an object, probably a revolver barrel, and it did not come about by Doc's falling in the street. This revelation, too, received no further investigation.

Findings of the coroners jury were not preserved, but it seems evident that Manning was acquitted on the grounds of self-defense. It seems equally evident, although the jury did not say so, that David King fired one of the death bullets, and in all probability struck Cummings over the head.

No further investigations took place because they did not seem useful. Regardless of who killed Doc, and the exact manner of his death, he brought it all on himself. Cummings had started the argument, and his life had been extinguished not so much by Manning and possibly King, as by his own hatreds, pugnacious temper and hard whiskey.

The Masons gave Doc a send-off in a small cemetery north of town. Meanwhile the whole community settled down to await the return of Dallas Stoudenmire.

Death of a marshal

Dallas Stoudenmire married Miss Isabella Sherrington at Columbus, Texas, in February of 1882. Although we know nothing about his bride, we do know that the marriage failed to calm his disposition, antagonisms fueled more and more by large consumptions of alcohol.

He disliked the Texas Rangers, accused them of being "untrustworthy and unreliable," saying they were more ready "to aggravate than to preserve the public peace," and they "took sides with the lawless rather than the law abiding portion of the town." He charged the rangers with riding into the village, getting drunk, and then shooting wildly in the streets as they rode back to camp.

The marshal also had a low opinion of ranger courage, saying they "ran most ingloriously when called to the scratch," and could be classified as "a bunch of thirty-dollar a month sons of bitches who would not fight."

This infuriated C. L. Hathaway, a red headed youthful ranger.

As a romantic, influenced by blood-and-thunder dime novels, Hathaway wore two long-barreled .45's low on his hip. The other rangers snickered and teased him unmercifully about all that hardware, but the good-natured boy took it all in stride.

One afternoon he rode into El Paso, caught the marshal out on the street in a sober condition, and snapped, "I understand you remarked that no Texas Ranger, thirty-dollar a month son of a bitch would fight. Well I am a ranger, I am not a thirty-dollar a month son of a bitch, and I will fight."

Stoudenmire looked down at Hathaway, suppressed a grin and apologized. "The Texas Rangers as a body of men are gentlemen," he said. The statement satisfied Hathaway, and he rode back to Ysleta and became the hero of the camp.

On other occasions, such confrontations turned out differently. While in a foul mood, Stoudenmire accosted Ranger Frank Beaumont in the street, and said, "Stop right there, Beaumont. I want to tell you what I think of you." And for what seemed like an eternity Stoudenmire cursed and abused Beaumont before finally turning into the Alamo Saloon.

Frank brooded about the chewing-out until he could stand the humiliation no longer, so he asked Frank Manning for the loan of a shotgun. After positioning himself on a barrel across the street from the saloon, Beaumont waited and waited, but Stoudenmire never came through the door. When darkness came, Beaumont began thinking more calmly and rationally, and he went home.

He learned later that Stoudenmire, upon entering the saloon, bellied up to the bar and drank himself unconscious. No one had the nerve to arouse him from his drunken slumber on the floor, so the town marshal, the fearless brawler and winner of many gunfights, slept there with his head beside the spittoon all afternoon and part of the evening.

As time went on, Stoudenmire nursed his hatred toward the Mannings. He suspected the brothers of plotting several recent attempts on his life, but couldn't prove it. And so he taunted the Mannings, daring them to fight him. A couple of times when he was in his cups, he set up targets on El Paso Street where he had killed Campbell, Hale and the innocent bystander. For those unfortunate enough to have missed his first performance, he drunkenly reenacted the shootings all over again.

Because of the feud, newspapers began printing law and order editorials. The El Paso *Lone Star* cried that the citizens stood on a volcano, that the streets could be "deluged with blood at any moment. Violence if allowed to break forth can only have the effect of paralyzing business and driving people from the city. Now is not the time to discuss the right or wrong of past issues."

Community leaders approached both factions. After three weeks of negotiations, the Manning brothers and Stoudenmire signed a peace treaty on April 16. The El Paso *Herald* printed a verbatim copy:

"We the undersigned parties having this day settled all differences and unfriendly feelings existing between us, hereby agree that we will hereafter meet and pass each other on friendly terms, and that bygones shall be bygones, and that we shall never allude in the future to any past animosities that have existed between us."

While the treaty quieted things down on the Stoudenmire-Manning fighting front, at least temporarily, it did nothing about reducing the marshal's heavy drinking and general belligerency. He even antagonized the religious folk by using the St. Clements church bell for target practice.

Politicians feared him, and they went to all kinds of extremes to tactfully ask him to curb his drinking. For instance, the council passed an ordinance making it illegal for "any" officer of the city to be guilty of drunkenness. Then, feeling wonderful over all this sin they had just abolished, the aldermen went a little further and made it unlawful for a male citizen to carry a gun, fight, drink, gamble, swear, disturb the peace, expose himself indecently, or "be seen in the company of a prostitute not his wife or some other relative."

None of these ordinances improved Stoudenmire's behavior. He got behind in his accounts (fine and fee money due the city), and the newspapers hinted that part of these funds financed the marshal's frequent bouts with the demons. George Washington Carrico, the El Paso *Times* editor, made some broad suggestions that Stoudenmire should go. Dallas stormed into his office and threatened to run him out of town.

The El Paso *Lone Star* printed an editorial calling upon the council to do its duty, "to make a proper investigation, to do it with open doors, and then remove or reinstate the marshal. If he has not done his duty, or if his continuance in office is a threat to the city, he ought to be removed. Public policy dictates that, even if a man be a good peace officer, if he be obnoxious in the community, or if his continuance in office is liable to provoke serious trouble, perhaps even a riot, he ought to be replaced. Let the city act only from a high sense of duty and quit dilly-dallying."

Stoudenmire's days were thereby numbered. On May 27, 1882, the council met to ask for his resignation. For good and sufficient reasons, the aldermen chose not to sit at the usual table for conducting business. Instead they opened the tall windows and sat in the sills, supposedly to catch the cool evening breezes, but in reality to position themselves for a quick escape should the marshal become violent.

Alderman Noah Flood placed a shotgun outside the window where he sat, and Alderman Phillips did not even attend. Since Stoudenmire had threatened to shoot him on sight, his absence was perhaps not strange.

When Stoudenmire appeared, he opened the meeting by going from window to window and staring each of the trembling figures in the eye. Finally he paused and snorted that he could not only straddle the mayor (Joseph Magoffin), but he could "straddle every goddamn alderman present too." He punctuated his profanities by occasionally removing his six-shooters and twirling them on his fingers. Magoffin coughed and adjourned the meeting without ever bringing it to order.

During the weekend Stoudenmire sobered up and rethought his position. Obviously he had to go, and he knew it. So on May 29, the following Monday, he wrote out his resignation, commenting that while he had suffered injustices from several of the politicians, he still wanted to apologize for his conduct at the last council meeting. He meant no disrespect.

The city fathers applauded his decision, passed several resolutions regarding his "loyal and faithful service" and moved on to other business. Alderman Ben Schuster nominated James B. Gillett, Stoudenmire's deputy, for the city marshal position. The council unanimously accepted the recommendation.

Stoudenmire should have left town. Instead, on July 13 he became a United States deputy marshal with headquarters in El Paso.

For the next couple of months El Paso stayed relatively quiet. Then on Sunday night, September 17, the Southern Pacific poured Stoudenmire off the train at the depot, and he staggered down to the Acme

Saloon. He asked C. C. Brooks, the bartender, to go see some girls with him.

Brooks refused, so Stoudenmire walked to the Manning Saloon, cracked open the door and peeked inside. He carried a warrant in his shirt pocket for a wanted man he thought might be there. Satisfied the man was not present, Dallas went into the red-light district to visit a working girl named Carrie. History does not record whether or not he went home that night. He later said he had plenty of sleep.

He awoke with a hangover the next morning, and after appearing on the streets, he heard the astonishing news that the Mannings were armed and looking for him. Someone had told them of Stoudenmire's visit to their establishment last night, and everyone had assumed that Dallas was looking for the brothers, not the wanted man.

As the city tensed for the expected bloodshed, peace emissaries moved back and forth between the two factions. Stoudenmire said he did not want to fight, but if he had to he would take the Mannings on one at a time or all at once. Doc and James expressed a similar reticence; Frank lamented that since he wasn't married, if he were killed there would be no one to regret his passing. So all in all it appeared the misunderstanding could be patched up.

At 5:30 in the afternoon on September 18, 1882, all agreed to meet in the Manning Saloon, have a drink together and sign another peace treaty.

As Stoudenmire stepped inside, only Jim and Doc Manning were present. "Where's Frank?" Dallas asked. Jim said he would go find him.

This left only Doc and Dallas, plus a few bystanders, and Stoudenmire called on Manning to have a drink. Doc left the billiard table and went to the bar as Stoudenmire said something to the effect that a lot of people were trying to cause trouble.

Doc snapped that Stoudenmire had not kept his part of the agreement, meaning the first peace treaty. "Whoever says that is a liar!" Dallas roared. Both men reached for their guns.

A bystander stepped between the two men and pushed them apart, a brave act on his part, but one which might have caused Stoudenmire's death. Off balance, he drew last. Doc's first bullet smashed into Stoudenmire's left arm, causing him to drop his weapon, severing an artery, and ricocheting into his chest.

Doc fired again. This time the bullet hit Stoudenmire squarely in the shirt pocket, where it lodged in some papers and a picture he carried. (One of those papers was the warrant he carried which started all the trouble.) The impact, even though the slug never broke the skin, still knocked the ex-city marshal through the bat-wing doors and out onto El Paso Street.

Outside on the sidewalk, Stoudenmire (who was left-handed), got out his other pistol with his right hand, and fired as Doc came through the door after him. His wild bullet struck Manning in the gun arm, causing the weapon to fly out into the street.

With Doc Manning now unarmed, Stoudenmire might have killed him had he himself not been so badly shot up. As he struggled to re-cock the pistol, Doc rushed him, pinned his arms to his side, and the two men wrestled along the sidewalk.

When Jim Manning heard the shooting he came running back in time to see the two men locked in a death embrace, grunting and swearing, Stoudenmire trying to shake the little doctor loose and kill him, the doctor struggling desperately to hang on and survive until help came.

The only weapon Jim had was a sawed off Colt with a missing trigger. He thumbed the hammer, aimed, fired and missed, the slug shattering a barber pole. He stepped closer, aimed and fired again. The bullet hit Stoudenmire an inch above and slightly to the rear of the left ear. It was all over. The doctor fell on top of his dead enemy, and began wildly beating Stoudenmire across the top of the head with the ex-marshal's own weapon.

Both James and Doc Manning went on trial for murder, and each was acquitted in separate Ysleta court cases.

On April 18, 1883, Frank Manning replaced James Gillett as the El Paso city marshal, but his tenure of office was short. In May he tried to shake down W. G. Walz, a merchant, and when Walz objected, Frank cracked him across the head with a heavy cane and threatened to shoot him. Frank was dismissed as marshal, and all of the Manning brothers left El Paso about this time.

Frank prospected in Arizona for many years, and as he grew older he became difficult to handle and was committed to the Arizona State Hospital in 1922. He died there on November 14, 1925.

Doc Manning moved to Flagstaff, Arizona, and lived for many

years as a respected physician. The arm Stoudenmire had shot remained crippled and nearly useless for the remainder of his life. He died at Flagstaff on March 9, 1925.

Jim took his wife, the very attractive Leonor Isabelle Arzate from Juarez, with him to Arizona and on to Washington state. His health gradually broke and he died of cancer and the effects of an old bullet wound. Death came in April of 1915, and he is buried in the Los Angeles Forest Lawn Cemetery.

Prior to Jim's death, the well-known journalist Stuart Lake offered to write his biography. Manning declined, and suggested Lake see Wyatt Earp. Thus Earp became famous; whereas James Manning is almost unknown in western annals.

As for Stoudenmire, he died with the shirt on his back, and that was about all. The El Paso Freemasons paid for a suit of burial clothes ($11.25) and coffin expenses ($4.50). The body went to Columbus, Texas for burial, and the grave site has long since been lost.

An era of violence in El Paso had now passed.

11

KING FISHER

FRONTIER DANDY

Some men become local legends in their time and place, but never achieve a national reputation. By all odds King Fisher should have become a better known figure than Billy the Kid or John Wesley Hardin. He had all the attributes: good looks, youth, style, color, deadliness and cold courage. Unfortunately he lacked a good press agent.

But if King Fisher did not achieve legendary status on a country-wide scale, he was at least King of the Hill in the Nueces Strip. Even today he is the subject of barroom and campfire gossip as men argue whether the good he did was worth the evil that he brought.

In his prime, King Fisher stood about six-foot tall and weighed approximately 186 pounds. He had strong white teeth, flashing eyes, black hair and mustache. One associate described him thus:

"Fisher was the most perfect specimen of a frontier dandy and desperado that I ever met. He was tall, beautifully proportioned and exceedingly handsome. He wore the finest clothing procurable, the picturesque, border, dime-novel kind. His broad-brimmed white Mexican sombrero was profusely ornamented with gold and silver lace. His fine buckskin Mexican short jacket was heavily embroidered with gold. His shirt was of the finest and thinnest linen and open at the

King Fisher . . . his enemies may have despised and feared him, but they never lost their respect.

throat, with a silk handkerchief knotted loosely about the wide collar. A brilliant crimson sash wound about his waist, and his legs were hidden by a wonderful pair of chaparejos, or chaps as cowboys called them—leather breeches to protect the legs while riding through the brush."

Naturally, Fisher's work outfit did not look like this, but even his day-to-day clothes were of good quality. For instance, his boots were of black patent leather with intricate trimming. On his hip hung a .45 Colt with a black gutta-percha handle and a blue-bronze steel cylinder and barrel. The weapon was a gift from Porfirio Diaz, who later became president of Mexico.

Under ordinary circumstances such an outfit might have got its owner laughed out of every cowcamp and cowtown in Texas, but nobody ever laughed at John King Fisher. His enemies may have despised and feared him, but they never lost their respect. Fisher wore his clothes in such a manner as to be impressive yet was not considered a showoff, a feat few other Texans could have accomplished.

Born John King Fisher in 1854 in Fannin County (later Collin County), Texas, he grew up disliking his stepmother. As a youngster she hung him by his suspenders in the open doorway and left him kicking, squirming and squalling until she had finished her chores.

When he was sixteen-years old, his family moved to Goliad and there King Fisher was arrested for horse stealing and for breaking and entering. A jury sentenced him to two years in the penitentiary, a term shortened to four months by the governor.

After leaving prison, Fisher drifted into the Nueces Strip, a no-man's land between the Rio Grande and the Nueces River, the latter emptying into the Gulf of Mexico at Corpus Christi. Lawlessness ran rampant through the strip, and it became the subject of congressional, as well as Mexican, inquiries and investigations. In a period known as the "terrible 1870's", hordes of outlaws, murderers, thugs, thieves from both sides of the border preyed upon each other as well as upon the few honest citizens with nerve enough to settle there.

In 1871, King Fisher moved to Pendencia, Texas, a ranching community east of Eagle Pass. Ranchers employed him to clean out the rustlers, and his reputation soared as a man of courage. In time he built his own ranch and established his own brand. However, he did not employ ordinary cowboys. Instead he hired desperate men from both sides of the border, especially from Mexico. Many were running from the law, and he gave them refuge as well as work. Fisher became a well-known figure in the territory as he rode about followed by his vaqueros, all heavily armed and dangerous. They did not like strangers, and a posted sign along one particular route read: "This is King Fisher's Road—Take the other one."

The town of Eagle Pass (named for the annual mass migration of Mexican eagles across the Rio Grande at this point) gradually became King Fisher's center of operations—part of the Fisher empire. Everyone knew him, and those who did not like him were at least discreet enough to keep their mouths shut.

Fisher never admitted to more than seven killings, and even these he rarely spoke about. In his most famous shootout he tangled with his own vaqueros. The men had brought stolen cattle in from Mexico, and everybody, Fisher included, went down to the corrals to change the brands or at least blotch them up so thoroughly that they would be unrecognizable.

The vaqueros believed Fisher should have paid them more. They planned to kill Fisher, and he knew it. So both factions nonchalantly continued branding and awaited their opportunity. It came when a vaquero jostled Fisher toward the fire. King cracked him across the head with a branding iron, killed him, and then shot three others, all perched like blackbirds on the fence. They too died instantly, and nothing was ever done about it.

By the mid 1870's the lawlessness of the Nueces Strip underwent a serious shakeup when the governor sent in Texas Rangers. In practically no time, fresh graveyards were created and the word went out that the badmen could either die or run. A special notice went to King Fisher's hired guns.

Texas Ranger Captain Leander H. McNelly, although dying of tuberculosis, took two squads of rangers and arrested Fisher. King and nine of his men surrendered without a fight, were shackled, tied to horses and taken to Eagle Pass for jailing. Upon arrival in town, no one seemed to know what the charges were, so everyone was released.

During the following year (1877) McNelly died and Captain Lee Hall took over. Hall also said he would break up the Fisher gang, and with his rangers enforcing the law, people gradually lost their fear and came forward to confess what they knew of King Fisher. As a result,

King found himself charged with three counts of horse stealing and one count of murder, the latter being for shooting William Dunovan, a little-known badman. No sooner had these charges been filed, than others were added. The rangers accused Fisher of killing Severin Flores and two other Mexicans known only as Estanislado and Pancho.

In order to keep King Fisher outside of his ordinary area of power and influence, the rangers transferred him to the "bat cave" jail in San Antonio. For five months he languished there until being released on $25,000 bail.

A personal struggle now went on between Fisher and Lee Hall, the former trying to stay out of prison, the latter trying to send him there for life. Altogether, Hall secured twenty-one indictments against Fisher, but he gave up after six juries in a row set Fisher free. The other charges were dropped when Hall married and retired from the rangers.

Fisher settled down to serious ranching, and being a more credible father to his three daughters and a better husband to his wife. A quiet life was not for him, however, and when the Uvalde County sheriff offered him a position as deputy, Fisher accepted. With his talents now on the side of the law, King became a diligent peace officer, tracking down Tom and Jim Hannehan, two accused robbers of the El Paso-San Antonio stage. When both men resisted arrest, King killed Tom, captured Jim and recovered the money.

As sometimes happens to ambitious sheriffs, the one who King Fisher worked for was soon suspected of dipping his hand in the public till. When indictments followed, Fisher took over as acting sheriff and then campaigned for the job in 1884.

In the meantime, the cattle business wasn't what it used to be. The invention of barbed wire ended the open range. Fence cutting wars broke out all across Texas and caused so much violence and bloodshed that the Texas legislature made fence cutting a felony. Fisher went to Austin for more information on the law.

While in Austin he bumped into his old friend Ben Thompson, one of the West's best known and most notorious gunmen, then serving as city marshal. Thompson had just returned from San Antonio where he shot and killed Jack Harris, proprietor of the Vaudeville Variety Theater, a dive specializing in all sorts of wicked entertainment.

After being acquitted of murder, Thompson returned to his job in Austin where he told Fisher all his troubles. King listened quietly, hesitating to pass judgment because Harris had also been his friend. When Fisher left for San Antonio, Thompson went along. Freud would have said he had a death wish.

San Antonio was an armed camp with policemen under orders to "kill him [Thompson] if he makes any trouble." And so the two men, Fisher simply an innocent bystander, went first to the Turner Hall Opera House, then to Gallagher's Saloon, and then to the Vaudeville Variety Theater.

Thompson and Fisher strolled casually upstairs, watched a show and started to leave. As they rose, someone pointed out Joe Foster, new manager of the theater and a close friend of the dead Harris. Thompson drunkenly walked over and tried to shake hands. When Foster refused, an argument started and threats were made. Slowly Thompson and Fisher backed into the stair hallway, and at that point they were ambushed.

Rifle and pistol fire boomed from everywhere, King Fisher being the only person who did not draw a weapon. Nevertheless, he was dead with thirteen bullets in his body; Thompson had nine. Thus passed from the Southwestern scene two of the most remarkable gunmen in history.

12

BUTCH CASSIDY

AND THE SUNDANCE KID

A MOVIE entitled "Butch Cassidy and the Sundance Kid" swept the country in 1970. Most reviewers rated it as great entertainment, and although it was historically accurate in only a few rare scenes, it did capture some of the glamor and excitement that those outlaws managed to project during their lifetimes.

Butch Cassidy and the Sundance Kid were only two members (but very important ones) operating mostly in Utah as part of the "Wild Bunch," otherwise known as the "Hole-in-the-Wall" gang. Around the turn of the century they headquartered at "Robbers Roost," the "Hole-in-the-Wall," or "Brown's Hole." These were not holes in the sense that we generally think of the word. They were regions, rugged areas composed of swift rivers and towering canyons. When badmen made a strike, they would disappear back inside these remote canyons as if they had vanished into a hole.

It could be said that many outlaws and several gangs comprised the Wild Bunch. Sometimes they operated together, and sometimes they operated independently. They rode into the holes whenever they felt like it, and they rode out in the same manner. At times there may have been a hundred or so men in the vicinity, and the next day there would be none.

*The Wild Bunch. Harry Longabaugh (Sundance Kid),
Bill Carver, Ben Kilpatrick, Harvey Logan (Kid Curry),
Robert L. Parker (Butch Cassidy).*

Butch Cassidy

*. . . Cassidy called his
outfit the "Train Robber's
Syndicate," but they are
remembered as the more
colorful and descriptive
"Wild Bunch."*

Therefore, the "Wild Bunch" must be considered the half-dozen or so men who actually made the name famous.

They were an intriguing group. Few except the Sundance Kid had much of a reputation for violence, and only one killing can be chalked up to him. Butch Cassidy never killed anyone.

The gang was an incredibly wide-ranging group of outlaws. They thought nothing of crossing the continent, or visiting other countries. They enjoyed life.

One of their habits was the way they switched names back and forth and adopted aliases. The practice drove lawmen to the brink of despair.

Butch Cassidy, leader of the Wild Bunch, was born Robert Leroy Parker in Circleville, Utah in 1866, the eldest of seven children. His father was a devout elder in the Mormon Church; none of the respectability rubbed off on the son. He fell in with a notorious horse thief named Mike Cassidy, and when Mike saw the law closing in, he skipped out to Mexico, leaving behind an impressionable lad who adopted the Cassidy name. Later he added the moniker of Butch.

Thus Butch Cassidy teamed up with Matt Warner, a youngster noted for his imagination and windy tales. Joining them were Bill and Tom McCarty, and together they robbed the San Miguel Valley Bank in Colorado on July 24, 1889. Afterwards the gang split up, with Cassidy heading for the Hole-in-the-Wall, and the others north toward Oregon where they dubbed themselves the "Invincible Three." Apparently they were not as invincible as believed, for they were all captured and put in prison. Matt Warner and Tom McCarty afterwards went straight. Bill McCarty still sought the easy life, and he and his nineteen-year-old son, Fred, teamed up to rob the Delta, Colorado bank. The townspeople shot the old man off his horse, and when Fred galloped back to help, they killed him too.

By the spring of 1890, Butch Cassidy operated a thriving business from the Hole-in-the-Wall in Wyoming. Other outlaws trusted him, and he had a sense of integrity and a strong personality. Stolen cattle were dispatched to buyers in Colorado and Utah. Small quantities of beef were sold locally.

Cassidy's rustling career ended when a tough sheriff cracked him across the skull with a revolver, and a judge gave him two years in the penitentiary. The governor freed him on January 19, 1896, on the promise to leave Wyoming and never return.

Over in Sundance, Wyoming, Harry Longabaugh had a reputation as a tough badman and rustler. No one is certain where he called home, although one story has it that he came north with a Texas trail herd and never returned. He had a moody, sullen disposition, and when drunk (which was often), he either fought or talked too much. Sometime around 1895 he killed a deputy sheriff and fled for refuge at the Hole-in-the-Wall where he became known as the Sundance Kid.

Another figure of significance was Harvey Logan, who was born in Kentucky sometime during the early 1870's. As he drifted west he became involved with a bunch of Wyoming cattle rustlers led by George "Flat Nose" Curry. Their many successes eventually led to an act of carelessness. Angry ranchers caught them red-handed in the process of changing brands on stolen cattle, disarmed the outlaws and threatened to kill them. However, several stockmen demurred so the rustlers signed a crude agreement whereby they promised to leave Wyoming forever. Under the circumstances, Curry, Logan and the others were very happy to sign.

They hastily, if somewhat nervously, scratched their X marks, were escorted to the eastern state line, given horses and personal belongings (but no guns), and told what would happen if they ever returned.

The gang now scattered, and Harvey Logan adopted the leader's name. From then on Logan would be Kid Curry. He drifted to Montana where on Christmas Eve, 1894, he blew several nasty holes in Pike Landusky, a United States deputy marshal. Kid Curry then left the state and headed for the Hole-in-the-Wall where he would share dual authority with Butch Cassidy.

Others of some importance in the gang were Bill Carver, Elza Lay, and Ben and George Kilpatrick. All of these men and more would form the backbone of the Wild Bunch, the most successful holdup men in western history.

The Wild Bunch also had women, and only Cassidy seems to have opposed their presence. He liked girls but never married. During his career, no special woman attracted his attention, and none have been particularly associated with his name except possibly Etta Place whom he may have shared with the Sundance Kid. As far as he was concerned, women and business did not mix. However, other members of the Wild Bunch did not agree, so they overruled him.

Laura Bullion, Annie Rogers and Etta Place became the three best known women of the Wild Bunch. Many other females wandered in and out of the hideouts but they were largely on a come-and-go basis.

Laura grew up near Knickerbocker, Texas, and by the age of sixteen she became the common law wife of Bill Carver during one of his infrequent trips to Bandera, Texas. It all ended when Bill stopped a bullet in Sonora. Following his untimely death, Ben Kilpatrick and the Sundance Kid allegedly rolled dice for the widow and Kilpatrick won.

Annie Rogers met Kid Curry in San Antonio and she followed him around for years before the Tennessee law put a temporary stop to his wanderings. Annie visited him in jail every day but the Kid thought she might hamper his chances for escape. He promised to meet her in San Antonio when free but after his escape he was killed before making it that far.

The most interesting female of the lot was Etta Place. According to legend she had beauty, wit and sophistication, a judgment which should be accepted with some tongue-in-cheek. Her hang-ups were outlaws. They brought her a lot of grief but they gave her interesting and exciting times too. She should have written her memoirs.

Etta became a special friend of the Sundance Kid and, although Butch Cassidy growled and grumbled, the Kid allowed her to accompany them wherever they went. During many robberies she held the horses and loaded the guns. She was the only woman to tag along when the gang fled to South America.

Under Cassidy's and Curry's leadership the outlaws were now ready to ride. Butch called his outfit the "Train Robber's Syndicate," a name which admittedly had a business-like ring. History bypassed that title, however, for the more colorful and descriptive "Wild Bunch." An incredible crime era began.

End of the Wild Bunch

On August 23, 1896, the Wild Bunch struck for the first time as an organized cohesive group. Cassidy and the others, plus several lesser assistants, held up the bank at Montpelier, Idaho and escaped. As robberies go, this one was a small job, but it gave the outlaws a taste of success and set the stage for spectacular transactions in the future.

Less than a year later, Cassidy and Elza Lay rode into Castle Gate, Utah, and asked for work in the mine. To all appearances the two were itinerant laborers astraddle swayback mares. Butch hooked his thumbs in his bib overalls, spat a stream of tobacco juice from a thicket of whiskers, and promised the foreman to return in the morning. Early the next day, arousing no attention, Cassidy and Lay sauntered into the paymaster's shack, shoved a revolver into the cashier's face, and grabbed $8,000. They tied up their man, carried the cumbersome money sacks to the horses and casually waved goodbye as they disappeared up the canyon.

The robbery created a sensation. It had been daring, it had been well planned, it had been accomplished easily and without violence. Furthermore, the Castle Gate holdup established Cassidy's reputation for leadership. Encouraged by this success, he led a raid on the bank at Belle Fouche, South Dakota, and $30,000 disappeared with the outlaws when they thundered out of town.

In those days there were basically five types of law enforcement officers or bodies. There were the town marshals who rarely left the city limits except to be buried. There were the sheriffs who rarely left the county lines except to pick up a prisoner. There were the United States marshals and deputy marshals whose effectiveness has been largely overrated by movies and television. There were the rangers such as those used in Texas and Arizona. Finally there were the Pinkerton detectives, a private investigative firm. None of these include the private agents such as Wells Fargo, the railroads and the stock associations. In some respects these agents were the most effective of all.

The Pinkertons started protecting President Lincoln during the Civil War. They have never been recognized as they deserved for their western exploits, and the probable reason is that Pinkerton became a synonym for strikebreakers in the days when strikebreaking meant busted heads and broken bones. They were a well trained, private police force usually employed by industry and government to solve the most difficult crimes. As a world famous body, they broke up more organized outlaw bands than any other single detective agency.

As law officers converged on the Hole-in-the-Wall (by now a well-known location), they found none of the Wild Bunch. They did not even find a visual description. No one could identify the young outlaws, and by switching names back and forth they literally kept the Pinkertons chasing shadows.

Still, the Wild Bunch thought it best to stay quiet for awhile. Cassidy and Lay went to work as ordinary cowboys on the WS Ranch in Alma, New Mexico. Butch worked hard, further developed his cattleman's talents, and became a reliable hand. Lay couldn't stay out of trouble. He and a few others robbed the Folsom, New Mexico train. Although the band got away, a posse caught them at Turkey Creek Canyon and a sharp fight ensued. Lay was captured and sentenced to life imprisonment.

Over in Clifton, Arizona, Kid Curry and Ben Kilpatrick held up the local bank and stole $12,000. In a remarkable bit of planning, the bandits made use of a deep and wide arroyo outside of town which extended for several miles each way. Curry's horse could jump it, but Ben's couldn't, so Kilpatrick waited on the far side while Curry committed the robbery alone. Moments later he came riding straight for the arroyo with a posse pounding right behind him. His horse cleared the chasm even with the extra weight of several thousand dollars stuffed in the saddlebags.

Kid Curry now had enough money to travel. He took a train for Savannah, Georgia and sailed for France. However, he did not stay long. Out of boredom he returned to his old haunts in southeastern Utah where he waited for several of his pals to return from a hitch with the Rough Riders in Cuba.

The gang regrouped after the Spanish American War, and hit the Union Pacific Railroad near Casper, Wyoming. In a masterful job they blew the express safe with three charges of dynamite, and gathered up $30,000 worth of currency.

Two days later and nearly a hundred miles down the road, the Wild Bunch camped against Curry's better judgment. The Sundance Kid complained that he was tired, that he had saddle sores, and that he wanted to rest. He did not realize, nor did anyone else, that they were in the center of one of the West's greatest manhunts. Posses and Pinkertons were swarming over the countryside, and surprisingly the outlaws and the lawmen had not yet collided.

When the Wild Bunch awoke the next morning, the law was everywhere except in the same sleeping bags. A posse stumbling around in the brush bumped into them as the outlaws prepared breakfast. During a short, stiff fight, Curry killed Sheriff Joe Hazen, and his death took the wind temporarily out of the attackers. While they regrouped, the bandits scattered like wild turkeys and no one saw them again for weeks.

The lawmen had at least identified Harvey Logan as Kid Curry, and word came that Lonnie Logan, a younger brother, might have been involved in the robbery. So one afternoon as Lonnie sat reading newspapers in an outdoor toilet, a posse killed him.

An infuriated Kid Curry called for a "spite robbery" of the Tipton, Missouri train, and his friends agreed. It went off without a hitch, but the angry bandits picked up only $50 in bills and three sacks of pennies. Curry poured the latter down a prairie dog hole, and so far as is known, those coins are still there today.

The Winnemucca, Nevada bank next attracted the Wild Bunch. For two days Cassidy hung around the community posing as a prospector, trying to make up his mind whether or not the bank could be successfully hit. After deciding it could, he worked out an escape plan which would get them safely across the 200-mile open stretch prior to reaching mountainous country.

The Wild Bunch scattered horses along the route, and then made a successful cash withdrawal of $32,000 from the Winnemucca bank on September 19, 1900. After escaping they caught a train to Fort Worth.

To celebrate their good fortune they had their picture taken, a now famous photo reproduced more times than any other such picture in western history. In fact, it was such a good shot that John Schwartz, the photographer, proudly placed an enlargement in his show window. A passing Pinkerton detective glanced in and recognized a few of the faces. For the Wild Bunch this was the beginning of the end. Now every lawman in the West knew their likeness.

Butch Cassidy suggested one more bank loan before leaving the state, so they rode over to Sonora, Texas where Bill Carver and another man went into town. The sheriff recognized them, and a shootout started. Carver died on the spot, and his companion absorbed fourteen bullets, but survived them all. The Wild Bunch, thoroughly shaken, disguised themselves as hobos and headed north for their old reliable Hole-in-the-Wall.

The gang planned on fleeing to South America, but first wanted one more big robbery. On July 3, 1901, they struck the Great Northern Railroad near Malta, Montana, and got away with over $50,000. For two weeks they hid out on an island in the Missouri River, and then scattered for the last time. Most would never meet again.

Ben Kilpatrick, the Tall Texan, dropped out first. St. Louis authorities arrested him and gave him fifteen years in the federal prison at Atlanta.

Kid Curry fled to Knoxville, Tennessee where police officers trapped him in a saloon. Although he broke loose by jumping from a third story window, the law caught him two days later and sentenced him to 130 years in jail.

Before leaving for prison, he escaped, made his way west, and fell in with three strangers looking for an easy way to make a living. They robbed the Denver and Rio Grande at Parachute, Colorado, but bad luck and a hard-riding posse dogged them. A wounded Curry ducked behind a rock, and waved the others on as he held everyone off. When officers finally rushed the barricade, they found him dead.

During this period Butch Cassidy tried to work out a deal with the Utah governor whereby he might retire without going to prison. Since no murder charges hung over his head, the governor and even the Union Pacific expressed interest. They arranged a meeting, but it fizzled when a storm blocked the roads. Cassidy figured the deal was off, so he turned his attention to South America.

He, the Sundance Kid and Etta Place (nominally the Kid's wife), sailed from New York to Buenos Aires. Near the Chilean border they bought a ranch and stocked it. During the next few years they occasionally made short American visits. Etta and Sundance once checked into a Denver hospital where she had an appendicitis operation. Nobody recognized them.

At this point their fate becomes vague and uncertain. Etta Place vanished. Rumors and some evidence indicate that Cassidy and Sundance might have returned to United States soil and lived out a quiet and peaceful existence.

We do know that the two outlaws robbed numerous banks and

mines in South America, and were the objects of intensive manhunts. The most historically accepted version of what finally happened is that they were ambushed by soldiers following a 1909 Bolivian mine holdup. Rifle fire wounded Sundance. Cassidy dragged him inside a compound, and the two men held the army off all day and all night. When morning came and the soldiers rushed the building, they found them dead. Cassidy had fired a shot into the head of Sundance, and used his last bullet on himself.

13

DAVE MATHER

A DEADLY SHOOTER

O F ALL THE ENIGMATIC GUNMEN trodding the sandy wastes of the Old West, Mysterious Dave Mather was one of the most interesting, as well as one of the most dangerous. He came honestly by the nickname of "Mysterious Dave." Folks knew him as a taciturn individual, sometimes drunk, always moody and deadly with a pistol.

Physically he was no great charmer to the eye. He stood about five-foot-nine, had a slender build, dark complexion, brooding eyes, and a so called "killer mustache" (the droopy kind). Like many men during, since and before his time, women both fascinated and frightened him.

Mather was born in Connecticut in 1845, supposedly a lineal descendant of the 17th century philosopher Cotton Mather. By 1873 his trail led into Arkansas where he earned a reputation as a cattle rustler and general nuisance. A year later he drifted north to near Dodge City, Kansas where he gambled and hunted buffalo for a living. Apparently the gambling wasn't too successful because an unhappy loser shoved a knife in his ribs and almost killed him. Following his recovery, Mysterious Dave became a part-time peace officer around Dodge.

During slow business nights Mather would sit alone in the saloons brooding and quietly drinking. Only rarely did he get drunk, and he had a peculiar test for his degree of sobriety. By law folks had to check their guns with the bartender, so every half-hour Dave would borrow his back for a few seconds, step to the bat-wing doors and fire a shot at the fire bell in the middle of Front Street. If the bell rang, he was still sober. If he missed, he paid up and went home.

Over the next few years he and Wyatt Earp became good friends. They moved into Mobeetie, Texas (now a Panhandle ghost town) in 1878, and in their buckboard lay a pile of gold bricks freshly painted. These sold for $100 apiece to the community's less intelligent citizens. According to the yarn Mather and Earp glibly wove, these gold bricks were from an old, recently discovered Spanish mine that the Indians had sealed up after slaughtering the priests and soldiers. Now these priceless pieces of treasure were being sold at bargain rates in order to obtain enough money for a new expedition into the remote area.

Surprisingly, the two "salesmen" sold a lot of those phony bricks. They might have sold many more if the sheriff had not bought one himself and later found out he'd been tricked. He ordered Mather and Earp out of town.

The partners split up and Mather went on to Las Vegas, New Mexico, a railroad and cattle center and one of the toughest towns in the territory. Justice of the Peace H. G. Neill, better known as "Hoodoo Brown," controlled the vice interests. Many of the West's most notorious gunmen used the town as an occasional headquarters. Among them were Billy the Kid, Tom Pickett, Dave Rudabaugh and Doc Holliday. The latter hung out his dental shingle, and often alternated between drilling holes in patients and drilling holes in enemies. The enemies he never charged, perhaps because he used shotgun slugs and the rate of recovery was almost zero.

Although there is some evidence that Mather sometimes held up a local train or stagecoach, he nevertheless was employed as a deputy marshal. In mid-January, 1880, came his first test as a lawman. Into town rode the Henry gang, a band of tough, swaggering youths. Tom Henry led them, and trailing behind were John Dorsey, James West and William "Big" Randall.

City Marshal Joe Carson, a forty-year-old Tennessee man, met them at the Close and Patterson Saloon and ordered the gang to obey the city ordinance by checking their guns with the bartender.

The gunmen snickered, so Carson and Mather came charging through the saloon door a half-hour later and that's when the lights went out. Carson was dead almost before he could swear. Tom Henry shot him in both arms, and the rest of the gang riddled him with bullets.

The gunmen unfortunately concentrated on the wrong man. Mather's guns were booming too. He instantly killed "Big" Randall, shot West twice through the body, and put a bullet through Henry's leg. In the confusion, Henry and John Dorsey, who were unscathed, escaped out the back door. When the lights came back on, Mather, also unscratched, sent Randall's remains to the cemetery, and West to jail. A doctor wanted West hospitalized, but Mather ignored him.

A manhunt started for the fugitives, and on February 6 both Dorsey and Henry were located and arrested in Mora, New Mexico, returned to Las Vegas and incarcerated with the dying, but still gasping, West.

Late that night Mather led a mob on the jail. Henry and Dorsey were roughly dragged outside. West was carried on a litter in order to keep his blood from dripping and smearing the vigilantes. The mob led all three to the plaza windmill and a platform across the lower level. A rope dangled from high above.

The doomed and trembling men were all less than twenty-one years old, and West pleaded for mercy. Someone grabbed Henry by the hair, forced him to look at the rope, and asked if he wasn't scared. Tom took a long look at the noose, choked momentarily, and finally muttered, "It's pretty tough to be hung, but I guess I can stand the consequences."

West was the first. The rope jerked him off his litter and high into the air. Since his hands were not tied, he slipped them under the rope. Pulling himself up, he began screaming for his mother. Then as his ill-fitting trousers dropped low on his waist, he cried, "Please button my pants."

At this moment Joe Carson's widow began shooting at the prisoners. Henry and Dorsey were shot down onto the platform, but neither were killed. Writhing in agony, Henry crawled to the platform's edge and begged someone to shoot him through the head. Within seconds Dorsey, Henry, and the dangling body of West were full of holes. A coroner noted dryly the next day that the dead men had met their just fate from the hands of parties unknown.

Not long afterwards, Mysterious Dave Mather left Las Vegas. For awhile he lived in Dodge City, then Colorado, then San Antonio, Texas. In Texas he tried to pass counterfeit money and the sheriff chased him out of the county. By some accounts he drifted to El Paso and became a deputy city marshal under Dallas Stoudenmire. If so, he did it under an assumed name.

He showed up in Dallas and became involved with Georgia Morgan, a black madam. Dave enjoyed her charms for several weeks, then stuffed his pockets full of her jewelry and disappeared again.

Back in Dodge City he became an assistant marshal and deputy sheriff, a position which brought him into contact with Mrs. Tom Nixon, a mother of several children, an invalid and, what was more important, the wife of another assistant marshal. On July 18, 1884, the jealous Tom Nixon and Mather tangled in a darkened hallway. Though neither man was wounded, Nixon rushed outside to proclaim triumphantly to the world that he had just killed Mysterious Dave Mather and that "he was glad."

Less than a week later, Mather walked up behind Nixon in a saloon and emptied a revolver into his back. A jury figured Tom got what was coming to him, and acquitted Mather.

During the shooting, a stray bullet killed a sleepy greyhound dog. After much deliberation, a jury finally concluded that the greyhound "came to its death by a bullet fired from a gun in the hands of Dave Mather, better known as Mysterious Dave, and that the shooting was justified as any dog should have known better than go to sleep in a Dodge City Saloon."

As for Dave Mather, the authorities asked him to move on. Mather nodded and left, becoming a wayward drifter across the plains and mountains of the West. He showed up in Lone Pine, Nebraska during the summer of 1887. What happened to him after that is a matter of pure speculation. He dropped out of sight, perhaps deliberately so. He was not known as Mysterious Dave without reason.

14

PAT GARRETT

Pat Garrett began as a buffalo hunter on the Texas plains. When the herds thinned in 1878, he moved to New Mexico and chased outlaws. Following this he became a land speculator, a Texas Ranger captain and a Pecos Valley visionary whose dreams and ideas nearly transformed that region. Next, he became an East Texas gentleman rancher, a New Mexico peace officer once again, and on to El Paso as Customs Collector. Finally, in 1908, he returned to Las Cruces, New Mexico where he was murdered under circumstances still mysterious and controversial. He died at the age of fifty-seven, best remembered as the tall slayer of Billy the Kid.

There was never a western sheriff quite like Garrett. He was an individualist, a dreamer, a man who never paid his bills but in most respects was as honest as anyone. Garrett was many things to many men, a quiet, sarcastic, introspective family man, loyal to his friends (no matter how odious) and an agnostic who actually understood the word. He was a complex man, at times tormented and subject to moods and depressions. His friends knew him as a great practical joker who had no sense of humor when the jocularity was reversed. Men despised him and praised him, for he aroused many emotions. All in all, Garrett was not the Southwest's most lovable human being, but he

Pat Garrett . . . best remembered as the tall slayer of Billy the Kid. He was a complex man, an individualist, a dreamer at times tormented and subject to moods and depressions.

was a tragic and a very misunderstood figure. He was a man of his times.

He was born Patrick Floyd Jarvis Garrett on June 5, 1850, in Chambers County, Alabama. The family moved to Claiborne Parish, Louisiana where he grew up on the family farm as the second of eight children. His education was ordinary. When both parents died at a relatively young age, he fell out with a brother-in-law who sold the family estate. In disgust Garrett saddled up and moved to Texas.

For awhile Garrett hired out as a trail driver, then teamed up with a young Kentuckian named Skelton Glenn. Together they moved to Fort Griffin, Texas (near Abilene) and hunted buffalo. Basically it seemed an amiable partnership. Garrett did the hunting and the killing, while Glenn and a few hired hands did the skinning. Soon the relationship began to sour.

In November of 1876 Glenn left for Camp Reynolds, a way-station for hunters, to get a gun repaired. On that day a fog set in, the weather turned chilly, and tempers took on an edge all over camp. Garrett in particular was in a bad mood. He couldn't buy trousers long enough to protect his skinny legs, and he wore heavy buffalo hides to take up the slack. On damp days such as this, the hides soaked up moisture and added extra weight. They chapped his calves and made an annoying slap every time he moved about.

Grundy Burns, the cook, carefully fed and coaxed the flickering fire with damp wood and buffalo chips before starting breakfast. As he nursed the flames along, he paid scant attention to the emergence of Joe Briscoe from a nearby arroyo. As an orphan, Briscoe grew up in the company of New Orleans nuns before running away to Fort Worth where he met Garrett. Briscoe needed a job, and Garrett employed him as a skinner.

On this particular morning Briscoe came walking out of the arroyo where he had found some captured rain water, and headed for the fire, his fingers practically frozen. Squatting down he tried to wash and dry a handkerchief, all the while mumbling—more to himself than anyone else—about the impossibility of getting anything clean. Garrett, trying to take some small comfort from the fire too, growled that no one but a damned Irishman would be stupid enough to wash anything in that muddy water.

The remark infuriated Briscoe. Ordinarily he would have paid no attention, or simply grinned and wisecracked back. This time he came up swinging, and a surprised Garrett promptly knocked him down. As the one-sided fight wore on with Garrett pummelling his man almost at will, Pat became ashamed of himself and tried to apologize and talk Briscoe into quitting. This made Briscoe even angrier. He couldn't even land a punch, and his opponent felt sorry for him.

He grabbed an ax and started chasing Garrett around the camp wagon. Around and around in the mud they raced, slipping and falling, all the time cursing and threatening and yelling for the other to stop. Finally Garrett grabbed the Winchester, turned and fired. The heavy slug knocked Briscoe sprawling into the campfire, where he quickly died.

In remorse, Garrett saddled a horse and rode to the point of exhaustion across the plains. On the following day, very haggard and shivering, he returned to camp and explained to Glenn what had happened. His partner suggested that he go into Fort Griffin and turn himself in to the authorities. Pat did so, but returned shortly afterwards saying that the officials had declined to prosecute.

As Garrett and Glenn resumed their hunting, the Plains Indians watched with obvious dismay. Their source of food was disappearing. One Comanche leader named Nigger Horse stormed the Glenn-Garrett camp with fifty braves and a white man who had been captured as a boy. Although no one was killed, the horses were stolen, the wagons and supplies burned, and over 800 hides destroyed.

Hunters from all over the region fled to Camp Reynolds where they milled about, fermenting corn and talking about how to teach the Indian a lesson. Garrett demurred, saying they should let the Indians move on. However, Glenn and the others packed themselves into creaking wagons and, carrying plenty of whiskey, but very little food and ammunition, drunkenly tracked their prey to Yellow House Canyon, now Lubbock, Texas. There the whites fought an incredibly inept battle, were completely routed and chased pell-mell back to Camp Reynolds. "The Hunters War," as the fiasco came to be called, was over.

By January of 1878, with the buffalo practically eliminated, Glenn and Garrett simply abandoned their wagons and rode west. Before long they arrived at Fort Sumner, New Mexico, where Garrett obtained a job and said goodby to Glenn. Pat felt at home here, and he awed the people with his six-foot, six-inch stove pipe length and build. Jokingly the Mexicans nicknamed him Juan Largo (Long John).

Although there were rumors that Garrett had previously married and then abandoned a wife near Sweetwater, Texas, he reportedly married a Juanita Gutierrez at Fort Sumner in 1877. She died a few months later, probably of a miscarriage. Two years later, Garrett went into the part-time hog business, only to be nearly killed by a rampaging sow. Apolinaria Gutierrez, presumably Juanita's sister, nursed him back to health and they were married in Anton Chico, New Mexico on January 14, 1880.

Apolinaria, the daughter of a well-to-do New Mexico freighter, bore Pat eight children and stood by him in the very turbulent times that followed. She was an intelligent, very attractive, well educated woman who spoke little English. Theirs was an interesting relationship, a loving but almost formal one by modern standards. Correspondence now in the possession of Jarvis Garrett, the surviving son, indicates that Pat kept Apolinaria in his thoughts and confidence. Letters penned to her during his frequent absences were long and affectionate, though he addressed her as "Dear Wife" and closed with a simple "Pat F. Garrett."

Destiny in Lincoln County

Pat Garrett took no part in the Lincoln County troubles which culminated in the 1878 burning of the McSween home and the escape of Billy the Kid. We have no inkling that Garrett even had a bent toward law enforcement until John Chisum wrote Governor Lew Wallace on April 15, 1879. Chisum urged that Garrett be appointed to lead a squad of men to Pope's Crossing on the Pecos and stop the movement of outlaws back and forth across the river.

While the New Mexico governor did not act on Chisum's suggestion, he gave encouragement to Garrett's candidacy for sheriff. Pat had recently been living in Roswell, and with strong support from the moneyed people, found himself touted as a "law and order" candidate, a man who would run the outlaws out of the country or bury them beneath its rocky soil. Both the nomination and the 1880 election were wild, tumultuous affairs, but Garrett emerged victoriously.

135

His subsequent pursuit, capture and killing of Billy the Kid has already been described and will be dealt with no further here. However, there are some intriguing sidelights. The Territory of New Mexico placed a $500 reward on the Kid's scruffy blond head but when Garrett tried to collect (and all lawmen dearly loved rewards), the acting governor refused payment on legal technicalities. This petty denial embarrassed the Territory. Indignant citizens began sending Garrett small amounts of money, the amount altogether totaling over a thousand dollars. Finally, the Territorial Legislature passed a special bill and paid the reward. Garrett would have emerged in excellent financial shape had he not bought so many drinks for legislators, and sat in so many poker games, that practically all of the cash went to pay his liquor and gambling debts.

In the meantime, Garrett asked his old friend Ash Upson to help him write a book about Billy the Kid and capitalize on America's craze about western figures. Ash was a former newspaper man, a garrulous, frequently quarrelsome, heavy drinking, stubborn old iconoclast who would become the best pal that Garrett ever had. Together they would write *The Authentic Life of Billy, the Kid, the Noted Desperado of the Southwest, Whose Deeds of Daring Have Made His Name a Terror in New Mexico, Arizona and Northern Mexico*. The prose hung together in the swashbuckling, wordy style of the day.

Upson wrote every word even though Garrett's name appeared as the author. And since Ash claimed to have known Billy the Kid in Silver City, New Mexico, he filled in many details of the Kid's early life, details now known to be false even though many writers and historians have accepted Upson's nonsense as if it were Holy Writ chiseled into stone. When the book reached the point where Garrett became sheriff and knew first hand of events, the facts became basically accurate and began to live up to the long and tedious title.

Charles W. Greene, editor of the Santa Fe *New Mexican,* undertook to publish the book, and the entire venture flopped. Greene knew as much about publishing books as Upson knew about the Kid's early career, which was practically nothing. Ash growled that Greene lacked the money, distribution facilities, and know-how to guarantee a nationwide sale.

As Garrett's dream of writing riches fell short, he dropped all plans about seeking reelection and turned his attention to becoming a New

Mexico Councilman (nowadays a state senator). Other candidates entered the race too, and newspaper battles soon raged. The *Rio Grande Republican* bitterly denounced Garrett, and printed several anonymous letters signed X. The unknown writer called Garrett an ungrateful man for campaigning against his friends. He denounced Pat as "illiterate," and said "the newspaper notoriety he received from his success in killing Billy the Kid has upset his brain."

A few days later Garrett lashed back, stating he was proud to oppose "the company of X and others of his tribe." He defended his "illiteracy," saying it was hardly fair to criticize him for something he could not control.

Garrett was a proud man, stung deeply by the assaults against his character and intelligence. He was determined to track down the real author of the X letter, and he suspected Lincoln attorney W. M. Roberts. Coming upon the lawyer in a saloon, Garrett asked him point blank about the matter, and received a negative reply. Garrett followed him outside, still pressing the matter. They argued for a few seconds, then Garrett jerked his long-barreled Colt .45 and bashed Roberts twice across the head, leaving the lawyer sprawled unconscious in the road. Whether or not he had located the Mr. X is a disputable point, but it is significant that no more anonymous letters denouncing Garrett showed up in the newspapers. It is also worth noting that Garrett lost the election.

As his political future fell apart, Garrett got a call from the high plains country around Tascosa, Texas (near Amarillo). The large ranchers were rapidly losing cowboy loyalty. Those "hired men" who prided themselves on "working for the brand" wanted more pay and better treatment. Their work had never been romantic (except in books). It was brutally hard, often dangerous, and had no security. Cowboys rode from sunup to sundown, sustained themselves on two meals a day, and received an average salary of $30 a month. Since these conditions were standard, no one griped. A cowboy improved himself by building a small spread of his own and stocking it with mavricks (unbranded strays) which ran wild on the open range.

The large ranchers opposed this practice, and claimed all cattle not even on their land. The cowboys agreed but asked for more salary since an important part of their income was being shut off. When the big cattlemen refused, their hired hands organized the first such cowboy strike in history. They demanded $50 a month for themselves, $50 a month for "good" cooks, and $75 a month for bosses.

The cowpokes sat out the strike in Tascosa, and within a month it was all over when the prostitutes and gamblers had all the money. As the beaten men drifted back to work, their employers might have been magnanimous, but were not. They blacklisted the strikers, many of whom drifted across the border into New Mexico and established the "Get Even Cattle Company." They rustled their former employers' stock.

The LS Ranch talked Governor Ireland into forming a company of Texas Rangers to deal with the outlawry. Pat Garrett would lead them. He would be paid $5,000 a year and be given $100 a month for each deputy. Garrett accepted the position in November of 1884, and he and his men quickly became known as the "LS Pat Garrett Rangers."

On a bitterly cold night of February, 1885, Garrett led his men toward an outlaw hideout on the Canadian River. He caught the wanted men by surprise, and after an all-day siege, talked them into surrendering. Three men were arrested, taken to Tascosa and locked up. Within a week the men escaped, but Garrett ignored their flight. He had become disillusioned, learning that he was hired to kill the men instead of capturing them. As he could not bring himself to do this, he resigned after six months and returned to Roswell where he cast his lot with one of the biggest irrigation schemes ever to hit the Southwest.

Pecos Valley visionary

The late 1880's saw the most productive era of Pat Garrett's life really begin. In the Pecos Valley near Roswell, New Mexico, man had always dreamed of how the land might be irrigated to grow crops of every description. Various schemes had been tried, with people recklessly borrowing money to finance their obligations, and just as recklessly repudiating their obligations to pay it back. It is no wonder that most of the early schemes failed; it is a wonder that any were successful at all.

It remained for Pat Garrett to come up with the most workable solution. He envisioned a series of dams along the Pecos, and in particular the Rio Hondo, its largest tributary. The water could then be flumed or ditched almost anywhere in the valley.

To finance the project, Garrett took as a partner Charles B. Eddy, wealthy New Mexico cattleman and financier, and Charles Greene, who apparently had learned nothing from the Billy the Kid publishing disaster. So these three men, Pat Garrett, the taciturn former sheriff whose imagination in the promotional field completely outran his abilities, and Charles B. Eddy, the tireless, often quarrelsome capitalist, teamed up with the equally imaginative and just as unknowledgeable Charles Greene. Slowly a plausible but far too expensive plan to irrigate the entire valley took shape.

On July 18, 1885, they organized the Pecos Valley Irrigation and Investment Company. Garrett and Eddy would handle the promotional work and ditch rights negotiations. Greene would be general manager.

The new corporation did not have enough capital. In September of 1888, after dickering with Chicago financiers, new blood was brought into the organization. There were now ten stockholders running the company, men of means with whom Garrett could not compete. The firm downgraded him to director.

It cited assets of $600,000, divided into six thousand shares of $100 each. Several small ditching corporations were bought out. An irrigation project called the Northern Canal started near present-day Roswell and extended south nearly forty miles, encompassing many smaller branches.

Twenty-mule teams pulled huge earth-ripping plows, and these were followed by "ditchers" which further gouged out the dirt. Behind came scrapers dragged by four to six animals. It was the biggest construction project ever to hit the Pecos Valley, and people came from miles away to watch it.

Expenses began to pile up. Construction time lagged. Payrolls were heavy. Stockholders underestimated the costs and overestimated their ability to pay. Assets turned out to be more paper than cash. In late 1889 Charles Eddy went to Colorado Springs, Colorado and talked to James John Hagerman, a builder of railroads. Bearded and grumpy, Hagerman did not like being called by either of his first two names. He definitely was not the sort of individual that one slapped on the back, and like Eddy, he was interested in projects, not people. While he did associate with his social and financial peers (and Eddy was one), he did not consider Pat Garrett an equal.

Hagerman and a small party took a train to Toyah, Texas, the nearest railroad stop to Roswell, where Garrett met them with a string of hacks and buggies. A few days later, Hagerman wrote out a $40,000 check and bailed the company out of its financial difficulties.

As for Pat Garrett, this infusion of new capital spelled the end of the ditch. In order to force the tall, ex-lawman out of the company, Hagerman reorganized everything, even changing the name from the Pecos Valley Irrigation and Investment Company to the Pecos Valley Irrigation and Improvement Company. He named the Northern Canal the Hagerman Canal. Pat Garrett, who had conceived the original idea, who had sunk all of his monies and his energies into these dreams, was now faced with assets dryer than some of the canals. With no fanfare, with no return on his investment, with no acknowledgement of his contributions, he was dismissed.

Perhaps it was just as well. The country underwent a small depression, floods shattered the Pecos River dams, farmers went bankrupt and could not pay their debts. Hagerman sunk another $150,000 into repairs, and the company staggered along for several years before sinking into receivership.

Pat Garrett turned again to politics. Chaves County was being split off from Lincoln County, and Garrett wanted to be its first sheriff. However, his old friend and occasional nemesis John W. Poe, who had been with him during the slaying of Billy the Kid, had come to Roswell and wanted to be sheriff too. Poe had a more affable personality, and won the election.

An angry Garrett left New Mexico. He sold everything and moved to Uvalde, Texas, taking not only his family, but the ever faithful, always crusty, heavy-drinking, profane Ash Upson. Though Upson's bouts with the demons were a continuing source of embarrassment to the Garrett family, Pat's wife was a remarkably tolerant and understanding woman. She always set a place for Ash at the table, even though he was often too far gone to find it.

Garrett passed the quietest years of his life in Uvalde. He spent more time with his children, especially a blind daughter, Elizabeth. He sent her to a school for the blind in Alamogordo, New Mexico, and all evidence indicates that she adored him. As his best known and most famous child, she became a popular public speaker, a good writer, an accomplished musician, and a close associate of Helen Keller. Elizabeth wrote "Oh Fair New Mexico" (the official state song), a tune entitled "El Paso," and a host of other melodies. Her spirit was vibrant and inspiring, and she was a credit to her father and the entire Southwest.

Pat loved to race horses, and he named one of his fastest mares after John Nance Garner, eventually vice president of the United States under Franklin D. Roosevelt. Little is known of this relationship, but in the 1950's, in response to a query from Pat's son, Oscar Garrett, John Garner scribbled shakily, "I knew your father as an honorable, honest, patriotic American. When the movies slander him, they slander their betters."

Garrett was restless in Uvalde, and he often spoke of leaving. On October 6, 1894, Ash Upson died and Garrett paid the funeral expenses. Then on February 1, 1896, Colonel Albert J. Fountain, who defended Billy the Kid at Mesilla, New Mexico, mysteriously disappeared in the White Sands. His nine-year-old son, Henry, vanished with him. The authorities feared murder. Once again the Territory of New Mexico needed Pat Garrett.

The Colonel Fountain Mystery

Colonel Albert J. Fountain and Albert Bacon Fall were the two most controversial individuals ever to hit New Mexico's Mesilla Valley. Their meeting created a thunderclap of violence and conflict, the reverberations of which still echo whenever two or more people get together and discuss the matter.

Fountain supposedly came from Staten Island, New York. After moving to the west coast as a soldier of fortune, he came to El Paso with the famed California Column during the Civil War. There he began his legal and political career, first by being elected as a Texas state senator from El Paso, then by being involved in the El Paso Salt War, and finally by killing a man during a downtown El Paso dispute.

Believing his future in Texas ended, Fountain moved to Mesilla,

141

New Mexico and organized a law enforcement body to fight Indians and rustlers. In the end the Army wiped out the Indians, but Fountain's forces, composed mostly of Mexican-Americans, broke up several outlaw gangs and drove the members from the territory. A few were killed while "trying to escape."

Fountain established the Mesilla *Independent,* a newspaper whose editorials criticized all of the fashionable sins of the day from crooked politicians to Catholic priests. The only sacred opinions were his own and those of the Republican Party. Modesty was not one of his virtues.

In 1887 the Kentuckian A. B. Fall, who would eventually go on to fame as Secretary of the Interior, and then topple from power during the Teapot Dome controversy, came to Las Cruces. He and Fountain were considerably alike. Both were proud and egocentric. They possessed courage and had answers for everything. In contrast Fountain was a born entertainer, a ham actor who loved speeches and parades, while Fall was more somber, preferring to work outside the limelight. Fountain was middle-aged, ambitious and power hungry; Fall was young, equally ambitious, and just as thirsty for political strength. Theirs became a classic case for two political titans battling in an arena where there was room for only one.

Fall established the *Independent Democrat* in Las Cruces. To further increase his power base, he teamed up with Oliver Lee, owner of a sprawling ranch near the mouth of Dog Canyon on the west side of New Mexico's Sacramento Mountains. Oliver Lee was probably the friendliest fellow who ever shot an enemy. Most people liked him then, and it's hard even now to find an unkind word.

As the struggle for political supremacy between Fall and Fountain reached its zenith, the focus switched to Oliver Lee. He controlled the Mesilla Valley muscle and the guns. Since many rumors tied Lee in with a rustling operation, the Southeastern New Mexico Livestock Association asked Fountain to look into the matter.

The investigation continued for months. Depositions were taken, cattle with altered brands were located. When enough evidence existed for an indictment, Fountain headed for Lincoln on January 12, 1896 to present his case to the grand jury. His wife asked him to take their nine-year-old son Henry along, figuring any enemies would not harm a small boy.

During the following two weeks the grand jury handed down several indictments, some involving Lee. When it was all over, the Colonel took Henry and headed home.

By February 1, he and young Henry were poised for the final dash to Mesilla. Yet, a nagging worry made him pause. Three unidentified riders had been following from a distance, and Fountain mentioned it to a mail carrier along the road. Although the carrier begged the Colonel to stay overnight at Luna's Well, Fountain considered it, then shook his head. His wife was expecting them, and little Henry had a head cold. Turning his team into the icy blasts whipping down from the Organ and the San Andreas Mountains, he and his son disappeared into eternity.

The Fountain family was frantic when the mail carrier came in the next day and asked where the Colonel was. Within hours large posses were out combing the back trails. They found where the Fountain horses had swerved off the road and galloped madly for a hundred yards or so across the desert. Judging by nearby footprints three men had apparently intercepted the buggy. Animal droppings and cigarette papers littered the ground, and near them was a large patch of dried blood.

Twelve miles away they found the abandoned buggy. Henry's hat and the Colonel's cartridge belt with twelve bullets missing lay on the floor. Hoofprints led toward the Jarilla Mountains where Orogrande is now, but the trail was lost when a large cattle herd moved across the path and effectively obliterated the tracks. The weary searchers turned homeward for additional food and clothing, and they built fires to keep from freezing.

Governor William T. "Poker Bill" Thornton of New Mexico offered a territorial reward of $2,000 for reliable information. Businessmen upped the ante to between eight and twelve thousand dollars. It was sufficient money to attract a first class lawman, since many observers believed that only an outsider would make an impartial investigation. On February 20, Governor Thornton, Pat Garrett and several New Mexico political figures met in an El Paso hotel room. Although Fall screamed foul and tried to block the proceedings, the officials hired Garrett as a territorial private detective until the Dona Ana sheriff could be prevailed upon to resign. The Pinkerton Detective Agency would assist in the investigation.

Complications set in. The sheriff had to be bribed into resigning.

Garrett believed that the Pinkertons were after the reward, and he co-operated very little with them. The agency still made a fairly exhaustive investigation, but dropped out in disgust after only a few months. The mystery now rested in the hands of Garrett.

As sheriff, Garrett moved slower than a mountain glacier. While he often spoke of developing his case, talk is about all he did during the first two years. Time went by and Thornton was replaced by Miguel Otero, who in turn prodded Garrett to act. In April of 1898, warrants were sworn out for the arrest of Oliver Lee, Jim Gililland and Bill McNew, all three of them ranchers.

Garrett admittedly did not have enough evidence for a conviction. What he really wanted was a confession, and planned to arrest Gililland or McNew and hold them in jail until they made a deal for their release. He did incarcerate McNew, but although the suspect spent several months behind bars, he never talked. Lee and Gililland went into hiding, and it was now up to Garrett to find them.

The trial

For a while it looked as if luck might be working for Garrett in his search for, and conviction of, Oliver Lee and Jim Gililland. Only A. B. Fall's legal talents stood between them and the hangman's rope, and when he left in June for the Spanish American War (much to his disgust he never made it to Cuba), the way seemed open to have the fugitives rounded up and executed before Fall returned.

Garrett received a tip that Lee and Gililland were hiding at Wildy Well, a line shack east of Orogrande, New Mexico. In the darkness of night, he rounded up deputies Jose Espalin, Ben Williams and Clint Llewellyn. An ex-schoolteacher named Kent Kearney volunteered to assist.

About 4 a.m. on July 12, the posse reined in half-a-mile short of Wildy Well. A flat-roofed adobe shack loomed in the false dawn, and nearby were a galvanized water tank and several outbuildings. The possemen approached closer, removed their shoes and tiptoed to the house. Loud snoring resounded from inside. Garrett took a deep breath, banged the door open, shouted "hands up," and cocked his revolver squarely under the frightened nose of the first person he saw. It turned out to be Mary Madison who lay beside her husband.

The Madison family were Lee employees, but none of Lee's instructions had prepared them for this. She screamed as a red-faced Pat Garrett demanded to know Lee's whereabouts. When no one admitted anything, Pat ordered a search of the buildings, all of which turned up empty. The posse might have left now except that a deputy observed the Madisons glancing nervously toward the house roof. Kearney placed a ladder on a shed, leaned it against the residence and climbed up. When he peeked over the top, shooting started.

Kearney tumbled from the ladder with a bullet in his shoulder and one in the thigh. From the roof Lee barely missed a shot at Garrett's head. The sheriff fired twice in return, sending gravel scattering from beneath Lee's stomach.

As Pat took cover, Espalin was pinned beside the house, unable to go inside. Williams ducked behind the water tank and lay there as cold water squirted down when the fugitives shot holes in the metal. The Madisons took refuge in the house cellar, forgetting their five-year-old daughter. She wandered aimlessly around throughout the battle.

Law enforcement had come upon hard times. Lee and Gililland dominated the battlefield and forced Garrett and his deputies to surrender. Lee permitted them to leave without their guns and shoes. Garrett promised to send a doctor back for Kearney. However, before the physician arrived, Mrs. Madison operated on the thigh wound to relieve his suffering. Although she successfully removed the slug, the patient bled to death.

Both Garrett and Lee told different versions of the story, and a good case can be built for each. Other than this, the facts were that a deputy was dead, one sheriff had been humiliated, two fugitives were loose and running, and the entire Southwest was in an uproar.

By this time the war in Cuba ended, and Fall returned to defend his clients. He realized that such an intolerable situation could not continue indefinitely. Sooner or later the implacable Garrett would either bring Oliver Lee to trial, or kill him.

Fall therefore convinced the railroads that a new county should be created with Alamagordo as its seat. Naturally its western limits would include the area where the Fountains were believed to have died, and thus jurisdiction would be removed from Sheriff Garrett. While Governor Otero did not show any enthusiasm for the undertaking,

Fall got around all this by naming the county after Otero.

Lee and Gililland surrendered to Eugene Manlove Rhodes, noted Southwest author, and the fugitives, in company with Rhodes, boarded a train headed for Las Cruces, the nearest railroad stop to Otero County. Also on this train were Garrett and the famed Texas Ranger Captain John R. Hughes. It is debatable whether or not Garrett and Hughes were aware of the outlaws' presence, but they made no attempt to interfere.

After Lee and Gililland entered custody, a trial took place in Hillsboro, New Mexico. People by the hundreds flocked to town, and tents of every size and description dotted the mountainsides. The onlookers sympathized with the defendants, and rumors were rampant that a jail break would be made if the men were judged guilty.

Fall took the initiative and handed out long-winded interviews to newsmen eager to justify their presence to faraway, cost-conscious editors. According to him this would be a battle of small interests against large interests, of poor ranchers against rich landholders, of a weak Democratic Party against the Republican juggernaut.

On May 29, 1899 the trial started and the prosecution charged that much of its evidence had been stolen. Fall said it never existed in the first place. With time and the crowds definitely on Fall's side, he was brilliant during the eighteen days that the trial lasted. His relentless cross-examinations confused and confounded the opposition. By the time most prosecution witnesses stepped down from the stand, Fall had them sounding like supporters for the defense.

Fall put his own people on the stand, and they refuted the evidence. Lee denied slaying Fountain. His mother, in one of the trial's more dramatic moments, testified that her son was a good boy. There were charges that Garrett planned to dynamite the Lee home, and to assassinate Lee once the fugitive was in custody. A. B. Fall pointed out the lack of bodies, and thus no conclusive evidence of murder.

During final arguments a prosecutor delivered a long, flowery address, punctuating it with frequent references from Dickens's *Pickwick Papers*. The translator, speaking to the Mexican jury, had trouble defining some of those phrases.

A. B. Fall spoke next, and he talked eloquently about the benefits of the jury system, and how it helped the little man. He called the prosecution witnesses "liars," and referred to the Dona Ana County officials as "a lot of broken down political hacks." He said, "You would not hang a yellow dog on the evidence presented here, much less two men." When he finished the courtroom burst into lengthy applause.

Prosecutor Tom Catron spoke last, knowing that it was all over, but not willing to give up. Bit by bit he went over every piece of evidence, every suspicious word spoken by the defendants. His arguments took two-and-a-half hours, and he, the jury and the prospectors were completely worn out when he finished.

The judge suggested that the jury retire and render its verdict in the morning, but Fall jumped to his feet and demanded that the twelve men try immediately for a decision. He prevailed, and fifteen minutes later it was all over. Lee and Gililland were acquitted.

A discouraged Pat Garrett dropped all interest in solving the Fountain murders. Instead, he served out the remainder of his term and became the El Paso Collector of Customs.

El Paso Customs Collector

In late 1901 the El Paso post of Customs Collector was vacant, and Garrett applied for the position. Since President Theodore Roosevelt prided himself on knowing many rugged western figures, he took Garrett's application under personal consideration.

As he did so, a torrent of letters and telegrams piled up on his Washington desk, critical items saying that "Garrett had made a name for himself as a killer." Fortunately for Pat, Roosevelt ignored most of these because they came primarily from disappointed Republican office seekers. On the plus side were numerous pieces of correspondence approving the selection, a large majority of them from El Paso businessmen.

To help his chances Garrett went to Washington where Roosevelt asked him to read a printed note, and if it suited him, to sign it. The note stated: "I the undersigned Patrick F. Garrett hereby give my word of honor, that if I am appointed Collector of Customs, that I will totally abstain from the use of intoxicating liquors during my term of office." Garrett read it, said it suited him exactly, and affixed his signature. Thus in seconds he demolished three serious Roosevelt misgivings. By repeating the words aloud he proved that he could read; by signing the statement he proved that he could write; and by both of these actions he took an oath not to drink.

Garrett won Roosevelt's approval and appeared before a Senate confirmation committee which questioned him about gambling habits. Pat looked the lawgivers straight in the eye and denied knowing the difference between a "straight flush" and "four of a kind." A month later an El Paso toastmaster quipped that "Here is the man whom the Senate worried about because he has the reputation of a poker player. Everyone in El Paso knows that Pat Garrett isn't a poker player. He just thinks he's a poker player."

Following the confirmation Garrett wrote the President and promised to "administer the law justly and conscientiously to all." Nevertheless, he was immediately in trouble with the Mexican Corralitos Cattle Company. Steers had always been appraised by age. The duty was $2 a head for calves less than a year old, and $3.75 for mature livestock. Ordinarily a specialist made the distinction, but Garrett did the work himself.

In April and May of 1902 the Mexican Corralitos people shipped over 3000 head through United States customs, and Garrett judged most of them as older than twelve months. The decision involved a lot of money, and the ranchers appealed it to the New York Board of Appraisers. They sent an investigator and otherwise tried the case by mail.

On August 22 the Board reached a "fair average estimate" and decided that only thirty percent were over one year. The judgment failed to please either party, but the ranchers accepted it while Garrett threatened to go all the way to the Supreme Court. He later backed down.

Meanwhile, I. A. Barnes, who represented an American importing firm doing business in Juarez, circulated a petition calling for Garrett's removal. Barnes recommended himself for the job. The petition stated that Garrett was rude and antagonistic, charges most likely correct considering the personality of the collector. Although the petition received what the newspapers called "the merry ha ha and the cold shoulder," it infuriated Secretary of the Treasury Shaw. He ordered Garrett to be more polite. Pat angrily wrote Roosevelt that he had always treated people with "the utmost courtesy."

Special Treasury Agent Joe Evans arrived in El Paso to investigate the situation and make recommendations. Evans suggested the government ask Garrett to refrain from appraising cattle, to hire a full-time specialist, and he recommended George Gaither, a well-known El Pasoan. The Treasury Department then forced Garrett to employ Gaither, and Pat did so under strong protest. After thirty days, Garrett dismissed him as incompetent.

A week later Garrett approached Gaither and Evans as they slouched against J. H. Nations Meat Market on San Antonio Street. "Did you tell anyone that I said your position was supposed to be permanent?" Garrett snarled to Gaither. "No, I did not," Gaither replied, "but you promised to do so if possible."

"You are a damned liar," Garrett roared, and Gaither struck him. The two grown, middle-aged men stood toe-to-toe slugging it out as bystanders separated them. Neither knocked the other down, but both were arrested and fined $5 for disturbing the peace. The El Paso *Times* chuckled that the whole thing bordered on the "comic opera style for a few minutes."

The Treasury Department employed Barnes, the same man who had tried to get rid of Garrett by circulating the petition, to investigate the fray. His report had the appearance of fairness, and he concluded that most El Pasoans "considered the fight a very disgraceful affair."

On May 14 Secretary Shaw directed Garrett to submit a prompt and full report on the subject. "You are advised that such conduct on your part is regarded as indefensible and deserves censure in the strongest terms," the letter said. Garrett replied that "although my side of the case has not been presented, and you say that I was entirely in the wrong and have no defense, I do not see where any report by me would be considered by you as justifiable for my conduct." He refused to defend himself, and that statement ended the fisticuffs affair.

Supporting Garrett was Tom Powers, proprietor of the notorious Coney Island Saloon where the First National Building is now. Powers was a one-eyed, happy-go-lucky Irishman who wanted to meet the President at the annual Rough Riders convention in San Antonio. Garrett agreed and introduced Powers to Roosevelt as a "West Texas cattleman." Everybody posed for pictures.

Practically before the negative dried, someone leaked the photos to

149

the press. Roosevelt growled furiously that he had been misled, and the El Paso papers correctly predicted that Garrett's two-year reappointment, due in January, was in danger.

Garrett's friends urged him to forsake Powers, but Pat refused. Instead he took Powers to Washington in December of 1905, to speak personally with the President. They were refused admittance even though El Pasoans sent a long string of additional endorsements. On the 15th, the President told Garrett that he would be out of work by the end of the month. Roosevelt was not discharging Garrett; the President was simply letting the regular term expire and not renewing it.

Pat still did not fully comprehend what had happened. Emerson Hough, well-known writer and friend of Garrett's, was asked to query the President for additional explanations. Over the next few weeks Hough and Roosevelt exchanged several letters, the President admitting that it was an annoying matter "to have Garrett introduce as an intimate friend a man well known as a professional gambler, and then have myself, Garrett and the gambler taken in a photograph together." Though pictures had not in themselves brought about Garrett's downfall, they had been the final straw. According to Roosevelt, the Secretary of Treasury was the one really responsible for Garrett's departure. Shaw said Garrett was inefficient, away from his office too much and "had bad habits."

With the news of his dismissal, Pat Garrett left El Paso and returned to Dona Ana County to a ranch he had purchased near Organ while serving as sheriff. His letters to Hough for the next two years reveal a sense of deep depression and impending tragedy. As early as March, 1906, he asked Hough to "pardon the unintelligent manner in which this letter is written for I am suffering great distress of mind and soul." The scene was obviously now being set for one of the truly great murder mysteries of our time.

The strange death of Pat Garrett

The last two years of Garrett's life were desperate indeed. He belonged nowhere. His enemies hated him, and his friends did not understand him. He was quarrelsome and insulting, brawling drunkenly on the streets and on the open range. He traded punches with Frank "Pancho" Amador, whose father built the Las Cruces Amador Hotel, and was shamefully thrashed by the much smaller man. Garrett reportedly even fought big Jim Baird, a neighboring rancher, and banged his Colt .45 across Baird's head.

Some people say that Garrett returned to Las Cruces in order to resume the investigation for the Fountain slayers. That is nonsense. He still believed Oliver Lee and Jim Gililland to be guilty. However, the Territory would never try them again no matter how much additional evidence turned up. Also, the reward offers had long ago evaporated. Garrett returned to his ranch, located on the opposite side of the San Andres from Organ, New Mexico, because he was broke and because he had no place else to go. He was so poor that Organ grocer L. B. Bentley wrote his name in the "deadbeat book" for a past due account amounting to less than $10.

In 1890 Garrett had co-signed a $1,000 bank note for George Curry. Curry defaulted, and instead of the bank filing suit against him, it took the hapless Garrett to court. However, the bank never quite got possession of the ranch because Garrett had previously mortgaged it to Las Cruces businessman Martin Lohman. When Garrett did not pay anything on the principal or the interest, Lohman discounted the note to W. W. Cox, owner of the San Augustine Ranch. With the bank and Cox now fighting with Garrett for money (neither of them really wanted the land), the county jumped into the act. Garrett owed back taxes for six years and couldn't meet the assessments. He watched in fury as the commissioners sold most of his livestock.

All this was too much for Cox. He rounded up Garrett's remaining steers and drove them onto the San Augustine range. In order to keep possession, he gave Garrett "one dollar and other valuable considerations" for everything. All that Garrett now owned was the shack where he and his family lived, and the land. The title even to that was shaky.

Events picked up momentum. On March 11, 1907, Poe Garrett (Pat's son) leased the Bear Canyon Ranch to Wayne Brazel and Print Rhode. Bear Canyon was a wilderness piece of property bordering Garrett's home ranch, and Brazel and Rhode were local cowboys with close personal and blood ties to Cox. Two months later Brazel and Rhode drove goats onto the land, and Garrett exploded in anger. He tried to cancel the lease and failed.

Into the confusion and hostility now stepped James B. Miller, better known as "Killin' Jim," or "Deacon Jim," depending upon whether he was murdering people or praying in church. He sought grazing land for Mexican cattle prior to shipping them to Oklahoma. He and a relative named Carl Adamson told Garrett they would buy the Bear Canyon property if Pat would get rid of the goats.

Miller even offered to purchase the 1200 animals which Brazel said he and his partner owned. When it came time for an accounting, though, there were 1800 goats. Brazel said he wouldn't give up the lease unless the extra 600 were bought, and Miller said he couldn't afford that many more.

An anguished Garrett asked everyone for a meeting in Las Cruces on February 29, 1908, to settle the matter. Carl Adamson came to Garrett's ranch, and the two men left for town early in the morning. As their double-horse drawn carriage wound through Organ and a mile or so beyond, they overtook Wayne Brazel on horseback. Together the three men headed for town, Adamson trying to keep the conversation light, and Garrett and Brazel getting very surly with each other.

Near Alameda Arroyo, Adamson stopped the carriage to relieve himself. Garrett hesitated, then decided to do the same thing. He stepped to the rear of the carriage, turned his back, removed his left glove, and unbuttoned his trousers. That was the old manhunter's position when a bullet slammed into the back of his head.

He died instantly, even though another bullet struck him in the body as he fell. Brazel and Adamson went into Las Cruces, leaving Garrett in the road. Brazel told the sheriff it was self-defense.

One of the intriguing aspects about this killing is that few people then, and even fewer people now, believe that Wayne Brazel did the slaying.

Governor Curry left immediately for Las Cruces. With him were James M. Hervey, attorney general, and Fred Fornoff, captain of the Territorial Mounted Police. They conducted a short investigation, and were themselves convinced that someone besides Brazel did the slaying. Their finger pointed toward Jim Miller, but Miller was never indicted and Brazel was.

Altogether over the years there have been many theories about who killed Garrett, and most historians believe Miller did it. There is another story which names Cox as the murderer, and an equally fine one that puts the blame on Print Rhode. The Garrett family thinks Adamson pulled the trigger.

Regardless of the trigger-man, everyone seems unanimous in the opinion that W. W. Cox paid a large amount of money to have Garrett killed. There are whispers of a secret hotel meeting in El Paso, a conference between A. B. Fall, Cox, Miller, Adamson and others. Cox allegedly offered a large sum of money to get the job done.

In my judgment Cox is not guilty of bribing anyone, and as for the secret hotel meeting, it never took place. There was no conspiracy to kill Pat Garrett. Brazel actually did the shooting. It was a simple case of fear and hate erupting into murder along a lonely New Mexico back road. The evidence for this conclusion is long and complex, little of it being previously revealed.

Approximately a year after Brazel's surrender, he went on trial for murder and was ably defended by Fall. A jury acquitted him after a few minutes deliberation. Following this, Brazel became a lonely and tragic figure. His wife died, and by 1915 he had completely dropped out of sight. There are stories that he died of a heart attack, that he was accidentally killed, and that he was slain in South America by a remnant of the Butch Cassidy gang. Nobody knows for sure, and thus we have another mystery.

As for Garrett, he was stretched out on five chairs in a Las Cruces undertaking parlor. Although burial was in the shabby Odd Fellows Cemetery, his body was moved across the street to the Masonic graveyard in 1957. A large stone marked GARRETT keeps its lonely vigil over the family plot. Here lies the man who was New Mexico, but you can search in vain throughout the entire state and find no other monument to his memory.

Barn in Ada, Oklahoma, 1909.
Jim Miller, Joe Allen, Berry Burrell and Jesse West.

Kustom Quality

Killin' Jim Miller

15

JIM MILLER

BUSHWHACKER

THE WELL-KNOWN HISTORIAN and folklorist C. L. Sonnichsen once described Jim Miller of Pecos, Texas as superior to all other badmen in one respect—"he had the best manners."

Jim Miller was not the familiar prototype of the Wild West gunman. Some folks called him "Deacon Jim" because of his regular church attendance, gentle nature and studious Bible reading. Other folks knew him as "Killin' Jim," a cold-blooded, almost inhuman individual who raised the art of bushwhacking and ambush to an exact science. His credentials were a shotgun and occasionally a rifle, and he claimed to have killed over fifty men, although that number cannot be documented. We know that he sold his trigger finger to the highest bidder, and in the Old West there were many men who bought it.

He was born in Van Buren, Arkansas on October 25, 1861, a youngster who carried through life large, egg-shaped knots behind his rather prominent ears. As a youth, he lived with his brother-in-law but at the age of twenty-two he severed their relationship with a shotgun blast. A jury gave him life imprisonment but the case was overturned on appeal and was never retried.

Miller drifted to Pecos, Texas in 1891, where he became a deputy sheriff. Sheriff Bud Frazer had some uncertainties about this man who killed his own relative and he knew of several pretty hairy stories linking Miller to other crimes, but nothing had been proven and deputies were hard to come by.

The Pecos townspeople took naturally to the likeable stranger who never smoked, never drank, never entered saloons, spoke softly and politely to women, never used tobacco or snuff, and rarely swore. Miller showed up in church every Sunday, loved those familiar hymns, and could be found in the "amen corner" every time a religious revival came to town. With sterling qualities such as this, people overlooked his idiosyncrasy of wearing a heavy, black frock coat. No one paid much attention to it in winter, but it did look strange all buttoned up in the middle of July.

After marrying Miss Sallie Clements, whose relatives were quick with a gun, but honest and hard-working, Miller entered the cattle business. Some folks wondered where he got the money, and more than a few ranchers with missing stock suspected rustling. Frazer's investigation cleared the deputy, but not everybody was convinced and the town split down the middle concerning Miller's activities.

As the relationship between Miller and a suspicious sheriff began to sour, Frazer left town on business. During his absence Miller permitted the criminal element to take over, and stories circulated to Frazer that Miller intended to kill him when he returned. Frazer spiked the plan by stopping off in El Paso and asking the noted Texas Ranger John R. Hughes to accompany him back to Pecos. Nobody in Pecos, of course, wanted to tangle with Hughes, and a few minutes after the ranger hit town Miller was in jail charged with plotting to commit murder. The trial took place in El Paso, and a jury acquitted Miller.

In 1894 Miller returned to Pecos where he purchased a hotel and announced that henceforth he would lead a quiet life. While churches welcomed the errant sinner back into the fold, Frazer was not so forgiving. On April 12 the two tangled in a gunfight in which by all rules of the game, Miller should have been killed.

Frazer walked up behind Miller, and when Deacon Jim turned around to see who was there, the sheriff fired. Amazingly the bullet bounced off the black coat. Determinedly the sheriff fired again and disabled Miller's right arm. Miller now had his own pistol out and blazing, but left-handed shooting was not his forte. He hit an innocent bystander. The frustrated Frazer lowered his aim then and shot Miller in the lower diaphragm, ending the gunfight. Frazer left and Miller was carried inside the hotel where an examination revealed why those bullets had bounced off the chest and why Jim had always worn that coat even in hot weather. A heavy iron plate was sewn into the lining.

Bud Frazer lost his reelection bid for sheriff, and left town for Eddy (Carlsbad), New Mexico. Behind him a slowly mending Miller boasted that he had run Frazer out of town, and that he would eventually kill him.

Six months later when Frazer returned on personal business, he and Miller met in the street by accident, and once again the six-shooters roared. Miller was hit in the right arm and in the leg. With the victim nearly helpless, Frazer rushed in closer and fired directly at Miller's heart. Unfortunately for the ex-sheriff, he still did not know about that iron plate, and the bullet simply bounced. This was too much for Frazer. He fled, leaving Miller in control of the battlefield.

Miller swore out a charge of attempted murder against Frazer, and the case went to trial in El Paso and resulted in a hung jury. In Colorado City the jurors were much more positive. They figured Miller had gotten what he deserved, so they set Frazer free.

Nothing further happened until September 13, 1896 when the feud ended at a gambling table in Toyah, Texas. From outside Miller laid a shotgun across the top of a saloon door, and with a single blast sent Frazer to the Promised Land.

Trial took place in Eastland, but the first jury could not reach a verdict. While waiting trial number two, the prisoner conducted prayer meetings, and when he went back to court, a preacher testified that Deacon Jim's conduct was as "exemplary as that of a minister of the Gospel." Miller was acquitted.

After the turn of the century Miller moved to Fort Worth where he entered the real estate promotion business with a man named Frank Fore. Fore was reasonably honest, and he threatened to tell a Fort Worth grand jury that Miller's land was in the Gulf of Mexico. So Miller cornered Fore in the washroom of the Delaware Hotel and shot him to death. As excited people gathered around to see what happened, Miller bent low over his former partner, and with tears streaming down his face, stated, "It's awful to have to kill a friend. I did everything I could to keep him from reaching for his gun." Naturally, old good-hearted Jim was acquitted once again of murder.

Over the next several years Miller's gun continued to bang and men continued to die. He earned lots of money and he always wore starched white shirts with stiff collars, a diamond stickpin and a diamond ring.

There were many rumors, and considerable evidence, that Miller killed Pat Garrett near Las Cruces, New Mexico. Since this episode has already been explored no further mention will be made of it here.

As things turned out, Miller was reaching the end of his line, or perhaps it would be more fitting to say he was about to reach the end of his rope. Interesting events were now blowing in the Oklahoma wind.

Over in Ada, Oklahoma, a feud between Angus Bobbitt and a faction led by Jesse West, Joe Allen and Berry Burrell, was about to boil over into violence. None of these figures had any halos, but Bobbitt might have been respectable. Although there were many facets to the trouble, basically it involved cattle and whiskey.

Miller did not know any of the four, but the West-Allen-Burrell people paid him $2,000 to get rid of Bobbitt. So one evening as the victim drove a wagon back to his ranch, Miller waylaid him. Killin' Jim simply cradled a shotgun in the crotch of an elm, waited until Bobbitt drove by, and pulled the trigger. Bobbitt lived for an hour, unable to identify his assassin.

In a territory where killings were almost as common as tumbleweeds, this murder touched a public nerve, perhaps because of its utter callousness, and people were outraged. Authorities lured Allen, West and Burrell back into the Territory and captured them. Miller was located in Fort Worth.

When lawmen arrested him, Miller said, "I never give police officers any trouble since I prefer taking my chances with the court." After forty or fifty killings by his own tally, his track record with a jury was running a hundred percent in favor of acquittal.

West, Burrell and Allen were frightened, but Miller remained lighthearted. He changed clothes every day, shaved twice a day, insisted upon fresh linen for his bed each morning, ordered porterhouse steaks from the local restaurant and always tipped the jailer with a five dollar bill. Meanwhile, letters and telegrams, many from preachers and prominent people, poured into town, all of them praising Miller as an upstanding citizen, a man of high moral character. Moman Pruiett, a famous criminal lawyer, said he was ready for the defense. The concerned people of Ada began to suspect that justice might not be served.

On Sunday, April 19, 1909, at 2 a.m., about forty vigilantes broke into the jail, clubbed the two guards and bound them with bailing wire. The four prisoners were removed from their cells.

West resisted, but was savagely beaten and dragged to the barn next door. Ropes were tossed over the rafters, and while the men begged for mercy, the vigilantes jerked them into eternity. West went first, followed by Burrell and Allen.

The mob saved Miller for last, and he acquiesced calmly. He asked to die in his black frock coat, and that was denied. Pulling off his diamond ring, he sent it to his wife in Fort Worth, and handed a diamond scarf pin to a guard named McCarthy who had been especially kind.

They put his hat on his head and tightened the noose around his neck. Then came a short pause for any last words. Deacon Jim smiled, shook his head, and said, "Let'er rip!"

*John Chisum . . . was every inch the
acknowledged master of a cattle domain larger
than many eastern states.*

16

CHISUM

CATTLE BARON

Men called him the Jinglebob King of the Pecos, and that he was. The big bones of his spare frame were strong, the skin sunbaked the color of old and supple leather. From the tip of his scuffy boots with the worn and faded trousers stuffed inside, to the thin-looking face with its long jaw, prominent nose, dark brown hair and bushy mustache, he was every inch the acknowledged master of a cattle domain larger than many eastern states.

John Chisum was not a gunman in the ordinary sense of the word. He rarely packed a six-shooter since cattle was his business, not manslaying. He qualifies for this book not because of his personal speed or accuracy with a weapon; such things never mattered to him, but because he associated with men who did live by the gun, and whose lives were, for better or for worse, tied together with his. The Billy the Kids, the Pat Garretts and enough other outlaws and lawmen to stock a five-square-mile graveyard, were frequent visitors to his ranch house near Roswell, New Mexico.

Madison County, Tennessee claimed him, the second of five children, and he was born there on August 15, 1824. When he was thirteen the family moved to Lamar County in East Texas near the Oklahoma line. Over the years he tried driving cattle into Arkansas and

161

Louisiana, but the insects and the mud and the swamps and the curling rivers stopped him and made the enterprise a losing proposition.

He ran twice for county clerk, got elected the second time, but gave it up when he met an eastern financier named Stephen Fowler. The capitalist looked Chisum over and said he would invest in cattle if he could find someone who knew anything about the animals. Chisum, of course, knew a lot, so in the spring of 1854 he and Fowler launched a ten-year partnership.

The partners grazed livestock where Fort Worth, Texas stands today, and for the first five years all went well. Then came the Civil War, the collapse of the Confederacy, Indian raids, the lack of cowboy help and drought. Fowler wasn't sure things would ever be the same again, so Chisum bought him out and moved to present-day San Angelo. He was now forty.

Chisum continued to turn his face westward. His brother Pitzer looked over the New Mexico Pecos River, found it good, and talked old John into moving there.

Chisum established his headquarters at Bosque Grande, thirty or forty miles downriver from Fort Sumner. He sold stock to the Bosque Redondo Indian Reservation and to numerous small ranchers and miners. Government contracts were a lucrative source, especially the military posts.

In addition, Chisum would put together herds for Charles Goodnight, a nearby rancher who made yearly drives to Dodge City and points north. However, in rounding up this assortment of cattle, Chisum did not always pay proper attention to the brands. Too often he simply absorbed another rancher's cattle on the verbal promise that the cattleman would be paid once the steers were marketed. And as sometimes happens in agreements such as this, John Chisum had a strong tendency toward absentmindedness. But when an irate rancher tracked him down, he never had trouble collecting. Old John just grinned and wrote out a check.

In early 1875 Chisum moved his headquarters to near present-day Roswell, New Mexico. First he built the Square House, eight small rooms surrounding a patio, a building of no structural size or significance. Later he replaced it with the Long House, an adobe structure 148 feet long and thirty-nine feet wide. To provide fresh water, he dug a "drinking ditch" from the South Spring River (a tributary of the Pecos) to his home. It flowed beneath the central hallway in the Long House and then curled on down to water his orchards and crops.

The dining room table sat twenty-six people, and rare was it when a chair stood empty. Tramping through his house at one time or another came governors, legislators, intellectuals, businessmen, army officers, common soldiers, buffalo hunters, outlaws, sheriffs and gold seekers. His niece Sallie, a sixteen-year-old with a big crush on her uncle, was the perfect Chisum hostess.

In such a luxurious home, one would have expected John Chisum to have an expensive room and office. Instead, his office was his bedroom: spare, neat and plain. In addition to a small bed, he kept a safe, a walnut writing desk and a big dictionary. Except for his women, John Chisum was not a complicated man.

He never married, although he had a lifelong reputation as a ladies' man. Several females at one time or another almost slipped the halter tight about his neck, but always he pulled away.

His first love was the Chisum empire. It extended 150 miles up and down the Pecos River, from mountain range to mountain range, almost a fifth of New Mexico. He held it by controlling the water, in this case the river. He never paid anyone for all this open range, but he claimed it and owned it by right of occupation.

At the height of his glory, seventy to eighty thousand cattle grazed on Chisum land. His Rail brand burned its way along a steer's left flank from the shoulder to the hip even though he was best known for the Jinglebob brand, an ear notch (which was a widespread method of branding) cut in such a way that the ear flopped in a distinctive manner.

These were the days when men rode for the brand, and were proud of their affiliation. They stood by the boss, and the boss stood by them. It was a unique loyalty, the likes of which we may never see again.

When a Chisum trail hand was slain, John nodded his head, and the murderer's horse was led out from beneath a cottonwood tree. Although John Chisum did tolerate small-time thefts, big-time rustling was a different matter. And of course Indians were always a nuisance, oftentimes a menace. The Chisum cowhands fought fire with fire, lead with lead.

John and his range boss Jim Highsaw rode into El Paso on the trail of stolen cattle and found their beeves ready to be slaughtered. High-

163

saw, reputedly a dangerous man, charged small rancher Dick Smith with the thefts and promptly shot him.

But of all Chisum's troubles, the worst was the Lincoln County War. He sympathized with the Tunstall-McSween faction, but did little to aid them and watched as they were ground under and buried beneath the rocky soil of Lincoln. Billy the Kid afterwards claimed that Chisum had hired him and others as gunmen but the cattleman heatedly denied it.

As time went on it became open season on John Chisum's cattle. Rustlers all over the territory picked away at his livestock. In desperation, Chisum wrote Governor Lew Wallace and recommended that Pat Garrett, a former buffalo hunter, be deputized to guard specific crossing points along the Pecos, that Garrett be empowered to intercept the outlaws, and if necessary kill them. Out of this effort came the election of Pat Garrett as sheriff, and his rendezvous with destiny less than two years later when Garrett surprised the Kid in a Fort Sumner bedroom and left him dead with a bullet in the heart.

Meanwhile, up in the Territorial capital the corrupt Santa Fe Ring, with Senator Tom Catron as its articulate spokesman, sought to bring Chisum to his knees. They hated John for his Pecos power, for his independence from political control, and for his support of Tunstall and McSween.

Various lawsuits charged Chisum with fraud, and in January of 1878, the authorities jailed him for several weeks in the Las Vegas, New Mexico jail. During his imprisonment he wrote an explanation and a vindication of his actions. This remarkable document has only recently been published in full, and it reveals Chisum as basically a straightforward man who trusted some old friends much more than he should have.

After his release he sold much of his stock to Hunter and Evans, a St. Louis firm with interests throughout the West. Basically, John made a good decision. Times were changing, and the days of free public land and open range were about over.

In 1883 a malignant tumor sprouted on the left side of his neck, grew to the size of a baseball and tilted his head to the right. When he could stand the discomfort no longer, he went to Kansas City, Missouri for an operation.

The doctors said the operation was a success and although in great pain, John started home. He made it as far as Las Vegas, when another tumor appeared. This one grew large almost overnight and kept him in agony. In desperation he returned to Kansas City, but this time the doctors said he was too weak to operate. They gave him medicine. Nothing helped.

Chisum could not speak above a whisper now, and with the spark of life flickering, he hoped the mineral baths at Eureka Springs, Arkansas might help. They didn't, and he died on December 22, 1884.

With his death at the age of sixty, a lot that was fine and noble and stubborn and persevering in this world died with him. Perhaps his best testament was the cowboys he left behind. Up until a few short years ago there were still a lot of men around who were proud to say they once worked for the Jinglebob brand. They had ridden the river with John Chisum.

Luke Short

Jim Courtright

17

LUKE SHORT &
JIM COURTRIGHT

A CLASSIC COMBINATION

Luke short was a gambler, not a gunman, but it is in the latter profession that his reputation rests. He and Jim Courtright, one of the most colorful gunfighters in the land, never caught much attention from frontier scholars even though their pistol duel in front of a Fort Worth shooting gallery in 1887 is one of the better known and most classic affairs of its kind.

Both men died young, but in their short years they packed in considerable living. An era came and went. Luke was born in Mississippi in 1854, the sixth of seven children. When he was two years old the family moved to Grayson County, Texas, where Luke ran away from home at the age of sixteen. He worked on a trail drive to Kansas, and somewhere along the way learned to shuffle cards much better than he learned to hustle cattle. He therefore began his rise to the top as a gambler.

When Short had his boots on he stood about five-foot-seven, and at his heaviest he weighed about 140 pounds. His hands were quick and he possessed a mathematical mind. The usual droopy mustache hung over the upper lip.

Luke was a fastidious dresser, a man about town in a Prince Albert coat, walking stick, and a high, silk hat. Local gossip had it that he bathed every day.

A sawed-off .45 Colt protruded from his hip pocket. Luke wasn't particularly accurate with the revolver, but for distances no further than the length of a card table he did not need to be.

He moved his residence often during the next few years. For awhile he scouted for the army, then took up with Wyatt Earp and Bat Masterson in Dodge City. He drifted to Nebraska and sold whiskey to the Indians.

By the time Short showed up in Tombstone, Arizona, his gambling reputation was established. Except possibly for a few Nebraska Indians, he had never killed anyone.

In Tombstone he and Charlie Storms tangled, the other man having the reputation of commiting several killings. The story is that Storms was drinking heavily and vowing to fertilize the parched Arizona soil with Short's blood. They met on February 25, 1881, as Luke and Bat Masterson left the Oriental Saloon. Storms waited on a street corner, grabbed Short, and reached for his gun at the same time.

Short being a little faster, to say nothing of being a little more sober, pulled his .45, shoved it against Storms' chest and jerked the trigger until it emptied. A grand jury considered the act justifiable and took no action. Luke Short went back to Dodge.

During the next few years a pseudo-reform element took office in Dodge, an element frowning on Luke and the three female "singers" who worked in his Long Branch Saloon. What happened next has come down in history as the "Dodge City War."

City Clerk Hartman arrested Short's girls in the Long Branch, and the next time Hartman and Short passed in the street, they took shots at each other. Therefore, a citizen's committee scooped Luke up, took him to the depot and gave him a choice of east or west bound trains. He took the one headed east.

For the next several months Short moved around Kansas like a pawn on a chessboard. His old friends Bat Masterson and Wyatt Earp took up his defense with Governor George Glick. Finally Luke simply returned to Dodge. Though the mayor screamed for the national guard to preserve order, and the newspapers predicted blood in the streets, nothing really happened. No shooting anyway.

On June 12, 1883, the Dodge City *Globe* noted: "Our city trouble is about over and things in general will be conducted as of old. All parties that have been run out have returned—no further effort will be made to drive them away.

"Gambling houses, we understand, will again be opened but with screened doors. A new dance hall was opened Saturday where all the Warriors met and settled their past differences and everything was made lovely and serene.

"The Mayor stood firm in his gambling Proclamation, but as his ardent supporters have gone over to his enemies he will stand without that ardent support he had calculated upon to help him enforce it.

"We have all along held that our Mayor was overadvised in the action he has taken and had he followed his own better judgment and not the advice of schemers and tricksters who had selfish interests at stake and not the best interest of this community he would have fared much better."

Nevertheless, things had changed in Dodge. Gambling was on its way out, and Short was a gambler. In November he moved to Fort Worth and to new trouble.

Longhaired Jim Courtright did not own Fort Worth, but he was its best known and most notorious citizen. He came originally from Iowa (other authorities say Illinois), and his name was Timothy Isaiah Courtright. He had to be tough to survive that, and it's worth noting that after he strapped on his guns and proved what a terror he could be, there was a noticeable decline in the number of people who called him Timothy.

Two-gun men in the West were rare, but Courtright had the bonafide credentials. With his long blond hair (not shoulder length as some writers have indicated) combed nicely toward the back, he cut a handsome figure on the street. Although not well known outside of Fort Worth, he had the reputation as a colorful and deadly gunman.

During the Civil War he served as a Federal scout under General Logan. Afterwards he became marshal of Fort Worth in the 1870's. Not much is known of his career but rumors had it that he and the mayor were shaking down the saloon owners and gamblers. That ended Courtright's career in Fort Worth, so he drifted west, allegedly to Mesilla, New Mexico, where he is supposed to have marshaled for awhile.

In 1883 he showed up in American Valley, New Mexico, where he and another gunslinger killed two men and then fled the state. Jim returned to Fort Worth where the rangers took him into custody. Hours later he escaped and went to South America, staying until 1886. Then he returned to Socorro, New Mexico, went to trial and was freed. The witnesses had disappeared.

After his acquittal, Longhaired Jim Courtright stopped for a short time in El Paso and demonstrated his prowess with the six-shooter in front of some properly awed citizens. Feeling pretty good, he headed back to Fort Worth.

Work in Fort Worth was a little hard to come by for a man who had only his gun-hand to sell. So in frustration he opened the Commercial Detective Agency and nearly went bankrupt.

The railroads bought his talents, and they used him as a strikebreaker. Several times Jim bullied the strikers, and on one occasion he and they exchanged several shots. Surprisingly nobody was killed.

When that trouble blew over and workers and management settled their differences, Jim buckled on his pistols and visited the gambling and saloon establishments demanding protection money. Most owners took a look at those guns, considered Courtright's reputation and paid up.

Everybody took protection except Luke Short. Since Luke owned the White Elephant, and was justifiably known as the Gambling King of Fort Worth, he naturally was a key figure in any local shakedown. Until Short buckled under, Courtright would not have the town under tight control.

Hard feelings flared between Short and Courtright, and the showdown came on the gloomy, overcast evening of February 8, 1887. For a week Courtright had been drinking steadily, and at 8 p.m. he stopped in front of the White Elephant and sent word inside for Short to come out and talk.

Always the dandy, Luke put on his flowered vest, his hat, checked his pocket six-gun, and stepped outside. The two engaged in conversation, and strolled down the street pausing in front of a shooting gallery.

Gradually the discussion heated up. Short had his thumbs hooked in the armholes of his vest when he dropped them to adjust his clothing, Courtright yelled, "Don't pull a gun on me!"

Instantly both men had six-shooters out, and Luke got off the first shot, one of the luckiest in frontier history. The bullet smashed Courtright's right thumb, and disabled the revolver.

Short fired again and again and again from practically point-blank range. Down went the longhaired gunfighter, unconscious by the time he hit the ground, dead within a few minutes.

The outcome stunned Fort Worth. Everyone expected a showdown sooner or later, but no one expected Luke Short to win. A rather sleazy David had slain Goliath.

Luke Short never went to trial, as the entire affair seemed like a clear-cut case of self-defense. Nevertheless, Short too was a dying man. He drank too much, ate too much, kept terrible hours, and gradually saw his health collapse. At thirty-six years of age, his kidneys started failing. In December of 1890 a shotgun blast from behind crippled his left hand and leg.

As time went on he knew he was dying from his own hard living and he paid $20 for an Oakwood Cemetery lot in Fort Worth. He also purchased a granite stone with the simple inscription of "Luke L. Short, 1854-1893."

He died of dropsy on September 8, a man who according to his biographer, had outlived his time in less than forty years.

18

JOHNSON COUNTY WAR

THE AMERICAN WEST had its share of grassland wars. They accounted for many feuds, and an untold number of deaths. Yet, by most accounts the violence was petty, involving only a few participants and sometimes a sheriff or two. The effects rarely had regional consequences, although a legacy of bitterness often hung on for generations.

But for sheer cussedness, bloodshed, courage and stupidity, no conflict ever equalled the Johnson County War in Wyoming, sometimes known as the "War on Powder River." It flared between the big cattleman and the little cowboy, two factions that had every reason to stick together.

Wyoming is a vast land of few people, and it has always been this way. The grass is high, the summers are mild, and the winters are frigid. It is cattle country, formerly open range, and from the 1870's to the 1890's largely controlled by foreign interests, especially Scottish and English. It is, and was, the land of the cowboy.

Some of the nation's largest ranches thrived during this period in Wyoming, but many were going bankrupt and did not know it. The trouble stemmed largely from mismanagement by absentee landlords. They took money out of the ranches; they plowed very little back in. Owners looked on the cowboy as a serf.

The Wyoming Stock Growers' Association dominated Wyoming.

It controlled the politicians, most of the newspapers and the courts. The association was largely made up of foreigners, the railroads and large businessmen, traditionally unsympathetic to cowboys.

A severe drought struck during the summer of 1886, weakening the livestock, and when the wind whistled off the snow-capped peaks that fall, everything that lived crumbled beneath it. Cattle turned their tails into the gale and drifted before it, stopping only when they hit an obstruction such as a fence or an arroyo filled with deep snow. There they piled up and died by the thousands. Except for the buffalo slaughter, the high plains had never seen, and would never see again, such massive and appalling death. When spring came at last, sixty percent of the animals were dead or dying. Wyoming was a disaster.

Big cattlemen now desperately needed loyal cowboys, and they tried to buy and sell them on short notice. When not needed, cowboys were discharged and told to ride. A so-called "fair but reduced scale of wages" went into effect.

The cowboys struck, demanding $40 a month for everybody. However, these fellows were too individualistic for their own good, and the strike soon broke.

Cattlemen who might have been charitable, decided to crush and humiliate, totally destroy the independent cowboy. They black-balled the strike leaders, thus forcing them to either leave the state, or homestead their own land and start their own cattle spreads. Mavericking (taking of unbranded cattle, usually calves abandoned or lost by the mothers) became widespread, a practice that infuriated the association. It prevailed upon the Wyoming legislature to pass a "maverick law" making such tactics illegal.

The big ranchers refused to honor the institution of "grub line riding," unless a cowboy paid fifty cents. (In winter, hungry and out of work cowboys rode the grub lines from ranch to ranch receiving free meals and shelter for the night, thus surviving until the roundups started again in the spring.) This directive closing down the grub lines stunned even the working cowboys. Cooks in particular could not ask the drifters for fifty cents and look them in the eye at the same time, knowing that the cowhands would often as not have to ride away hungry.

These harsh measures forced many an honest cowboy into killing and rustling stock, or even mavericking, in order to survive. And as he did that, the Cattle Growers' Association tried to crack down even harder. According to the association, Wyoming was split between honest men and rustlers. A rustler included not only those caught stealing cows, but those whose homesteads included steers "everyone knew they couldn't afford."

The association hired detectives, men who either bullied or took the cowboys to court. The latter rarely worked, however, because juries were invariably made up of other cowboys who promptly voted for acquittal. Therefore, measures grew even tougher. In 1899 Ella Watson, better known as "Cattle Kate," and James Averell, a postmaster, justice of the peace and storekeeper, were lynched by agents of the cattlemen (strangled might be a better word) in a bungled execution. Bushwhacking became a common practice. Johnson County, reputed to be a stronghold of the rustlers, underwent a reign of terror.

In anger and frustration, the association plotted to burn northern Wyoming free of rustlers, especially the town of Buffalo, the county seat of Johnson County. They drew up a death list allegedly containing the names of seventy men.

Agents for the cattlemen showed up in Paris and Lamar counties in Texas where they recruited twenty-two gunfighters. These hired killers were promised $5 a day and expenses, plus a $50 bonus for every rustler slain.

The "Cheyenne Ring" (actually elements of the powerful Stock Growers' Association) financed the operation, and top politicians from the governor down were involved at least to the extent of knowing what was going on.

Approximately fifty men made up the invasion army. Actual killings would be done by the Texas gunmen, but these rough characters would be led by fifteen or twenty top cattlemen. Also included were three teamsters, a surgeon, and two newspapermen, one from Cheyenne and the other from Chicago.

Oddly, it never occurred to these invaders that the countryside would view them as anything other than instruments of justice. Nobody seemed to understand that they might be the ones to be trapped and wiped out. So certain were they of success, they took special care to neutralize the state militia should some local sheriff attempt to call on it to restore order. And to make certain the outside world knew nothing of this bloody episode until it ended, the invaders cut most of the telegraph lines.

The "secret" invasion train (about as secret in Cheyenne as a Wyoming cloudburst) pulled out of Cheyenne on Tuesday, April 5, 1892. Behind its blacked out windows were the invaders, horses, supplies, wagons, and enough ammunition to kill everyone in three states. Hours later the train chugged into Casper and unloaded. By early morning, farmers plowing their fields recalled seeing the string of mounted riders silhouetted against the ridge line. A few of the nesters remembered shaking with apprehension and fear.

In an assassination plot of awesome proportions, the invaders planned to ride the Powder River country into Buffalo, county seat of Johnson County. They would execute the sheriff and county commissioners, then kill the rustlers one at a time wherever they could be found.

When the invaders reached sixty-five miles north of Casper, they changed their plans. Word came to them that Nate Champion, the best known cattle rustler in Wyoming (an assumption of the invaders, and not a fact, since Champion had never been indicted and was not wanted anywhere by the law), and over a dozen other suspected rustlers were holed up at the KC Ranch. The invaders, most of whom were now drunk, very weary, and beginning to quarrel among themselves, decided to skip Buffalo for the time being until they took care of Champion and his friends.

That night the invaders rode through a snowstorm, and when morning came they had the KC Ranch surrounded. Inside the house were two teamsters who stopped for the night, along with Nate Champion and a partner, Nick Ray.

At dawn the teamsters stepped outside, and since they were innocent, the invaders silently took them prisoners. When the teamsters did not return in a few minutes, Nick Ray came out of the house and glanced around suspiciously. Without warning a number of rifles cracked, and he fell. Crawling on his hands and knees he headed for the doorway, where another bullet struck him in the back. Champion dashed outside and dragged him in.

The siege was now on, and heavy gunfire raked the windows and doors. Champion fired back, but could not get any clear shots. Occasionally he paused to write a diary, one describing his own frustrations, his partner's agony and death. Describing the shooting as coming from the stable, the river and the back of the house, he wrote, "Boys, the bullets are coming in like hail."

As the invaders concentrated on the house, another alleged rustler, Jack Flagg, came by in a buckboard and nearly got himself killed too. He escaped only by cutting the horses loose from the tracings, and riding one of them pell-mell into Buffalo.

The invaders now had to make a big decision. Should they continue with the present siege, or should they skip Champion for the larger objective, the burning of Buffalo. Incredibly, these killers decided to stick with Champion and kill him first since they already had him trapped. They still believed in their own invincibility.

Late that afternoon the invaders shoved a wagon loaded with hay and pine-knots up against the wood house and set it afire. Champion wrote in his diary: "It's not night yet. The house is all fired. Goodbye boys, if I never see you again."

Outside a tight cordon of rifles covered the house. With so much flame and smoke billowing forth, many of the Texans figured Champion could not survive and might have already committed suicide.

Suddenly a stocking-footed man sprinted from the burning doorway and into the snow. In his hands he held a rifle; a revolver protruded from his belt. Gunfire came from everywhere, and down he went. Nate Champion, King of the Rustlers and the bravest man in Wyoming, lay dead. A rough boot rolled him over on his back, and someone scrawled a note saying "cattle thieves beware" and pinned it to his bloody shirt.

The invaders backed off about half-a-mile from the burning cabin, the sizzle of Nick Ray's body, and prepared what they described as "a hearty meal."

Late that night they resumed their march toward Buffalo, the Texas gunslingers and the Wyoming cattlemen still confident of their overwhelming strength. As they proceeded along, a Texan accidentally shot himself in the knee and became the first casualty. He died of gangrene.

By this time the countryside swarmed with armed men, and sympathetic large ranchers warned the cattlemen that Buffalo was an armed camp, with rustlers gathering there by the hundreds. The news shocked the invaders into realizing the kind of death trap they were in, and they retreated to the TA Ranch, fifteen miles from Buffalo where they built fortifications. A wire went out to Cheyenne asking the state militia for protection, but due to the patched and cut telegraph lines, the message arrived in such a garbled condition that politicians there suspected it came from the Johnson County authorities, and they sent no assistance.

Before long three or four hundred small ranchers (rustlers to the invaders) had the TA Ranch surrounded and were firing into it. Unfortunately, only a cannon ball would penetrate those heavy walls, so the ranchers tried to borrow one from the military at Fort McKinney and were politely turned down. Undeterred, they rigged a wagon shield protected by thick logs. It took fifteen men to roll it forward, but once it got in close enough, dynamite bombs could be thrown.

In the meantime, Governor Barber gradually realized that the invaders were on the verge of being destroyed. He tried to get the state militia out, and when they refused to budge, he frantically wired President Benjamin Harrison and asked for a United States military intervention to prevent a state-wide rustler insurrection.

And as in the movies, the army arrived just as the small ranchers were getting their barricade in close enough to throw their explosives. The invaders happily surrendered to the army and were taken as prisoners to Fort McKinney.

Incredibly, after all this gunfire, only one man had been wounded, and he would die. A Texan, crawling along with a cocked pistol stuck in his belt, accidentally caught the trigger on a twig, and the weapon discharged, the bullet striking him in the groin.

On Sunday morning, April 17, the invaders, now prisoners and under heavy guard, were moved out of Fort McKinney and headed for Cheyenne, where some of them were placed in the penitentiary, more for their own protection than anything else. By August the state released the Texans and told them to return for eventual trial. Of course, none of them did.

The cattlemen defendants went on trial in Laramie County (Cheyenne) because, according to the judge, that community had "no bias or prejudice." Then the judge dismissed the cases.

In spite of a few additional murders and bushwhacking which attempted to settle old scores, Johnson County and indeed all of Wyoming adopted an attitude of forget and forgive. No doubt this was the best way. There had been enough pathetic sacrifices to a lost cause.

*Buffalo Bill . . . was a fighter . . . and a lover . . .
and damned good at both.*

19

BUFFALO BILL

THE REMARKABLE SHOWMAN

ONLY THE SLIMMEST of technicalities permits Buffalo Bill to appear on these pages for he was not a gunfighter. He is included because he is a significant part of the Wild West gunfighting legend.

Early pulps tied him closely to the exploits of Wild Bill Hickok and the facts about them are only now being untangled. Movies and TV scripts usually feature Buffalo Bill with guns tied low, a terror to bad-men and Indians alike. In truth the real Buffalo Bill has yet to stand up. When he does rise we shall see a vain and complex man, a remark-able showman, a fine scout, and a westerner of great courage who did more to establish the Wild West tradition than any other man in his time. Even with the fable and tinsel stripped away, he stands as a unique, authentic American folk-hero.

William F. Cody (Buffalo Bill) was born in Scott County, Iowa in 1846, and as a young man signed on to ride for the Pony Express. In spite of its high-flying publicity, it was never much more than a pub-licity gimmick. A letter previously took twenty-five days to reach the west coast from Missouri, and it traveled the southern route through El Paso. Mail contracts were worth $600,000 a year, and the firm of Russell, Majors and Waddell wanted them. They established the Pony Express to dramatize that the mail could be delivered quicker (the

Express took eight to ten days), and that a central route made more practical sense than the longer southern journey. It cost nearly $100,000 before the corrals could be opened. The operation consistently lost money and it went quietly out of business after a year-and-a-half.

Ironically, the Pony Express owes much of its glorification to Bill Cody whom some writers dispute even rode for the company. (Cody was fourteen when the enterprise started; sixteen when it folded.) If he actually was so employed, he played no important or outstanding part.

Years later when he organized the Wild West Show, he incorporated a Pony Express ride as the big scene. The old scout would come thundering across the grass-covered city parks, leaning low in the saddle, shooting painted Indians and wicked outlaws by the score as they vainly tried to intercept the U.S. mail. Audiences loved it.

Following the Pony Express failure, Cody joined the army. As he worded it, "While under the influence of bad whiskey, I awoke to find myself a soldier in the 7th Kansas." About all that can be said regarding his Civil War exploits is that he enlisted as a private and never got demoted. His unit saw little action.

A young lady named Louisa Frederici now caught his attention. Bill wrangled an introduction by pulling a chair out from under her at a party, and she later got even by marrying him. Neither believed their marriage to be made in heaven. She nagged a lot and Cody no doubt had much of it coming since he never stayed home, was consistently unfaithful, and wasn't much of a father to their three children. When their first child was born, he made it to the scene just in time to help name the baby.

Meanwhile, the army called, and Cody signed as a scout for the 7th Cavalry. The Sioux were straying from the reservations, and General Custer wanted to round them up. Cody guided the way and performed bravely in several sharp engagements. When peace came in 1867, he went to work as a buffalo hunter for the Union Pacific.

During the next year or two, he shot buffalo by the thousands, and while he was more successful than most hunters, his exploits attracted only occasional and light attention. Folks called him Buffalo Bill, but the plains were full of Buffalo Bills, most of them as little known as he.

He quit the railroad and again scouted for the army. One morning as he lay drunk under a wagon, sleeping off his latest visit to the post sutler, an eastern writer named Ned Buntline crawled beneath the vehicle and awakened him. As one of the West's most intriguing characters, the stranger had a permanent crick in his neck, put there by a Tennessee mob that objected to his unorthodox habits of acquiring new wives without divorcing the former ones. He had come west to lecture on the evils of drink, a subject of much first-hand knowledge to him. Back on the Atlantic coast readers knew him as America's leading pulp writer, a specialist in hairy-legged, blood-thirsty tales of high adventure. His discussions with Cody now made history. As one biographer so aptly expressed it, "Buntline was a writer in search of a hero, and Cody was a hero in search of a role."

For the next few weeks Buntline accompanied Cody on all expeditions, writing down stories the scout told him, elaborating every sentence, paying attention to the facts only when they could not be avoided. Before the year ended Buntline rushed a book into print entitled *Buffalo Bill: King of the Border Men.* He subtitled it *The Wildest and Truest Story I Ever Wrote.*

Other "non-fiction" books on the same subject flooded the market. Buntline wrote one entitled *Buffalo Bill and His Daring Adventures in the Romantic Wild West.* The Wide Awake Library published *In the Wild West With the King of Scouts.* There was a double-header book entitled *Buffalo Bill: the Buckskin King,* or *Wild Nell: the Amazon of the West.* Cody himself published several autobiographies, and in addition he came out with a book (probably ghosted by Buntline) entitled *The Dread Shot Four,* or *My Pards of the Plains.* (The word "Pard" got a lot of literary mileage in the pulps.)

Numerous Buffalo Bill books and magazine articles hit the stands within the next few decades, and they all shared three common characteristics. 1) They were terribly written. 2) They always ended with the old scout wiping out a band of painted savages, or sending a gang of black-hearted outlaws into tail-dragging retreat. 3) The meanest whites or redskins were always dispatched in manly hand-to-hand combat with gory bowie knives. It is difficult for 20th century people to understand how folks could believe those tales. One explanation is that the country was semiliterate. It had not yet learned to be skeptical. The printed word was accepted just as if it were Holy Writ chiseled into rock. Following the Civil War there was a general period of depression. Americans hungered for heroes, men who were brave and who did not possess doubt or fear. We were in a remarkable transitional era which once past would never come our way again.

General Phillip H. Sheridan, the runty soldier who built a reputation during the Civil War, asked Bill to become his chief of scouts. Since the title called for pay equal to that of a full colonel, he carried the request to its logical conclusion. With that kind of salary he was entitled to that kind of rank. From then on he was Colonel Cody. In his defense, there were many civilians with the title of Colonel, very few of whom had a more legitimate claim to it than he did.

As his fame spread, easterners and Europeans clamored to come west and meet him, to employ his talents for the shooting of buffalo. Bill asked and received top pay as guide (and story teller), and knowing that the dudes expected a flamboyant individual, which he was already, he dressed to fit the part.

Teddy Roosevelt sought his services, as did the Grand Duke Alexis of Russia. The United States Army often provided an escort. Special trains were outfitted whereby buffalo might be shot from the coach windows and even from the cow-catcher. One particular expedition had sixteen wagons packed with baggage, supplies and liquid refreshments. The campgrounds were easily identified for years by the number of empty liquor bottles scattered around.

The rich invited him east where they could more easily fawn over him. Bill saw himself portrayed on stage as the greatest white man alive.

As he took his bows around the country, Sheridan telegraphed him to come west immediately. The Sioux were bolting the reservations again, and several clashes had already occurred. On April 26, 1872, Cody and a military detachment of six men located an Indian camp on the banks of the Nebraska Loup River. They crept to within fifty yards and charged, killing three Indians. When several warriors made it to the other side of the stream, Bill rode his horse across and started after them. Cody shot two more Indians, and the others got away. This action won Buffalo Bill the Medal of Honor.

During the summer and fall, Cody's old friend Ned Buntline urged him to go east and play himself on the stage. It did not take much convincing, and soon Bill appeared in a New York play entitled *The Scouts of the Prairie,* or *Red Deviltry as It Is.* In a three-act drama there was a temperance lecture (delivered by Buntline, naturally), a prairie fire, a scene of unrequited love, the dying moans of a tortured trapper, an oath of vengeance, a scalp dance, and of course a knife fight. The Boston *Journal* said that "The play is an extraordinary production of more wild Indians, scalping knives and gun powder to the square inch than any drama in history."

However, much of Buffalo Bill's greatest achievements still lay before him. Over the horizon was his fabled fight with Yellow Hair, the world famous Wild West Show, and enough heartbreak for several men.

During the late 1860's and 1870's Buffalo Bill Cody led a double life in terms of careers. From fall until spring he appeared on the eastern stage with a troupe called the "Buffalo Bill Combination." The lead actors were Cody, Pawnee Bill, Texas Jack and Wild Bill Hickok.

On stage they united to defeat badmen and Indians alike. Off stage they bickered about importance and billing notices. Hickok rarely argued about such matters, but he was a problem. He usually had to be half-drunk to perform. His careless pistol fire often powder burned the women's legs and, although the audiences loved it, the antics added fuel to his backstage unpopularity.

In the summers Cody returned to his former occupation as a guide for hunting parties or as a scout for the army. For a while he served with Col. Anson Mills (who built the El Paso Mills Building), and in 1868 became chief of scouts for the 5th Cavalry. Within the next few years he took part in no less than fourteen Indian battles. He did so while alternating this bloody work with his eastern stage appearances.

On the day of his most famous battle, he donned a tightfitting, black-velvet suit trimmed with a red sash, lace and silver buttons. No doubt he was looking ahead to his next stage appearance, and he wanted his audience to know that during moments of combat, this was what the well-dressed scout wore.

Cody's fight with Yellow Hair would be the most misunderstood event in his career. Some historians doubt the incident even took place, but the facts indicate that it did.

Yellow Hair (not Yellow Hand) was an obscure Cheyenne subchief so named because of a blonde woman he had recently scalped. Historically the clash with Cody was of no significance. It achieved fame only because of the heavy emphasis Buffalo Bill placed on it in most of his autobiographies. He alluded to it often in his stage appearances too.

The meeting happened more accidentally than deliberately. They stumbled upon each other while crossing the crest of a hill from opposite sides. Without exchanging words or insults both men charged and fired their weapons. The Indian bullet went wild, but Cody's tore through Yellow Hair's leg and killed his horse. Bill's horse stepped into a hole and fell. As both men scrambled about frantically, the Indian fired again, missed, and was in turn shot through the head.

According to Buffalo Bill's written account, Yellow Hair "reeled and fell, but before he had fairly touched the ground I was upon him, knife in hand, and had driven the keen edge to the hilt in his heart. Jerking his war bonnet off, I scientifically scalped him in about ten seconds."

Waving his bloody trophy in the air, Cody shouted, "This one's for Custer."

He sent the grisly hairpiece to his wife in an innocent looking package. She opened the box, saw the scalp, smelled it, and promptly fainted.

Following the death of Yellow Hair, Buffalo Bill's scouting career gradually closed. Though the army paid him $150 a month as "Chief Scout of the Big Horn and Yellowstone Expedition," he had his eye on the stage. Thus in 1877 Cody began the first of his many "farewell tours." He gave them for the next thirty-eight years.

As time went on Cody gave more thought to an old idea, the creation of a Wild West Show. Oddly, he made his greatest impact not so much in Europe (which gave his crusade respectability), nor even in the East, but in the West. The tradition of horse-mounted Indians and the U.S. Cavalry owes its influence to Cody's pageant. The ten-gallon hat did not really come into Western use until Buffalo Bill assured everyone that it was of authentic frontier garb. Westerners who should have known better went to his show, saw cowboys with two guns tied low, rustlers, highwaymen and Indians, fancy roping and trick shooting that nobody other than a professional could have done, and declared it all genuine.

The Wild West Show began in 1883 with broken-down Indians, broken-down cowboys and broken-down buffaloes. Yet it was a success because nothing quite like it had been seen before. In most places the show made money. Chicago turned out a good crowd, as did most eastern cities. The West was always good for a sellout. Then came New Orleans where it rained for forty-one straight days. When the water finally stopped falling, the Wild West Show had deficits of $60,000.

With the show faltering, Buffalo Bill hired Annie Oakley, and overnight "Little Miss Sure Shot" became a sensation. Annie stayed on the show for years with nothing more than a hand-shake contract with Cody. Those who knew Annie considered her to be a "real person," kind, understanding and practical.

Cody hired Sitting Bull and a host of other Indians to play the same parts they had been playing for years. They painted their faces, yelled, screamed and looked threatening. Then the military came rushing out and "shot" them down. Still, most of them liked their parts. Cody treated them fairly, and the Indians were a good investment.

Meanwhile in Europe, Queen Victoria was celebrating her Golden Jubilee. The Crowned Heads wanted an American Exposition, a portion of which would be the Buffalo Bill Wild West Show. As it turned out, the other participants were ignored and Buffalo Bill became a world figure. This 1887 overseas trip pushed his prestige to new heights even in the United States.

About 20,000 Europeans crowded his first performance. The show went on for months to record attendances. Royalty fell all over itself to tramp through the mud and inspect the stables. They all clamored for a ride in the Deadwood Stage. When it wasn't held up by masked outlaws, everyone was disappointed.

In the year of his most resounding success, Buffalo Bill returned to the United States a troubled man. Drink had sapped much of his energies. He admitted he was an alcoholic. His domestic life underwent a serious crisis. His jealous and waspish wife Louisa resented the manner in which he passionately kissed his showgirls hello and goodbye. She didn't think it benefitted a western hero to have his name linked romantically with female royalty and American actresses. Cody complained in turn that after years of sending his wife money, she had invested it in property bearing her own name.

The last straw came when a daughter died. Mrs. Cody vowed to denounce her husband at the gravesite. A weary Buffalo Bill filed another of his many suits for divorce. She contested it. After a messy trial filled with charges and countercharges, the judge denied the divorce and ordered most of the testimony stricken from the record.

Other troubles dogged the performer. A 1901 train wreck killed 110 of his horses and seriously injured Annie Oakley. After several operations and a long convalescence, she returned to the circuit with much of her shooting skill intact. However, she never regained her old zip and cheerfulness.

During these years Cody had paid little attention to administrative and financial management. As a result he gradually lost control not only of the show, but his soul as well. Others now owned him. With steep debts plaguing his every movement, he became the attraction and star of his own spectacle, but not the owner.

Business managers cheated him and kept him in such bad financial straits that he desperately wrote the government, saying that he had heard of a $10-a-month stipend going to Medal of Honor winners. Cody fortunately died before learning that the United States had stripped him of the medal on the grounds that being a civilian he was not eligible to receive it in the first place.

The final appearances continued for year after dreary year. He suffered from neuritis, rheumatism and prostate trouble, and at times around the country he had to be helped on and off his horse. He visited El Paso with the Sells-Floto Circus on November 5-6, 1915.

The El Paso *Times* covered the entire affair, and reported that except for a subdued voice, he looked tall and erect, the picture of health when he stepped off the train and was met by El Paso Mayor Tom Lea and a host of other dignitaries. The 16th U.S. Infantry from Ft. Bliss took charge of the celebration. A military band cranked up "For He's A Jolly Good Fellow" and "There'll Be A Hot Time In The Old Town Tonight." From somewhere in the rear a soldier shouted, "First Scalp for Custer," and the old hero waved and smiled.

Major George H. McMaster organized a smoker at Camp Cotton near the present Paisano Drive overpass. A large party took place in the Sheldon Hotel (now the Plaza), dutifully attended by General Pershing and as many people who could squeeze through the door.

With tears streaming down his face, Cody paused for "moving pictures" with Colonel Charles Taylor, an old Indian fighter himself and then reminisced about local men he had known, ancestors of present soldiers at Ft. Bliss and civilians in El Paso. He spoke of how things used to be when he roamed this area in his youth (he never did). Over and over he repeated, "This is the happiest day of my life." No one doubted his sincerity.

A huge parade wound through downtown El Paso on November 6, and ended at the show grounds at Magoffin and Dallas streets. When the performances began that afternoon, the seventy-year-old Cody sprang into the saddle just as if he were going after Yellow Hair. El Paso's own Harry Ponsford, who was there, said that the standing-room-only crowd gave him a thunderous ovation.

This was the next-to-last public appearance for Buffalo Bill. The show moved on to Albuquerque. From there Bill went to join his wife in Denver. He had put off the prostate operation for too long. He lived every day in pain. Finally, on January 10, 1917, the weary old scout was called to appear before his final critic.

*Wild Bill Hickok . . . most of his female friends
had more miles on them than the Union Pacific.*

20

WILD BILL HICKOK

I N THE OPINION of many knowledgeable historians. Wild Bill Hickok was the most dangerous gunman who ever lived. An exact tally of men who fell before his pistols is impossible to say. A minimum of ten might be a good estimate; or a maximum of twenty. None of this literally takes into account the Indians or Confederate soldiers.

His blond hair tumbled to his shoulders, and he had a passion for fancy vests, ruffled shirts, long-tailed coats and highly polished shoes. He stood six-foot-two with broad shoulders and slim hips. The nose was aquiline, the voice high-pitched. Although there is no evidence he ever liked anything other than girls, Wild Bill Hickok was the most effeminate gunfighter who ever lived.

His mother named him James Butler Hickok on the day of his birth, May 27, 1837, in Troy Grove, Illinois. He came from a long line of God-fearing Vermonters.

He grew up in Troy Grove, and got enough education to at least count to twenty on his fingers and toes. For the first seventeen years of his life, he showed no indication of the manslayer he later became.

At the age of eighteen he and a teamster entered into a fistfight, and both tumbled into a canal. Bill climbed out, did not see the teamster, and incorrectly thought he killed him. He fled the village to escape the consequences.

Hickok turned up next in Leavenworth, Kansas, where sectional rivalries, hatreds and prejudice were already leading to unparalleled guerrilla fighting and mass murder.

Sharps rifles poured into Kansas, weapons better known as "Beecher's Bibles," in honor of the half-crazed Reverend Henry Ward Beecher who believed a judicious amount of gunfire would open the gates to heaven. Hickok sold his services to an irregular army known as "Free-Staters" until 1857.

For the next several years he took up housekeeping with various ladies, worked as a teamster on the Santa Fe Trail and shot a few buffalo. He and Buffalo Bill met and became friends, a meeting later to have far-reaching effects on both their lives.

In 1861 Hickok went to work for the Pony Express and Overland Express station in Rock Creek, Nebraska. Here he came in contact with David McCanles, a North Carolinian who teased Hickok unmercifully about his girlish build and feminine features. McCanles occasionally roughed up Hickok, claiming it was all in good fun.

Trouble really came to a head when Hickok started courting McCanles' woman. McCanles came to the station door accompanied by his young son and two male friends, and made some demands about being paid for the equipment there since the property had at one time belonged to him. After the usual profanities were exchanged, McCanles stepped inside and ordered Hickok to come out from behind a curtain. Instead, Hickok fired, and McCanles fell dead.

His two friends, James Woods and James Gordon, came running when they heard the gunfire. When Gordon entered the door, Hickok shot him, chased him outside and shot him again. He also shot down Woods.

Woods ran a short ways and fell in a weed patch where the stationmaster's wife, Mrs. Wellman, clubbed him to death with a hoe. Other station employees chased Gordon until the exhausted man fell against a large tree where his pursuers shotgunned him to death.

A judge released all of these manslayers on the grounds of self-defense, and while this incident did not create too much attention at the time, it did later on. When Hickok's fame began to spread, writers looked back on the Rock Creek fight, and with no little help from

190

Hickok, turned it into the greatest mass slaughter in Western history with Wild Bill Hickok polishing off a dozen of the West's most dangerous desperados.

Hickok left Rock Creek shortly afterwards, and in October of 1861 signed on with the Union Army as a wagon master and scout. The military records are rather skimpy concerning his services, but then they give very little information concerning the services of most soldiers, especially scouts. We do know that during this time, the name "Wild Bill" became as much a part of him as his flowing mustache.

Then came the affair with Dave Tutt, a twenty-six-year-old gambler. He and Hickok gambled, Hickok lost and couldn't pay up. For security Tutt took Wild Bill's pocket watch. Hickok growled that if Tutt so much as used the timepiece, he would kill him.

The two antagonists met on the afternoon of July 21, 1865, in the Springfield, Missouri public square. Tutt wore the watch proudly for all to see. Drawing their pistols they advanced upon each other, and when about seventy-five yards away, commenced firing. Tutt missed. Wild Bill laid the barrel across the left forearm to steady the weapon, and fired. Down went his opponent, dead practically before striking the ground. Hickok was acquitted.

Resuming his military duties, Hickok became great friends with General George Custer and worked as one of Custer's principal scouts. Custer admired Hickok, played poker with him, and might have come to know him better had it not been for Custer's rendezvous with Sitting Bull at Little Big Horn.

Much of what we know, or think we know, about Hickok's scouting experiences came from an interview he had with Henry Stanley, correspondent for the New York *Herald* who later went to Africa and "found" Dr. Livingstone. Hickok blithely told the gullible Stanley that he had personally slain over 100 men.

For the next few years Wild Bill Hickok was in and out of the army. He ran for sheriff of Ellsworth, Kansas, and lost. Returning to the army, an Indian lanced him in the foot during a skirmish in eastern Colorado. By 1869 he was in Hays City, Kansas, a cattle trail town, a railroad town, a military town; a tough community with all of the ingredients for trouble.

He ran for sheriff, this time got elected, and killed a man named Bill Mulrey on August 24. A month later he put two slugs in a teamster and sent him to Boot Hill. However, it was on July 17, 1870, that the real trouble came. Several members of the 7th U. S. Cavalry caught him off guard in Drum's Saloon, knocked him to the floor and began kicking him. Hickok drew his pistols from his belt or sash (he never wore holsters), killed one private and seriously wounded another.

Bill decided this might be a good time to resign as sheriff, so he dragged his battered body to the train station and went to Ellsworth to recuperate. After recovering, he rode to Abilene, Kansas and was appointed city marshal on April 15, 1871, at $150 a month, plus one-fourth of all fines assessed against persons he arrested.

Frankly, as a law enforcement officer Wild Bill Hickok would have made a good dog catcher. He spent most of his time at the gambling tables or with the ladies of the evening. A newspaper complained that Hickok allowed Abilene to be overrun with gamblers, con men, prostitutes and pimps.

But if Hickok wasn't worrying about enforcing the law, he was worried about assassination. He refused to sit with his back to a door or window. He entered buildings by back doors or side entrances, pausing once inside to study the faces of those around him. He scattered newspapers around the floor of his bedroom at night so he could hear someone prowling around.

Reportedly John Wesley Hardin, well-known Texas gunman, after causing trouble in a saloon, surrendered his weapons to Hickok by offering them butts forward. When Hickok reached for them, Hardin performed the so called "Road Agents Spin", and thus had the drop on Hickok. Most historians doubt the story, as there is not the slightest evidence except Hardin's word on the matter, but it is worth noting that Hardin did not hang around Abilene long after that.

In spite of these distractions, the Bull's Head Saloon gave Hickok the most trouble. Phil Coe and Ben Thompson, gamblers and gunmen, were the proprietors and what brought matters to a head was the over-size painting of a Texas Longhorn painted in full, perhaps too full, masculinity. Most Abilene townspeople were offended by the sign, and they demanded the animal's anatomy be altered. So Hickok stood by with a shotgun on his arm while the necessary deletions were made.

In spite of many threats, Thompson eventually left town, and Coe sold his interest in the saloon although he remained on as a gambler. Ordinarily this would have eased the tension between Hickok and Coe, except that they were both courting the same woman. Rumors circulated around town that each planned to kill the other.

One afternoon, Hickok heard that his girl, Jesse, was openly consorting with Coe in a saloon. He rushed over, and according to some stories, angrily slapped her to the floor. Coe, who was unarmed, and whose gallantry stopped short of suicide, did not interfere.

On October 5 the trouble finally came to a head. Many cowboys were in town, fighting, drinking, carousing, and only Mike Williams, a special policeman, offered Hickok his assistance.

Coe, too, was celebrating the end of the cattle season, and for unexplained reasons he carried a revolver. When he and a party of friends neared the Alamo Saloon, a vicious dog tried to bite him, and he took a shot at it and missed. Seconds later Hickok appeared on the scene demanding to know who had been doing the shooting. Coe explained.

Wild Bill drew two pistols and shot Coe twice in the stomach. Coe returned the fire, one bullet tearing through Hickok's coat. With his opponent now lying in the dirt thrashing in agony, Hickok heard footsteps coming up behind him. Turning swiftly, he fired again and killed Deputy Mike Williams.

In those days, almost nobody survived stomach wounds. Coe died three days later, happy to be out of his misery. As for Williams, Hickok paid the funeral expenses. There wasn't much else he could do.

Abilene had had enough. The city fathers told the Texans there could be no more cattle drives. They also dismissed Hickok as city marshal, stating that the community was "no longer in need of his services." The council did not say thanks, and it did not offer any recommendations or pass any high sounding platitudes in praise of his services.

Hickok was out. Never again would he be a peace officer. From now on the road of life would be all downhill.

Aces and eights

When Wild Bill Hickok picked up his last town marshal paycheck and letter of dismissal from Abilene, Kansas, he did what most other notable western characters such as Buffalo Bill were already doing; he crossed the Mississippi to show the easterners his stuff. Americans thirsted for heroes and Bill had the credentials.

The east coast thrived on the penny dreadfuls, the pulps of their time. The covers portrayed barrel-chested, noble looking Americans, slashed from numerous knives, holding their ground against bloodthirsty Indians, villainous outlaws and evil Mexicans. Here was America in its purest form, and if those stories weren't true, they should have been.

Easterners wanted Wild West shows too. Indoors or outdoors, these melodramas played to packed houses. Wild Bill saw no reason why he shouldn't pick up some of this easy money. Recently he had done well at the gambling tables, and with a poke of gold in his pocket he organized and directed "The Daring Buffalo Chase of the Plains" in the early 1870's.

First he hired some cowboys to lasso those rambunctious animals, and that became quite a problem since the buffalo had a short, thick neck, short horns and a head customarily held close to the ground. Finally they roped six, dragged them on board a train, and headed east to make their fortune. In the party were four Comanches, three cowboys, six buffaloes, a bear, a monkey and Wild Bill. The show opened at Niagara Falls on July 20.

The show itself had an enclosure, but the audience did not, which meant that the paying customers weren't paying. Hickok would have to depend on generous donations.

The buffaloes, so frisky out West, now acted like contented Jersey cows. That is, until Wild Bill fired a shot to see if he couldn't stir them up a little. Things immediately perked up. The buffaloes started to run in circles with the Comanches screaming in pursuit, and that's the way it might have stayed had not some stray dogs mixed into the turmoil. Several small boys followed the dogs, and then some adults obviously under the influence went after the boys.

Buffaloes broke through the wire fence and stampeded the audience. Someone turned the bear and the monkey loose. The bear did not attack anybody, but did help itself to a sausage vendor's wares. Altogether it took Hickok and his cowboys several hours to corral the buffaloes, the bear and the monkey, besides restore order. All of this of course ended the performance, and when Bill passed the hat, he picked up a total of $123.86, for a thousand dollar investment. There was nothing to do except sell the buffaloes to a butcher shop and pay the expenses home for everybody.

His old friend Buffalo Bill Cody came to his rescue. Cody needed a third party for his dramatic play entitled *Scouts of the Prairies,* and Wild Bill was just the man. The play itself never won any awards, the more unkindly critics saying it "could have begun in the middle and gone forward or backward and it would not have made any difference."

Wild Bill took third billing right behind Buffalo Bill Cody and J. R. (Texas Jack) Omohundro. Roughly the plot went like this: The scouts came out onto the stage and in deep manly voices told of their daring and heroic deeds in saving damsels, the U. S. Mail and all sorts of things. This was difficult for Hickok because he did not have a deep, manly voice. He squeaked. But the show went on, the scouts went through their act, and the scene erupted with a cowardly Indian or outlaw raid complete with blazing guns, clouds of choking smoke and buckets of ketchup. The New York *Herald* said "everything was so wonderfully bad it was almost good."

The actors made money, but Hickok wasn't happy. He thought it a little silly to stand in front of an audience and shout these less than immortal phrases: "Fear not, fair maid! By heavens you are safe at last with Wild Bill, who is ever ready to risk his life and die, if need be, in defense of weak and helpless womanhood."

As a result, Bill began forgetting his lines. He quipped and told jokes in front of the audience. When the Indians attacked, and he had to defend the maidens, instead of firing over everyone's head, he shot low and powderburned a lot of legs. Not only did the redskins jump a little higher, but the ladies did some fancy skipping about too.

Wild Bill drank a lot. In addition he became rather affectionate with the ladies backstage, and at times even got a little friendlier on stage than the script called for. So it was no surprise when in March of 1874 he said goodbye to Cody and the troupe and went west again.

He returned with the old inner fires still burning, but with the furnace showing the effects of wear and tear. Instead of being known as "Wild Bill" Hickok, he should have been known as "Weak Eyes" Hickok. Some writers believe his eyesight went bad because of gonorrhea, which is a possibility since most of his female friends had more miles on them than the Union Pacific.

So now he was nearly forty, going bald and wearing glasses. His reflexes were bad, although that allegedly did not stop him from killing three buffalo hunters in Wyoming. Like a candle burning at both ends, he sensed his own life nearing its termination. In an effort, possibly, to give his existence some meaning, he married the fifty-year-old (or older) Agnes Lake, who had been chasing him around the country for years and patiently waiting for him to tire of his long string of female companions.

They tied the knot in Cheyenne on March 5, 1876, and spent their honeymoon in Cincinnati. A month later Bill said something to his wife about getting himself a grubstake in the western goldfields and sending for her. He left, and she never saw him again.

He returned to Cheyenne in June, where he met Martha Jane Cannary, historically better known as "Calamity Jane." She could drive a stage, wrestle a buffalo, chew tobacco and cuss like a wagon master. She dressed in men's clothes and was as masculine as Wild Bill was effeminate. One look at her picture, and you know why the West was wild. While many stories have linked her romantically with Hickok, it is not likely that she shared anything more with him than his whiskey bottle.

But the gold fields did not produce for Hickok, and he drifted into Deadwood, South Dakota where he dropped all pretense of pick and shovel work and returned to the cards. His face had a deeper and sadder look, and he more than once spoke of a premonition of death, saying Deadwood would be his last camp.

On the afternoon of August 2, 1876, he strolled into the Number Ten Saloon, saw a poker game in progress near the center of the room, and sat down in the only vacant chair, one with its back toward the door. Twice he asked Charlie Rich, another player, to change places, but Rich felt lucky where he was and wouldn't move.

Hickok's luck went bad. He borrowed money from the bartender to continue. At 4:10 he had his best cards of the afternoon, but never lived to play them out. Twenty-five-year-old Jack McCall from Kentucky, an ex-buffalo hunter, slipped through the door, pulled a pistol, screamed "Take that!" and fired.

Wild Bill died instantly with a bullet in the back of his head. He sat rigid for some seconds, then fell backwards to the floor. From his hand tumbled four cards, two aces and two eights, to be henceforth known as the famous "Dead Man's Hand."

In the uproar that followed, McCall snapped his pistol twice at bystanders and it misfired both times. One can only conjecture what might have happened if the firing pin had struck on those faulty cartridges when he pointed it at Hickok.

McCall ran to a butcher shop, hid and waited for the authorities to find and arrest him. In the questioning that followed, a believable story never did surface. At first McCall swore Hickok had killed his brother. When he could not prove it, McCall next said he and Hickok had quarreled, that Wild Bill had insulted and abused him. However, the evidence showed Hickok had actually grubstaked him and demonstrated unusual kindness regarding a gambling debt. So, never being a man to run out of yarns, McCall accused others around town of paying him to commit the murder. That was never proven either, and so the reason for Wild Bill's death is still unknown.

What we do know is that Jack McCall went on trial for murder the day after Hickok's death, and was acquitted. Unproven rumors say the judge and jury were bribed.

The army roared over the acquittal, remembering Hickok's services as a scout during the Indian wars. It demanded a trial in a United States court, citing the fact of Deadwood being an illegal town built upon land ceded to the Sioux Nation by treaty. On August 29, United States marshals rearrested McCall and took him to Yankton, Dakota Territory for trial. He pleaded "not guilty."

On December 4 the trial finally started. It ended two days later with a verdict of guilty as charged. On January 3, 1877, the judge, after some ramblings regarding the teaching and prayers of a mother, sentenced Jack McCall to be hanged by the neck on the first day of March.

After the review courts upheld the verdict, McCall, through his two very competent attorneys, applied to President Ulysses Grant for a pardon or at least a commutation of the sentence to life imprisonment. Governor John L. Pinnington of the Dakota Territory signed and endorsed the petition, defending McCall somewhat by stating that on the day of the murder the accused was so drunk he fell down three times while crossing the street to the saloon.

All of this impressed the president not at all. He refused the pardon.

With the end in sight, Jack McCall took to reading the Bible and receiving regular visits from a priest. He accepted the Catholic faith, and to all appearances went to his death with a clear conscience.

At 9 a.m. on the appointed day, a carriage took him to the scaffold where a small crowd waited in the drizzling rain. At 10:15 the trap door slammed open, and he dropped through. Afterwards, the noose stubbornly refused to come off his neck, so the marshal cut the rope a foot or so away and the body went to the grave with the makeshift necktie still intact.

As for Wild Bill, his friends buried him the day after his death. Three years later they dug him up, pronounced him in good shape, and reinterred him at Deadwood where he rests today, still a tourist attraction.

21

CLAY ALLISON

WILD WOLF OF THE WASHITA

IF EVER A PSYCHOTIC, deranged gunman lived, that man had to be
Clay Allison. Oddly enough Allison is little known in the annals of
western blood-letting. No one has ever written a reliable, definitive
biography, perhaps because there was so much killing that parts of it
would be unbelievable.

Allison claimed Tennessee as his home. Born in 1840, he might
have spent his life as a dirt farmer had the Civil War not intervened.
Though his service record is sketchy, he gained a lot of experience in
killing and liked what he learned. Scouting (which was about the same
as spying in those days) seemed to be his forte. A story goes that the
Federals captured and sentenced him to be shot. On the eve of his
execution he murdered a guard and escaped.

The Confederate Army said Allison had an erratic mental condition dating back to a head wound he received in his youth. The Tennessee Light Artillery described him as suicidal and discharged him
after one year on the grounds that "emotional or physical excitement
produces paroxysmal or a mixed character, partly epileptic and partly
maniacal."

Clay took his medical discharge and simply enlisted in a unit which
didn't care if he fought calmly or in a blind rage, so long as he fought.

*Clay Allison . . . discharged from the army for
maniacal tendencies . . . never let insanity
interfere with a killing.*

He went west following the war, all the way to Texas where he and another man became embroiled in an argument. Reportedly they dug a grave, agreeing that they would strip naked, jump in and fight to the death with bowie knives. A tombstone, to be engraved later, was moved to the site. However, common sense or the lack of a suitable day kept delaying the showdown until both men finally dropped the matter.

Instead Allison went to see Oliver Loving and Charles Goodnight about a job. The two cattlemen were impressed by the tall stranger with the dark wavy hair and fierce blue eyes. They put him to work as a trail herder. Two weeks later as they passed a small town, Allison, who had been drinking, rode down its main street wearing nothing but a sombrero, boots and gun belt. The sheriff tried to arrest him for indecent exposure, but Allison gave the officer a strong smell of a smoking gun barrel and the lawman changed his mind.

His antics earned him the nickname of "Wild Wolf of the Washita," and Allison did his best to live up to it. By the summer of 1870 he had settled in Colfax County, New Mexico (near Cimarron), and established a small ranch. Before long he came in contact with Chuck Colbert, a widely-known local desperado with seven notches on his pistol. The nature of their disagreement is unknown. It is enough that both men enjoyed their reputations. Like little boys playing King-of-the-Hill, they decided that only one would stand on top.

Colbert wanted Allison to be notch number eight. Maybe Allison wanted Colbert to be notch number one.

The two spent a day together racing horses, and that evening went to a hotel for dinner before settling down to the more serious business. As they ate, Colbert became over-anxious and slowly eased his revolver out of his holster, nonchalantly raised it from under the wooden planks and with a big smile of victory, pulled the trigger. But he did not lift the gun up far enough. The bullet struck the table edge and ricocheted across the room instead of going straight.

Allison being a little more calm and deliberate, shot Colbert squarely between the eyes. When asked why he didn't kill his man earlier, Allison replied that he did not wish to send Colbert to hell on an empty stomach.

Of course, not all of Clay's victims died by the gun. He lynched a few to break the monotony.

Near Elizabethtown, New Mexico, lived Charles Kennedy, a somber man who murdered miners and travelers who stopped at his cabin for a night's lodging. His wife never questioned his errant behavior until he also killed their infant daughter. She reported it to the authorities and Allison happened to be with the posse that brought Kennedy in. Later investigation turned up enough bones buried in the Kennedy backyard to fill a bushel bucket, but the medical examiner couldn't judge if they were animal or human.

As far as Allison was concerned, the man had already been tried and found guilty. A few dark nights later he and several friends took the murderer to the town slaughterhouse and hanged him.

Not long afterwards a Methodist minister named F. J. Tolby, an outspoken critic of the Santa Fe Ring, was brutally slain. Rumors implicated Cruz Vega, a local ne'er-do-well. Since Vega understandably could not recall what happened, Allison and his trusty friends threw a rope over a telephone pole crosstie and assisted Vega with his faulty memory.

After being hoisted up and down a few times, Vega's recollections substantially improved, enough anyway to implicate another man. However, as he was already up in the air, the vigilantes rode off and left him dangling.

Still, Vega was not without friends. Francisco "Pancho" Griego vowed to kill Allison in retaliation. No one disputed Griego's ability since only a month earlier he had killed three of Uncle Sam's soldiers in a wild saloon brawl. He announced himself as ready for Allison. Clay merely smiled, bought the man a drink then steered him over into a corner of the barroom and shot him dead.

This killing in 1876 prompted Governor Samuel Axtell to place a $500 reward on Allison's head, and when no one, especially the local police officers, tried to collect it, the newspaper printed a critical editorial. That afternoon the high-strung manslayer stormed through the newspaper office, dumping presses and type into the Cimarron River. One part of the next day's paper had already been printed, so he marked the blank side with the words CLAY ALLISON'S EDITION, and sold these issues on the streets for 25¢ a copy. On the following day he sobered up and paid $200 in damages.

The authorities finally had to do something when Allison murdered three Negro soldiers of the 9th Cavalry. Even then Sheriff

Isaac Rinehart wouldn't move without plenty of protection and he found it with a detachment of soldiers whom he organized into a posse. They quietly arrested Allison, although Clay still managed to show his contempt for them all, especially the sheriff. On the way to the Taos jail, he jerked the sombrero off Rinehart's head, spat tobacco juice into it, and jammed it back on.

When Allison went to trial the charges were dismissed for lack of evidence, and not long thereafter, in fact three days before Christmas, 1876, Clay and his brother John were celebrating the holidays at Las Animas, Colorado. Both were full of Christmas cheer, but short on brotherhood and fellowship that evening at the dance. Witnesses complained that the brothers were rude and insulting, and found it amusing to step on feet.

Constable Charles Farber and two deputies armed themselves with shotguns and started shooting as soon as they entered the dance hall. John Allison, his back turned, went down first, but survived his wounds. From across the room Clay shot the constable four times, instantly killing him and chasing away the other officers. Later he submitted to arrest, primarily because his brother needed medical attention. When the trial eventually came up, no witnesses appeared.

Farber's death may have been Allison's last killing. Clay married, fathered two children, and gradually moderated his behavior. Sometimes, however, the old bravado still flared, like the time in St. Louis when he threatened to kill a man whom he did not even know.

Though it may have been, and probably was idle boasting, the threats got back to the man. Without saying who he was, he sidled up to the gunman and began idle conversation. When Clay just as casually reached for his pistol pocket, the stranger knocked him down and beat him so unmercifully that Allison decided maybe he wouldn't kill him after all.

On another occasion, Allison saw a dentist for a toothache, but the nervous doctor extracted the wrong one. An infuriated Allison shoved the dentist into his chair, jerked one of the doctor's molars and was busily pulling a second when a crowd intervened.

But all men have to go sometime, and Allison's demise was as ironic as it was inglorious. He had purchased a ranch near Pecos, Texas and gone to town for supplies. On his way home he foolishly stood up to whip the horses, and as they lurched forward, a sack of grain tumbled from the wagon. In grabbing for it, Allison fell also. The heavy wheels rolled across his neck, broke it, and the "Wild Wolf of the Washita" was dead at the age of forty-seven on July 3, 1887.

22

TEXAS RANGERS

THE TEXAS RANGERS were organized primarily to fight Indians and Mexicans. Only after Texas had grown in population and had been engulfed in a wave of lawlessness, did the rangers turn their attention to outlaws.

The name "ranger" in the early days referred to an individual who ranged across a large expanse of territory, traveling light, ready to fight at a moment's notice. Officially they thought of themselves not only as rangers, but militia, mounted volunteers, spies and mounted gunmen.

In 1823 Stephen F. Austin first formed bands of "rangers" to protect settlers along the Brazos River, but it was not until 1835 that the Texas General Council gave recognition, assigning them the difficult task of defending the frontier against the Indians. One company of twenty-five men patrolled east of the Trinity River, another between the Trinity and the Brazos, and the third between the Brazos and the Colorado.

When Sam Houston became the first President of the Republic of Texas, he made friends with the Indians. Because he was a strict economy man in his conduct of governmental affairs, he reduced the Texas army to a bare minimum, destroying it as an effective fighting force.

After Houston served two terms, Mirabeau Lamar became Presi-

Tough Breed . . . these Texas Rangers look as tough as they probably were. Rifles, pistols and knives were obvious tools of the trade.

dent and a different concept of power occupied the Texas capital. Houston loved Indians; Lamar despised them. The new President rebuilt the military but his efforts went to naught when Houston took over again as President. This time the old general not only reduced and practically abolished the army; he even sold the navy.

To keep at bay those Indians who were "unreasonable," he signed into law on January 29, 1842, an act authorizing a company of mounted men to "act as rangers" on the southern frontier. A year later he approved legislation for two companies of "spies" on the southwestern region.

The human material for the "rangers and spies" were largely adventurers and rabble. At times they brought credit upon the Texas republic, and at times they disgraced it. Most were brave and intrepid, and for awhile they cleared Texas of Cherokees and Comanches. If they were involved in such stupid blunders as the Meir expedition, or in such shameful episodes as the Council House slaughter of Comanche chiefs, it can be said in their defense that the era in which they lived was full of such mistakes and tragedies.

When the long simmering Mexican War broke out, the American armies for the first time fought guerrillas. The Mexican irregulars were a nuisance, not a threat, but in order to disperse them, General Taylor called for several mounted Texas Regiments, or in other words, rangers.

Taylor used them as anti-guerrilla forces and scouts, and during this period the rangers started their reluctance to take prisoners. Mexicans who could not account for their presence were usually shot on the spot. A lot of innocent people died, but the number of Mexican guerrilla operations diminished too. Nevertheless, this random killing of civilians appalled Taylor, and he referred to the rangers as a "lawless set" who have "scarcely made one expedition without unwarrantably killing a Mexican."

As the American armies drove deeper into Mexico, the reputation of the Texas Rangers became known far out of proportion to their strength and effective fire power. Even when the armies entered Mexico City, huge throngs crowded the streets, anxious to see what *Los diablos Tejanos,* the Texas Devils, looked like.

In Mexico City the rangers scattered around the town, drinking, chasing girls, sightseeing. Every day a few wound up dead, the murderers ducking back into the dark streets and buildings. A few of the rangers decided to put a stop to the killings, and as they walked down the street, if someone threw a rock, muttered curses, or simply brushed against them, the rangers pulled their pistols and executed the guilty on the spot. In one day alone eighty bodies were left sprawled in the streets. General Scott promptly found work for the rangers to do outside of the city, and not long afterwards they were returned to Texas.

The Texas Rangers went out of business for the next decade; after Texas entered the Union, the United States Army took over the job of protecting the frontiers. The Governor did call out the rangers for service against Indian uprisings in 1855, 1856-57, neglecting to tell them in the process that the state treasury was empty. The rangers would have to furnish their equipment, and then wait for future legislators to pay them. Texas would soon learn that if it expected honest and capable service, it would have to support the financial burden.

Almost none of the rangers distinguished themselves. A few companies tangled with the Indians and were routed. The most incredible occurrance came on October 2, 1855, when a ranger force joined a filibustering party near Eagle Pass. One hundred and eleven men crossed the Rio Grande, captured Piedras Negras on the 4th, and then fought an inconclusive engagement with a large Indian and Mexican force. During the night the Mexicans were reinforced, so with the Rio Grande waters running high, the Americans plundered and put Piedras Negras to the torch before straggling back across the river.

Mexican towns were not the only places burning. The Comanches were running rampant, destroying outlying ranches and farms. In desperation the Texas legislature voted money for a thorough chastisement of the Indian. In January of 1858, Governor Hardin R. Runnels commissioned John S. "Rip" Ford as "supreme commander" of Texas forces.

Ford broke his command into four detachments, and in April crossed the Red River into Indian Territory (Oklahoma) where on May 12 he struck the Comanche camp in full fury. In bitter fighting that raged from early morning through late afternoon, Old Iron Shirt, a Comanche chief whose name and reputation derived from a coat of mail he wore, believed he and his followers were invincible. They weren't.

Ford's 200-plus men engaged over 300 warriors, killing seventy-six and capturing 300 horses and eighteen women and children. The rangers had four casualties, two being wounded. This campaign plus engagements by the U. S. Army effectively broke the back of Indian power in Texas.

As the Indian menace waned, Juan N. Cortina, a Mexican of medium height, fair complexion, green eyes, brown hair and red beard, vowed to redress popular Mexican grievances in the lower Rio Grande Valley near Brownsville.

To some people Cortina was a murderer, to others a liberator. While Cortina never achieved Pancho Villa's fame the two had much in common.

With his band of followers (some say bandits, others say soldiers) he terrorized the valley so that Americans in Brownsville asked regular Mexican troops for protection, the first and only such occurrence in history. (The Mexicans responded.)

Several bodies of rangers and the United States Army hurried south to assist. Captain W. G. Tobin and his command of Texas Rangers arrived first, which was regrettable because they should have arrived last or not at all. They drank too much and removed a lieutenant of Cortina from jail and lynched him. The rangers themselves were later ambushed and several were slain. Probably the best thing that happened was when Captain Tobin fell out of a carriage and broke his neck.

Down from Austin came Rip Ford and a body of rangers that grew larger as it neared Brownsville. They crossed the Rio Grande, and in a series of sharp engagements they rolled the Mexican bandits up into a ball and shot them to pieces.

Colonel Robert E. Lee moved in to restore order. He passed many destroyed and abandoned buildings and farms, noting that "Those spared by Cortina have been burned by the Texans."

As the war ended in the Rio Grande Valley, Cortina retired to become a brigadier general in the Mexican Army, and later the Governor of Tamaulipas.

Meanwhile, General Sam Houston got the idea he would organize an army of Texas Rangers, invade Mexico, bite off a chunk, annex it to Texas, and a grateful nation would elect him President of the United States. Some historians believe he thought he could avert the coming Civil War in this manner, and maybe he could have. Crazier things have happened.

The war he sought to prevent actually came before he could get started, and during that conflict the rangers dropped practically from sight. Texas entered one of the darkest periods of its history.

After the war, the carpetbag Governor F. J. Davis replaced the rangers with the hated Texas State Police. In fairness the state police were never as bad as often painted, but they were not as effective as they might have been. They lacked public support, and when the *State Journal* published a "Roll of Honor" on April 11, 1873, naming twelve policemen slain in the line of duty, a state legislator published a "Roll of Horror," a list of seventeen men murdered by the State Police.

But better days were coming. The citizens elected a Democratic legislature. It appealed the State Police law, and when the Governor vetoed the bill, it was passed over his veto.

So the rangers were back in. The period of their greatest glory lay right before them.

One cannot study Texas Ranger history without being astonished at the number of killings by those men. An accurate count of the dead is impossible to compute, but the figures (counting Indians, Mexicans and Anglos) would run into the hundreds, and there is a story behind every one. Some have been told, some will be told, but the vast majority will simply be forgotten. The details bleached away with the bones.

Rangers never had a uniform, nor did they wear a badge. Generally they furnished their own weapons and their own horse. They were an arm of Texas government and were also abused by that same power. For instance, ranger companies (except for the commissioned officers) were usually recruited locally and paid $30 a month and board. When they were killed, and a lot of them were, the state shoveled them into the ground as cheaply as possible. And when the troubles which they had been hired to quell were finally settled, they were unceremoniously discharged and told if they wanted to reenlist at another trouble spot, they could pay their own transportation.

In 1874 the Texas legislature created two distinct ranger forces for protection primarily against Indians and Mexican bandits. For awhile outlaws took on secondary importance. Captain L. H. Mc-

Nelly commanded a force to suppress troubles along the Mexican border. Major John B. Jones would lead the Frontier Battalion and control Indians.

McNelly, a thin and wiry little man, went into Nueces County to stop the killing and thieving. Mexican rustlers had been slipping across the Rio Grande for livestock.

McNelly hired Jesus Sandoval ("Old Casuse" the rangers called him) as a guide and translator, and as rustlers were caught crossing the river, Casuse would slip a rope around their necks, toss it over a tree limb and haul them up and down a few times in order to make them talk, which they always did. After all possible information had been extracted, the luckless individuals were lynched.

In order to completely stop the rustling, the rangers struck at its source. They crossed the Rio Grande to a ranch house headquarters, charged and killed several Mexicans during the stiff fight. Unfortunately they struck and killed innocent people in the wrong place. So they galloped south to the correct location and clashed with the Mexican Army which chased McNelly's men back to the river bank.

McNelly's health deteriorated after this, and he retired from the rangers to die at the age of thirty-three on September 4, 1877.

Captain Lee Hall and John B. Armstrong took over his duties, and during their tenure the Texas adjutant general published a crime book, better known as the "Ranger Bible," or "Fugitives from Justice in Texas." Its long lists of wanted men led directly to hundreds of these individuals being captured and imprisoned or killed.

Armstrong ran roughshod over criminals, and in particular he wanted the elusive John Wesley Hardin, one of the West's best known fugitives. After considerable detective work he tracked Hardin to Alabama, killed one of his followers, and took Wes prisoner. Hardin went to jail for fifteen years, and upon release showed up in El Paso where he practiced law before being shot dead by Uncle John Selman.

In the meantime the Frontier Battalion under the astute command of Major John B. Jones, made its presence felt. Thirty days after he took over, he had five companies in the field. For the first six months he chased Indians before turning his attention to white outlaws.

He gave special attention to brand changers: a U easily became an O, a P became a B or an R, an L became a B.

Sometimes Hall would get information on a particular rustler, wait until he returned home, and then break in at dawn, a time of least resistance. According to W. P. Webb, foremost historian of the Texas Rangers, "On those occasions the rangers often came in contact with the womenfolk of the outlaws from whom they received terrible tongue-lashings for searching their houses and arresting their men."

Jones went next to Lampasas, scene of the boiling Horrell-Higgins feud. The ranger captain entered the county with seven men, and within three days had arrested twice that number and forced both sides to sign a peace treaty.

Gradually the rangers moved into West Texas. On January 29, 1881, ranger commander George W. Baylor, ambushed a war party of Indians in the bitter cold near Sierra Blanca and killed four warriors, two women and two children. Thus ended the last Indian fight in Texas.

And with this particular fight, an era ended. There were no more frontiers. The rangers were becoming more and more a police force, moving from one trouble spot to another, hunting cattle thieves, bank robbers and fence cutters.

The Frontier Battalion closed itself out after nearly twenty years. According to regulations, only commissioned officers could make arrests. Ordinary rangers were not permitted that privilege. The question went to the Texas attorney general for a decision, and he agreed. In 1900 the Frontier Battalion faded out of existence.

A year later the Governor reorganized the rangers on roughly the same outlines. Captains chose their own men, and there were four companies of not more than twenty each. Captain John R. Hughes took charge of Company D at El Paso; Captain W. J. McDonald took Company B at Amarillo; Captain J. H. Rogers Company C at Fort Hancock, and Captain J. A. Brooks Company A at Alice.

In 1935 the rangers reorganized as a part of the Department of Public Safety, charged with the protection of life and property and the investigation of major crimes and insurrections. Nowadays they have an official uniform, a white dress shirt, black tie, silver grey Stetson, tan western cut trousers, matching long coat or short jacket, black belt, black gun holster, black cowboy boots and a .357 revolver. They are the elite of Texas' investigative forces, a group of eighty-two men, known and respected around the world.

23

BLOOD & SALT

MEN CHOOSE STRANGE GODS to die for. They kill each other because of different ideas or philosophies, different dreams, soup that's too hot, or a love that's too cold. Name a subject and somewhere, somehow, men have fought to possess it. It might have been a woman, it might have been gold, it might have been oil. In El Paso during the middle and late 1800's it was salt.

There were two local salt wars, the first being so little known that only a few historians and buffs are aware that it even happened. Writers have dubbed it the "Magoffin Salt War," and the events took place in December of 1853.

Its short period of fury circulated around James Wiley Magoffin who was born in Kentucky in 1799. He left home at an early age, and after a series of adventures which included being shipwrecked, he emerged in the early 1830's as the American Consul at Saltillo, Mexico. There he met and married a San Antonio, Texas woman named María Gertrudis de los Santos Valdez de Veramendí. Shortly afterwards they moved to Ciudad Chihuahua where at least one, and possibly two, sons were born.

For many years Magoffin traded between Chihuahua City and Santa Fe, the enterprise ending when Mexican President Santa Anna stopped it. Magoffin then moved to Missouri and organized wagon trains between Independence and Santa Fe. A few years later the powerful Missouri Senator Thomas Hart Benton introduced Magoffin to President Polk. The apparent results of their conversation was that Magoffin became highly instrumental in the transfer of the El Paso Southwest to the United States, during the war with Mexico.

After helping arrange the Spanish surrender at Santa Fe, Magoffin came to Paso del Norte (Juarez) in September of 1846. As advance man for Colonel Alexander Doniphan, Magoffin paved the way for the peaceful arrival of the American Army. However, Chihuahua Governor Angel Trias took a different view of Magoffin's activities. He called them treasonous, and it was only by the narrowest of margins that Magoffin escaped being shot. The Mexicans slapped irons on Magoffin's wrists, and incarcerated him for nine months in Chihuahua and Durango prisons.

Upon his release, Magoffin settled across the river from Paso del Norte and established Magoffinsville. The splendid home he built, the vast gardens that grew around, were situated in El Paso somewhere in the present-day vicinity of Piedras and Alameda streets, or a few blocks farther west. The river curled in the area, and dense bosques (thickets) a mile wide covered the river bottoms. Two or three miles away, across Indian-infested countryside, was downtown El Paso, then usually called Franklin or Smithsville. To the east lay the isolated communities of Ysleta, Socorro and San Elizario. They were the "big" towns on the American side of the river, and San Elizario was the county seat.

Don Santiago, as the Mexicans called Magoffin, had the widest circle of friends in the valley. Following the death of his first wife in Missouri, he married her sister. Together they lived in an adobe hacienda of immense proportions (no longer standing), and it was known far and wide as the cultural and hospitality center of this region. (The building should not be confused with the present Magoffin homestead, built by his son Joseph.)

Throughout the years the genial Don Santiago became known, loved and respected for his generosity, wit, companionship and business acumen. In December of 1853, the Post Opposite El Paso (soon to be known as Fort Bliss) reactivated, and Magoffin quartered the soldiers on his property. He became the post sutler.

That same month James Magoffin learned that a caravan of *sali-*

neros (salt gatherers) were leaving Doña Ana (a small and very old community about ten miles north of Las Cruces, New Mexico) on December 6. According to reports, the group was headed for the salt springs on the east slope of the San Andres Mountains. Since Magoffin claimed some kind of interest or ownership of those beds, he strongly believed that the centuries-old precedent of free salt meant nothing. Those who took the mineral should pay him for it.

The white-haired Magoffin angrily demanded that Sheriff Jerry Snyder (officed in San Elizario) do something, and the lawman raised a posse of seventeen Americans, ten Mexicans and one Englishman. From somewhere Snyder also obtained a howitzer, and although the records are silent concerning how he obtained it, there isn't much doubt that Fort Bliss furnished the weapon. Whether or not the military turned its back and pretended not to hear as it rattled out of sight is beside the point. It is important that here was one of the few such posses in history to drag a cannon along.

Magoffin and Company planned to intercept the salt gatherers as they crossed San Augustine Pass going east. The posse camped two or three days on the approximate site of the present-day White Sands Missile Range headquarters, and were disappointed when no one showed up. Either the caravan had come through earlier, or it had gone another route. The only thing left to do was catch the *salineros* on their way back from the salt springs.

The posse rode north to Chino Pond and waited for the New Mexicans. On December 16, a wagon train composed of 127 men and twenty-six cumbersome two-wheeled carts, better known as *carretas,* rumbled south toward the fresh water. At about three in the afternoon, Sheriff Snyder served his papers. He demanded that the salt gatherers either pay the fee or submit to arrest and be taken to El Paso County for trial.

In those days when life alternated between dreary monotony and absolute tedium, men took their humor where they could find it. The fact that an upstart Texas sheriff thought he could arrest New Mexicans, or that he could make them pay for free salt, struck the *salineros* as very funny. As they guffawed, a red-faced Snyder spurred his horse back to the pond. He would take possession of the water hole, deny it to the New Mexicans, and through thirst, force them to either pay up or surrender.

Undisturbed, the salt gatherers halted a short distance away, and freed their oxen from the spans. As the animals ambled forward, the excited Texans rushed out to either capture the oxen, or at least prevent them from drinking. The New Mexicans shouted *"Cuidado! Cuidado!"* (Be careful! Be careful!) Somebody fired a shot, and the wild melee began.

Magoffin's outnumbered Texans should have ingloriously lost, and no doubt would have had not one of them remembered the howitzer. It boomed two or three times; the fire belched and the smoke rolled.

The cannon balls didn't hit anything except desert some distance away, but the noise scared everyone. The *salineros* fled in one direction, and the posse in another, the lawmen having enough presence of mind to take the oxen, the salt and the carts with them. Although some accounts mention three men as being killed, more reliable estimates place only one man as hurt, none slain.

With the spoils in tow, the posse headed south toward the Texas line and safety. From that time on, all of the fighting took place in court. The Territorial Court of New Mexico denied Magoffin's right to tax the salt beds. Instead the District Court indicted James Magoffin for "assault with intent to kill," and a reward of $2,000 went on his white head, although it was not a dead or alive notice.

Warrants for "unlawful assembly" went out for Samuel Magoffin (the son), Gabriel Valdez (possibly Magoffin's brother-in-law), Frederick Percy (the Englishman), Jeremiah Snyder (the sheriff), and Bigfoot Wallace, easily one of the best known and most famous Texans of his time.

New Mexico's Governor David Merriwether tried unsuccessfully to extradite everyone, especially James Magoffin, but all of the former possemen stayed discreetly out of the Territory and gave no one an opportunity to arrest them. As the uproar died down, Magoffin returned the oxen to their rightful owners and made restitution for damages. Not long afterwards, all charges were thrown out of court. Thus ended one of the El Paso Southwest's most intriguing episodes.

This is not to say that salt was no longer a factor in local economics or politics. Beneath the shadow of Guadalupe Peak almost ninety miles to the east lay other, more productive salt beds. The forthcoming struggle for their possession would lead to a blood-bath the likes of which El Paso County had never seen. Because of it, the political foundations of two nations would be shaken, and the United States and Mexico would stand once again on the brink of war.

The El Paso Salt Ring

The El Paso Salt War of the 1870's was far different from the Magoffin Salt War of twenty-five years earlier. Times had changed. Ysleta held title to the county seat, and while the mainstream of history was slowly slipping past San Elizario, that little community was headed for a convulsive outburst of hate which would forever etch its name in the El Paso County Hall of Violence. The Mexicans were the dynamite; and the Anglos were the fuse.

The Salt War cannot be understood without considering the conditions which prevailed in El Paso County. The most significant and outstanding fact was this area's remoteness. As an island in a sea of sand, El Paso was hundreds of miles and decades in time from most ports of civilization. While the stagecoaches rumbled in and out several times a week, occasionally on schedule, El Paso was still months away by wagon train from San Antonio, the main stopover for eastern traffic heading west.

A population of approximately 6000 persons lived in Juarez (still Paso del Norte). About the same number lived on the American bank of the Rio Grande, most of them scattered from Hart's Mill (the present-day Hacienda Cafe) to San Elizario. Of this number, El Paso had about 700 souls.

Nevertheless, El Paso dominated the American scene. Regional commerce centered here, most of it controlled by the eighty or so Anglos. Of these individuals, practically all spoke fluent Spanish, it being the language of trade and business. However, several of these same gentlemen had trouble speaking English. El Paso had a polyglot collection of Germans, Canadians and Italians.

El Paso Street rippled through the center of town, and was so-named because it led to El Paso (Juarez), Mexico. Somewhere south of present-day Paisano Drive it petered out, and became a trail leading through the thickets to the river. The north end of the street termi-

217

nated (as did the town) at the Plaza, presently in the front of and to the left of the Plaza Theatre. An *acequia* (irrigation ditch) flowed down San Francisco Street and across the Plaza. On its banks grew an ash tree, which has come down through history as the famous "newspaper tree" because of the many notices, want ads, threats and bad poetry posted upon it.

Looking down El Paso Street from the Plaza one could see an unbroken line of adobe, white-washed, flat-roofed, one-story buildings, a great many being saloons. All had corrals out back. At the present site of the Paso del Norte Hotel stood Ben Dowell's Saloon, the favorite such establishment in the city. More deals were probably cooked in this saloon than anywhere else in the Southwest.

Culture in El Paso clashed as much as it blended. The schools were an incredibly complex problem. Anglos wanted the so-called Free Schools; while the Mexicans, led by the Catholic Church, insisted upon retaining the religious system of teaching. Neither side showed much willingness to compromise.

The border meant nothing. Men crossed back and forth as they had for centuries, and without passports or visas. This region was a law unto itself and it rigidly believed in an eye for an eye, a tooth for a tooth.

The troubles and frustrations began to crystalize with the salt beds lying near Guadalupe Peak nearly 100 miles away. *Salineros* drove their two-wheeled carts into the shallow lakes and shoveled the salt onto the wooden floors. Water drained through the cracks in the boards, and the salt dried in dirty-looking heaps. This enterprise became a favorite way for the border population to earn a few coppers, a slang term for Mexican pennies, which in those days had value. (The standard unit of commerce in El Paso was the Mexican peso, and not the American dollar.)

Greed and racism gradually became factors in the salt trade. Since the lakes were on public land, and therefore free to the salt gatherers, an El Paso Salt Ring formed to file claim on the property and to charge a fee for every *fanega* (two and one half bushels) of salt taken. The ring leaders were El Paso Republicans by the name of W. W. Mills, A. J. Fountain, Gaylord Judd Clarke, A. H. French, B. F. Williams and J. M. Lujan.

Of the six, Mills and Fountain were initially the most important.

Mills was an arrogant, haughty, brilliant man who largely changed the face of El Paso and helped bring it into the 20th century. Fountain was a shrewd, ambitious, equally brilliant and vain attorney who sought a political empire.

Also deserving of mention were Louis Cardis, an elegant, respected Italian who was occasionally honest, and Father Antonio Borajo, the San Elizario priest. These two men controlled the Mexican vote, and naturally preferred not to be openly identified with the Salt Ring so long as they received their share of the profits. While Father Borajo had many fine and good qualities which should not be overlooked or forgotten in the tumultuous events that followed, he nevertheless, as Cardis once described him, "had salt lakes on the brain."

As sometimes happens in partnerships composed of ambitious and hungry men, there came a falling out. Mills and Fountain split up when each supported different political candidates for governor, and Fountain won. He went off to Austin as a state senator, while Mills brooded at home in El Paso and wrote poison-pen letters to newspapers throughout the state. He accused Fountain of everything from impersonating a federal officer to embezzlement. A grand jury indicted Fountain on eighteen counts of criminal charges, a sting of humiliation which Fountain never forgot or forgave even though he was acquitted.

He turned with vengeance on Mills and formed, in cooperation with Gaylord Clarke and French, an Anti-Salt Ring. Fountain vowed to and did expel Mills and his cronies from salt bed ownership. Borajo and Cardis now wanted Fountain to claim the lakes for himself and make it a three way split. That compromise fell through.

On December 7, 1870, B. F. Williams, loaded with Pass Whiskey (a locally brewed liquor), spent an hour or so in Ben Dowell's Saloon verbally assaulting Fountain, French and Clarke. When Fountain learned of it, he grabbed his walking cane and headed for the barroom where Williams, in a furious rage, reached for his derringer. He fired two times as Fountain commenced raining blows upon him with the cane. One bullet struck Fountain in the left arm, another bounced off the top of his head, and a third hit squarely in the chest, penetrating five letters and glancing off a pocket watch before plowing along his side and breaking a rib.

Williams ran to his residence a few doors away while Fountain staggered outside and told Clarke and French what happened. The wounded man then walked home as steadily as he could and picked up his rifle.

Clarke and French organized a small posse and headed for the Williams place. There, Clarke and three men began chopping away with axes at the heavy front door. French hastily posted three men at the rear, and was in the process of deploying another three guards in front when everyone suddenly dropped everything and ran. There stood Williams with a double-barreled shotgun held at hip level.

Williams fired at Clarke who ducked behind an adobe pillar supporting the roof overhang. The first blast missed, so Williams rushed in closer. He and Clarke shifted around the pillar until Clarke finally jumped the wrong way. When he did, the shotgun roared again and he died practically on the spot.

From about a half-block away, Fountain witnessed the killing. Cocking his rifle, he paused and shot Williams down in the street. French then rushed over and fired a revolver bullet into the dying man's head. Thus began, and ended, round one of the El Paso Salt War.

The death of Cardis

The double killing of Gaylord Judd Clarke and B. F. Williams increased the bitterness between all factions involved in the salt struggle. New personalities became involved, and pressures for additional violence soared.

However, A. J. Fountain had had enough. He dropped out of the salt dispute after finishing his legislative term in 1874, and moved with his family to Mesilla, New Mexico. During the next few years he won additional fame as the political opponent of A. B. Fall. Eventually Fountain and his nine-year-old son Henry disappeared near the White Sands, and the mystery of their deaths has never been solved.

The Republican Party controlled El Paso in those days, it being a carpetbag holdover from the Civil War reconstruction period. Mills and Fountain were the two captains, but their feud completely shattered Republican unity and created a political leadership vacuum.

Into the breach stepped Charles W. Howard, a stocky newcomer whom the Mexicans would hate and learn to call *"El Indio"* (the Indian) because of his dark complexion. As a combative, former Missouri lawyer, Howard would bring the blessings of the Democrats to West Texas.

Louis Cardis and Father Borajo joined forces with Howard, and the trio became a political powerhouse. Howard became district attorney, Cardis the state legislator; and Borajo guaranteed their elections by making sure his Mexican parishioners voted the right way. When Cardis reached Austin, he helped remove S. B. Newcomb as the El Paso district judge, and the position went to Howard who promptly filed on the salt beds in the name of his father-in-law.

But as the Republicans fell out among themselves in their hour of greatest success, so the Democrats did also. No one is quite certain what happened. Howard, Cardis and Borajo had an agreement regarding salt profits, an understanding that shattered when Howard accused his two partners of "monstrous schemes." He never explained what those schemes were, but it could have been that they wanted more money while he wanted it all.

The break left Cardis and Borajo fuming in helpless rage. Neither had ever admitted any complicity in the salt intrigues to their Mexican followers. Whereas they had previously instructed their people to pay these "lawful" fees they now denounced the tax as a gringo effort to further impoverish the poor.

In the midst of this uproar, the Holy See in Rome decreed that the Rio Grande, at least the West Texas portion, would divide the lines of authority between the Bishop of Durango and the Diocese at Tucson. Borajo therefore should have reported to Durango for a fresh assignment. Instead he refused to budge, and defied all attempts to remove him.

Bishop J. B. Salpointe came in from Arizona to check on the matter, and to the Bishop's amazement, a mob led by Borajo stopped his carriage in Socorro, Texas. The San Elizario priest reportedly called Salpointe some "hard names," and suggested that he go no further. Salpointe did go on, but had to camp on the ground when he reached his destination because Borajo had threatened the people with dire consequences if the Bishop were well received.

The Bishop returned to Arizona with Borajo's taunts of "Protestant, *pelado* and thief" still ringing in his ears. Nevertheless, the

221

church still had the final say even if it took the Durango Bishop to say it. He ordered Borajo transferred to the Mexican parish of Guadalupe, several miles downstream on the Rio Grande from San Elizario.

With only Cardis left to fight, Howard gradually gained the upper hand. Twice he caught Cardis in the streets and beat him with his fists. Such was his power that he ordered two San Elizario Mexicans arrested for talking about taking salt without paying for it. The accused might have walked away free during the trial, had not one of them angrily blurted out in Spanish to the judge that he would take the salt if he wanted to.

The conviction aroused angry mutterings in San Elizario, including threats against Howard's life. He therefore went to Ysleta, where a noisy crowd demanded his appearance. Regardless of what has been said about Howard, no one ever disputed his courage, and in early El Paso this attribute covered up a multitude of sins.

He jammed his shirt down inside his trousers, and stomped out to talk with the mob. He had hardly spoken when the seventy or eighty armed men, shouting and jeering, dragged him through the Ysleta streets, lifted him on a horse, and took him to San Elizario as a prisoner.

According to Howard, "a sullen, ferocious looking body of men," roughly 200 strong, were waiting in the village plaza. For three days Howard stayed under tight security while everyone debated the question of whether or not to shoot him. If the new parish priest Father Pierre Bourgade had not intervened, an execution certainly would have taken place.

Cardis suggested mercy, a recommendation he would not have made had he foreseen what lay ahead. He thought it best that Howard sign a written statement, one which not only confessed to past errors, but which promised that he would leave the country within twenty-four hours and never return. Howard signed the document, and Father Bourgade escorted him to the waiting carriage.

He drove practically without stopping to Fountain's house in Mesilla where he telegraphed the Texas governor that a Mexican invasion was imminent. Back in Ysleta, Sheriff Charles Kerber considered plans for obtaining troops on short notice from New Mexico's Fort Craig. (Fort Bliss, formerly known as Camp Concordia, had been abandoned since January.)

These messages put the Governor in a quandary. Neither troops nor the Texas Rangers could arrive in less than a month. However, on October 9, 1877, Cardis wired that peace had been established "mainly through my efforts."

Cardis had hardly quit patting himself on the back before his time on earth was up. Howard returned to El Paso with bitterness and humiliation eating his guts out. He blamed Cardis for everything, writing that, "I can think of nothing on Earth or Hell bad enough for him."

Howard expected Cardis to be in the Solomon Schutz store on San Francisco Street, and his guess was correct. The plump Italian who usually wore a Prince Albert coat and a black bow tie sat in a rocking chair with his back toward the store entrance when his executioner walked in. Joseph Schutz called out, "How do you do, Judge Howard," an obvious warning for Cardis who immediately jumped up and ducked behind the bookkeeper's desk. The flimsy piece of furniture wasn't much protection from a double-barreled shotgun.

A few words were exchanged, and then Howard shot Cardis in the stomach. As he staggered away from the desk, another charge struck him in the chest. Cardis died almost before hitting the floor.

Charles Howard walked outside the store, chucked two empty shotgun shells into the street, and went down to the Customs Office for advice from Inspector Joseph Magoffin. Joseph told him to get out of town, and so Howard went back to Mesilla.

The community was stunned. Many men did not like Cardis and were glad to see him dead; however, a cold-blooded murder such as this could have serious repercussions. Solomon Schutz sent the following telegram to Colonel Edward Hatch at Fort Bayard, New Mexico, the nearest army post to El Paso: "Don Luis Cardis was killed by Charles Howard, and we are expecting a terrible catastrophe in the county, as threats have been made that every American would be killed if harm came to Cardis. Can you send immediate help for God's sake?"

The Texas Rangers ride

Following the death of Louis Cardis, Governor Hubbard ordered Major John B. Jones, a famed Texas Ranger, out of Austin and to El Paso for an investigation. Since no rails went to West Texas, Jones caught a train to Topeka, Kansas and then to Santa Fe. A stage carried him in to Mesilla where he conferred with Fountain and Howard.

Two days later he arrived in El Paso, and found all sorts of rumors floating about. He read a message written by several San Elizario Anglos: "Some eight or ten of us have got together, and will fight till we die; we are in Atkinson's house — send us help for the honor of the gringos." A postscript to the sheriff stated: "Help us Charlie for Christ's sake, and we will do our damndest in the meantime."

Jones went to the house of Mauro Lujan in San Elizario and spoke with the Mexican leaders. Apparently the Americans were in no immediate danger and all the Mexicans wanted was justice. They produced a copy of the United States Constitution, and showed Jones the 1st and 2nd Amendments which guaranteed them the right of free assembly and to bear firearms. The ranger patiently explained the difference between a legal assembly and a mob, and he also assured them that when and if Howard returned to Texas, he would be arrested and charged with murder.

The guarantee might have calmed down everyone if Jones had not planned to organize a company of Texas Rangers to keep the peace. This disturbed the Mexicans, and after talking it over among themselves, they questioned Jones again. No, he would not allow them to raise their own law enforcement body, and yes, the rangers would be recruited locally because there was no place else to get them. Mexicans could enlist if they were American citizens and could prove it. (Rangers practically always recruited locally in order to save expenses. When a company transferred, it either discharged the officers on the spot or required them to pay their own transportation costs to the new post.)

In middle November, 1877, Jones commissioned John B. Tays, a brother to the Reverend Joseph W. Tays of St. Clements Church, as a lieutenant in the Texas Rangers, and gave him authority to raise a body of men. While nobody ever said that John Tays was the brightest individual in El Paso County, he was basically an honest and decent human being.

However, the ranger recruits would have disgraced a penitentiary. Over half came out of New Mexico, some already running from the law. Howard himself sent down at least two men from Mesilla. Hard looking characters like these frightened the people they were hired to protect, as much as those they were hired to suppress. El Paso breathed a sigh of relief when they rode down to San Elizario for duty.

Jones simply gritted his teeth. If these were the best men Tays could find, so be it. Admittedly the available choices were not prime. To help calm the situation he commissioned Joe Magoffin and Guadalupe Carbajal, the latter being a justice of the peace, to arrest Howard, charge him with murder, set bond at $4,000, and release him until the trial. Magoffin went even further and cautioned Howard to stay out of town pending a court date. Had that advice been heeded, it might have prevented much bloodshed. In the meantime Jones returned to Austin.

In early December, Mexican wagons left almost daily for the salt beds. Howard screamed that if anyone took his salt without paying the fee, he would prosecute. To back up his threat he stormed down to San Elizario.

Upon learning of Howard's mission, Tays rode to Ysleta to provide an escort, but on his way in he encountered a Mexican force from across the river. Since to Tays this amounted to an armed invasion, he telegraphed Captain Thomas Blair at Fort Bayard to come on the run. Late the following evening Blair and fourteen soldiers arrived at the outskirts of San Elizario, only to have their right of way contested by a body of hostile Mexicans. An argument followed, and Blair evidently doubted he could fight his way through. The Mexicans denied being aliens, so this gave the captain an excuse to withdraw gracefully. He wired his commanding officer that the dispute was local and greatly exaggerated. Meanwhile Governor Hubbard telegraphed President Hayes for military assistance to repel a Mexican invasion.

When Howard arrived in San Elizario, he left the rangers and went straight to the home of Charles Ellis, a prosperous storekeeper. The house is still partly intact, and has often been mistakenly referred to as the Spanish Governor's mansion or Viceroy's Palace.

Shortly after Howard went inside, a disturbance occurred up the street and Ellis went to investigate. As he mingled with the crowd, the Mexicans recognized and killed him. They dragged his body through the village on a rope, cut his throat and stabbed him twice through the heart.

That night the ranger headquarters underwent a siege, and its twenty-five or so rangers figured they had very little chance if help did not arrive soon. When dawn came, things looked quiet, so Sergeant

C. E. Mortimer cautiously ventured outside on patrol. A rifleman hiding inside a house shot him down in the street. Although Tays performed bravely in dashing out and dragging him back into the headquarters building, Mortimer died that afternoon.

Firing continued all day. Rioters looted the Ellis store, removed the merchandise and killed Miguel Garcia. As wagon loads of San Elizario goods were disappearing across the Rio Grande, two mothers came down from El Paso and bullied the Mexican leadership into releasing the women and children taking refuge inside ranger headquarters. They almost got away with Billy Marsh, the youngest ranger in the fort, but before the group vanished from town, the Mexicans had second thoughts about Billy being loose, and took him prisoner.

Deputy Sheriff Andrew Loomis of Pecos wanted out of that death trap too. According to him, the affair was none of his business. Tays therefore hung out a flag of truce, and the Mexicans allowed him to depart.

The siege dragged on from Wednesday night to the following Monday morning when the Mexicans dug rifle pits and breastworks. Stating that they had undermined the structure, the Mexicans demanded that Tays "Give up Howard, or we will blow up the building." They modified their ultimatum by promising that "If Howard gives himself up willingly, and if he gives up all claim to the salt lakes, no harm will come to him."

When Tays relayed the message to Howard, the attorney nodded his head and said, "I will go. It is the only chance to save your lives. But they will kill me." Turning to John McBride, his San Elizario agent, Howard said, "Take care of my money and papers. Goodbye boys." He shook hands with those near him, and then casually stepped out of the building as if he were going to lunch.

Tays went along to negotiate for Howard as best he could. A half-hour later John Atkinson, a San Elizario businessman sympathetic to Howard, appeared at ranger headquarters saying, "Everything is peacefully arranged. Come with me. Tays is waiting for you."

As the rangers stepped outside and walked down the street, they were disarmed and shoved into a one room building. Most of them were too tired to even curse. They sank onto the dirt floor in a worn-out sleep.

Back at the Mexican headquarters, Tays argued for Howard's life while the Mexicans yawned and waited for word that the rangers were locked up. Then the leader Chico Barela waved his hand, and Tays was dragged off to join his friends. For the first and only time in history, a Texas Ranger Company had been taken captive.

The executions at San Elizario

Charles Howard lived a life of political intrigue and deceit. He sought power and he crushed those who opposed his efforts. For him there was only the intoxication of success, or the consequences of defeat. Men of both races hated and feared him. Yet his bravery redeemed and washed away a lot of sins, and it is the one outstanding quality which makes him appear a bigger and more likeable man across the intervening century since his death.

His chief opponent was Francisco "Chico" Barela, an Ysleta farmer and salt-gatherer. He had light skin, brown hair and blue eyes, a complexion totally different from the average Mexican. He also had a daughter engaged to Louis Cardis, reputedly a man of many loves and sweethearts. When Howard killed Cardis, Barela swore vengeance.

With his enemies now in his power, Barela hesitated. Should he keep his promise and turn them loose, or should he hand them over to the mob? He asked Father Borajo, now living in Guadalupe, Mexico, for advice, and was allegedly told, "Shoot all the gringos and I will absolve you." From that moment on there was never any question regarding Howard's fate.

Howard and his two San Elizario associates John Atkinson and John McBride were readied for prompt execution. The husky lawyer went first, standing erect and level-headed as a dozen or so Mexicans led him into the street where nearly a thousand men had been drinking and shouting his name for hours. Now they lapsed into a sullen silence as he was marched to a vacant space between two houses. Howard glowered, snapping his dark eyes at the menacing five rifles pointing at his chest. He gave the command, "Fire!"

The guns cracked and he fell, writhing in the dirt. As he rolled about in agony, horse thief Jesus Telles swung a machete at Howard's neck. The dying man twisted aside at the last second, and the heavy blade continued its arc, stopping at Telles's own foot. He and the others watched in stupefied amazement as two of his own toes flipped skyward in somersaulting curls.

Other men rushed in to finish the botched execution. They hacked and chopped until life finally left Howard's body.

John Atkinson was led forward next. He reminded the crowd of its promise of mercy, but they howled back "kill him." Atkinson yelled, "Then let me die with honor. When I give the word, fire at my heart." Jerking off his coat and shirt, he too gave the command of "Fire!", and once again the firing squad did a sloppy job. All five bullets struck him in the stomach, and instead of falling he simply reeled backwards. "Higher," he screamed, and he cursed them.

Two more shots knocked him down, but still did not kill him. As he thrashed about in agony, he motioned for Jesus Garcia to shoot him through the head. Garcia complied.

McBride took his turn next. Unlike the others, he said nothing, and the records are silent concerning the speediness of his death. Perhaps there was nothing else to say.

The bodies were stripped, mutilated and tossed into an old well. Chanting, "Death to all gringos," the Mexicans considered executing the rangers. Two troublemakers from Mexico were especially vociferous in demanding additional American blood, and might have succeeded had not Chico Barela opposed it. He released the rangers, gave them horses but no weapons, escorted them as far north as Ysleta, and warned them not to return. In the meantime the mob destroyed and almost totally plundered San Elizario. Wagon loads of looted household goods and store merchandise disappeared across the Rio Grande into Mexico.

By the time the embarrassed and bedraggled rangers returned to El Paso, help was pouring into town. Colonel Edward Hatch brought troops in from New Mexico on the basis that this was no longer a civil disturbance, but an armed, illegal, outlaw invasion from Mexico.

John Kinney, self-styled King of the Cattle Rustlers, led a crew of Silver City rabble-rousers and incorporated them into Sheriff Charles Kerber's posse. Most of these new arrivals had such odious reputations that Tays would not enlist them in the rangers.

The army marched towards San Elizario followed by the rangers and Kerber's posse. Behind them rattled a wagonload of coffins.

At Ysleta the rangers and posse arrested Crescencio Irigoyen and

228

Santiago Duran. The two prisoners were bound hand and foot with leather straps and seated on the caskets. However, when the partisans reached Socorro, the captives weren't with them. Tays wrote that they were "killed while trying to escape." The bodies were left lying in the road where they fell.

In Socorro the rangers and posse had a field day. Jesus Telles, who had chopped off his own toes while trying to sever Howard's head, saw them coming and dashed for the mission. He never made it.

Farmer Cruz Chavez was shot to death, no one being certain what part if any, he played in the mob action. A man named Nunez supposedly fired on the rangers from the window of his home. Moments later Nunez was dead, and his wife left gasping with a bullet through her lungs.

All armed resistance evaporated as the innocent as well as the guilty fled before the vengeful rangers and posse. An army captain angrily wrote Sheriff Kerber that men, women and children are "perishing for want of food and from exposure to the cold in and around Saragossa (Zaragoza), Mexico."

Atrocities mounted against the Mexicans, and there were numerous charges of rape, theft, assault and looting. When the lawmen weren't abusing Mexicans, they were fighting among themselves. On New Year's Day, 1878, Sergeant J. C. Ford killed Sergeant Frazer following a heated argument. More killings would have taken place had not Tays hastily mustered out the rangers on January 10.

Congress demanded an official investigation. Governor Hubbard appointed Major John B. Jones, a Texas Ranger, as one member of the board, and President Hayes named Colonel John H. King of the 9th Infantry and Lt. Colonel William H. Lewis of the 19th Infantry. They made an official report on March 16.

The army placed the damages at $12,000, while Jones said it was closer to $31,000. Mexico would be asked to surrender fugitives, and to make reparations. The board agreed that a military post should be reestablished at El Paso, and that it should be manned by at least 200 soldiers. From this recommendation, Fort Bliss was activated again.

An El Paso Grand Jury indicted Chico Barela, Sisto Salcido, Luciano Fresquez, Agaton Porras, Desiderio Apodaca and Jesus Garcia. All fled to Mexico, and no serious attempts were ever made to extradite them.

C. L. Sonnichsen, well-known Southwestern historian, documented the El Paso Salt War in a book by the same name which is published by the Texas Western Press.

Sonnichsen had this to say: "El Paso and Juarez are cities now where a quarter of a million Americans rub elbows with an equal number of Mexican citizens . . . and we are proud of the good understanding we have reached after a century and more of close contact. We have our troubles and our grievances, but the record on the whole is good. The Salt War was part of the growing pains we had to endure in developing the ability to live together." He closed with the cogent statement that "The Salt War, like all wars, was wasteful and unnecessary, unless to prove to a pessimist that men can die bravely in a bad cause."

He might also have noted that goodness and evil, compassion and brutality, love and hate, have no religious, economic, cultural or ethnic boundaries. The Salt War is not just a story of Americans vs. Mexicans, or Anglos vs. brown-skinned people, or even Protestant vs. Catholic. It is a story of well-intentioned men on all sides who gave way to misguided prejudice.

24

JOHN LARN

TEXAS KILLER

Most residents of Shackleford County, Texas (near Abilene) refuse to talk of John Larn.

Practically every reference to him has been obliterated from the printed record. Larn is a memory all would rather forget. As a trusted member of the establishment, he was many things to many men: efficient, cruel, kind, pleasant and barbaric.

Other accounts marked him as an evil, gun-slinging genius who finally died in a cloud of hate-filled gunsmoke while locked in his own jail. Some of his close relatives performed the execution.

Larn came out of Mobile, Alabama, and drifted into Colorado where he murdered a cattleman who objected to his "borrowing" a horse without asking. A couple of months later he shot the sheriff who tried to arrest him.

Staying on the move, he drifted to Fort Griffin, Texas, and hired out on a trail drive to New Mexico. Along the way he killed three men and threw their bodies into the Pecos River to "feed the catfish."

Returning to Fort Griffin, Larn had a falling out with the trail boss and led several disgruntled drovers in a rampage through the camp. Two men were killed and seven wounded. Since it was commonly understood that the dead men had been rustling cattle, not much sympathy was wasted on their sudden demise.

Before long Larn had obtained employment with Joe Matthews, a leading rancher in the area. Just like in a movie script, Larn soon married one of the boss's daughters. As a husband, he was considerate and faithful. He did not drink, smoke or swear in her presence. Of course, he never did any killing in his wife's presence either.

Larn established his own ranch along the Clear Fork of the Brazos River and fostered an interesting relationship with John Selman. Of the two, Selman was crude, Larn much more polished and smooth. Yet in the final analysis Selman proved the wiser. While still two jumps ahead of the hangman's noose, Selman moved to El Paso and to one of the West's most controversial showdowns. Larn stayed to die.

In one of the classic struggles for power, the big ranchers fought the small farmers in Shackleford County. Cattle barons accused the grangers of stealing livestock (a partly correct assumption) and of fencing off the range (an entirely correct assumption).

In February 1876, when Larn was perhaps twenty-five years old and had two more years to live, he ran for sheriff, was elected, and set out to clean up the county. On April 2 he caught horse thief Joe Watson, most of his gang, and his wife Sally who supplemented the family income by working as a prostitute. In their possession were twenty-six stolen horses. Larn decided the time had come to set an example. Within minutes he lynched Watson, "Reddy," "Larapie Dan," and "Doc" McBride. A note pinned to the clothes of the latter read, "He said his name was McBride, but he was a liar as well as a thief."

As for Sally, Larn sent her home before the hangings and said her husband would join her shortly. He did, but very dead.

Two other gang members escaped to Dodge City, Kansas where Larn, with a warrant in his pocket, caught up with them. Soon after he brought them back and locked them in the Fort Griffin jail, vigilantes removed the pair to some handy trees along the river bank and lynched them too. By December, eleven other rustlers, or alleged rustlers, had been jerked into eternity. The valley of the Clear Fork now showed all the appearances of being a peaceful area.

It might have stayed that way had not Larn and Selman become restless and started to rustle a few cattle themselves. Occasionally they even shot their hired help in order to keep down expenses.

Two stone masons built a rock fence on Larn's property, but before being paid were found floating in the river. The circumstances appeared strange to the coroner, but he hesitated to call it murder since things like this did happen now and then. Several other equally strange disappearances then took place, part of them traceable to Larn. When Joe Matthews asked his son-in-law to act more responsibly, Larn mocked him.

A shootout caused the final split in the vigilante relationships. Bill Bland and Charlie Reed, two Larn partisans on a spree, rode into Fort Griffin. Reining up in front of the Beehive Saloon, they dismounted and swaggered through the bat-wing doors.

As the boys merrily shot out the lights, Deputy Sheriff Bill Cruger and County Attorney Jefferies tried to arrest them. When the smoke cleared, Bland was dead, Reed had been chased out of town, and Jefferies and Cruger were both wounded, the former, seriously. An innocent bystander lay on the floor with a hole in his head. Lieutenant Dan Barron of the 10th Cavalry sat slumped in a chair, groaning and dying.

Due to heavy community pressure, Larn resigned and concentrated on rustling. His night riders shot up the homes of grangers and ranchers alike. The Governor issued a proclamation against the killings, and sent Texas Rangers to enforce it. However, the rangers spent much of their time avoiding ambushes, especially after they learned Larn had thrown some hides bearing another man's brand into a water hole near his slaughter pens. After dragging the river, an unspecified number of items turned up, enough to force Larn to answer charges.

In a twist of fate Larn met his chief accuser in Fort Griffin. After a short conversation the would-be witness decided to leave town for his health. With his disappearance the case against Larn collapsed. Tight-lipped ranchers growled that more severe measures would be taken.

Grangers and ranchers teamed up to achieve identical ends. A farmer testified that Larn and Selman had chased him for miles along the river bank, and tried to kill him. This gave Sheriff Cruger an excuse to arrest Larn, but to be on the safe side, he deputized the Reynolds family as a posse. The Reynolds were related to Mrs. Larn.

John Larn stepped outside his large, rambling home that morning in June, 1878, and walked toward the barn. Riders were loping in from the east, but he recognized his wife's relatives among them and paid little attention. With his gunbelt hanging across a fence rail, the most dangerous gunman in Texas was arrested while sitting on a three-legged stool and milking a cow.

Cruger planned to get Selman too, but the wily gunman was warned and slipped out of the country after failing to get word to his partner. The deputies tied Larn and put him on a buckboard for the trip to town. Mrs. Larn went along, for whatever her husband's faults, she confidently believed in his innocence.

Since Larn had many friends in Fort Griffin, the posse took him to the county seat of Albany. Chained hand and foot, Larn walked under heavy guard to a wooden shack jail while his wife frantically sought an attorney.

Her efforts were too late, and perhaps indirectly caused his death. Things had gone too far now for Larn's release on bail. No one would feel safe.

About ten that evening, vigilantes overpowered the guard, John Poe, who would later be with Pat Garrett at the slaying of Billy the Kid. Poe's reluctance to adequately protect Larn stemmed from his own membership in the vigilantes.

Nine masked men stomped into the jail. The prisoner heard them coming, knew what it was all about, and rose to face them. "Larn," a man named Reynolds said, "we've decided not to hang you."

Larn understood, faintly smiled and said nothing. Then nine rifles cracked in the night air.

25

BASS OUTLAW

Bass outlaw (not to be confused with Sam Bass) was the nicest fellow in El Paso when sober, but he was a homicidal maniac when drunk. Unfortunately for those who knew him, he drank quite a bit.

In his boots he stood about five-foot-four, and if you added the heft of his revolver, he weighed about 150 pounds. In an age where masculinity counted for about everything, Bass had a deep inferiority complex regarding his size. He continuously had to prove his manhood.

Although a misfit in the Texas Rangers, he stayed a long time and was even promoted. The rangers kept him because good men were hard to find, the hours were long, the pay small, the duty dangerous. But the rangers also kept him because the man had charm, especially when sober. Ranger Alonzo Oden described him as an officer and friend who "could laugh louder, ride longer, and cuss harder than the rest of us; but could be more sympathetic, more tender, more patient than all of us when necessary." The evaluation ended with: "Bass had one weakness which proved stronger than all his virtues. He couldn't leave liquor alone. None of us could handle him, none of us could reason with him, we just stayed nearby until he sobered up."

Outlaw (his real name) killed a man in Georgia sometime before 1885 and immediately left the state. When he reached Alpine, Texas,

*Bass Outlaw . . . with a chip on both shoulders and a
flask in his pocket, he was always ready for a fight.*

he enlisted in the Texas Rangers, and in 1890 was promoted to corporal. Two years later he became sergeant, filling a vacancy left by Charles H. Fusselman, killed shortly before by horse thieves on the east side of the Franklin Mountains near the present Trans Mountain Road. Outlaw might have risen higher in rank had not Captain Frank Jones forced his resignation because of excessive drinking while on duty.

For awhile Outlaw hunted buried treasure near Sanderson, Texas, the scene of a former passenger train holdup where the outlaws escaped with fifty or sixty thousand dollars. For weeks Captain Jones, Outlaw, and other rangers played cat-and-mouse with the robbers, finally overtaking them near Ozona, Texas, where the leader was shot. The wounded man rode into a dense thicket, wrote out a will, and blew his brains out. Though the other outlaws were captured, none would confess to what happened to the money. The stolen Wells-Fargo money sacks were being used to hold coffee and sugar, a clear indication that the money had been hidden somewhere, probably buried.

Outlaw searched the canebrake repeatedly for the treasure, but never found it and neither did anyone else. He turned to United States Marshal Richard Ware for a job, and was accepted.

On April 5, 1894, Ware and Outlaw were in El Paso attending court. With them was a deputy marshal who had been serving subpoenas. As a rule the man who did this also took the fees, and since Dick Ware had not given Outlaw any work, Bass began to sulk. And when he began to sulk, he also began to drink.

Outlaw wandered up Utah Street (now South Mesa) where he bumped into Constable John Selman and Frank Collinson, the latter a former buffalo hunter. The two men patiently listened to Outlaw's complaints, his threats against Ware, and advised him to sober up.

Bass waved the suggestions aside, and the three of them walked to the house of Tillie Howard, El Paso's best known and most flamboyant madam. Selman and Collinson sat in the parlor while Bass wandered to the back. Seconds later a gunshot roared and Selman glanced over at Collinson and remarked, "Bass must have dropped his gun."

Outside in the backyard Tillie Howard frantically blew on her police whistle, standard procedure when brothels had trouble and needed police assistance. The noise startled Outlaw, and he rushed across the yard to take it away from her. At that same instant John Selman walked out on the back porch.

Texas Ranger Joe McKidrict also heard the whistle. He was stationed with Company D at Ysleta, and was in the neighborhood only by chance. He ran down the street and hurdled the back fence. "Bass, why did you shoot?" he shouted.

"Do you want some too," Outlaw snarled. He shot McKidrict through the head, and in the back after he had fallen.

For an instant everyone (including Outlaw) stood aghast. Old John Selman reacted first by leaping off the porch and drawing his pistol. As he hit the ground, Outlaw fired almost directly into his face, the explosion causing deep powder burns. The bullet missed by inches, and Selman reeled backwards, snapping off a shot almost by instinct at the blurred figure facing him. Outlaw sagged as the slug struck him above the heart.

Outlaw did not go down, nor did Selman. The constable stood there in the yard helplessly holding his eyes, unable to do more, while Outlaw staggered backwards. Desperately the little man tried to raise his gun and kill Selman. Finally as he backed into the fence, he was able to steady his gun and snap off two shots with incredible accuracy. One bullet hit Selman just above the right knee, and the other severed an artery in the thigh.

Bass fell over the fence, wobbled out onto the street and surrendered to Frank McMahon, another Texas Ranger. McMahon and a bystander helped Outlaw into the Barnum Show Saloon where Dr. T. S. Turner laid him on the bar. Concluding that nothing could be done, the Doctor transferred Outlaw to a backroom prostitute's bed where Bass died four hours later. Bass knew that he was dying, and he called over and over, "Oh God, help!" Then he asked, "Where are my friends?" Nobody answered.

Joe McKidrict was sent to Austin for burial. His real name happened to be Joe Coolly. He changed it to keep his mother from learning his whereabouts.

John Selman struggled into a carriage after the shooting and went to see Dr. Alward White who confined him to bed for two weeks. Selman spent the rest of his life (which wasn't long) with a cane. Though he never recovered the full use of his eyes, and was nearly blind at night, he became meaner by the day and finally put three slugs in John Wesley Hardin, the most dangerous gunman in Texas—perhaps in the West.

Old John Selman went on trial in October of 1894 for the murder of Bass Outlaw. Judge C. N. Buckler instructed a verdict of not guilty.

James Gillett . . . survived everything but his wife's fury.

26

JAMES GILLETT

TEXAS RANGER

ONE OF THE BETTER KNOWN Texas Rangers was Jim Gillett, a man of courage, intelligence and resourcefulness. Within his limitations, he epitomized the near perfect lawman, and set standards equalled but never exceeded to this day.

He was born on November 4, 1856, in Austin, Texas, the son of a Kentuckian who traveled west to the Lone Star State and became a lawyer, legislator and soldier, fighting in both the Mexican and Civil wars. Nineteen years later young Jim signed on as a $40 a month Texas Ranger, a trade to which he dedicated a significant portion of his life.

Menardville became his first duty station, but instead of fighting Indians, he and his buddies spent most of their leisure time playing cards and pitching horseshoes. During his first year he engaged in only one Indian scrap, and before long was ordered to assist in smothering the Mason County War (more of a feud). He even stood guard for awhile over the notorious John Wesley Hardin, a gunman standing trial for murder. (The jury handed Hardin a sentence of twenty-five years in the state penitentiary at Huntsville.)

Always on the move, Gillett rode into Tom Green County, where he tracked down and killed Dick Dublin, a local desperado. Dublin had over $700 riding on his curly head, and Gillett happily thought of himself as a rich man until learning the reward went only with a live and kicking Dublin, not a dead one.

Gillett participated in the search for Sam Bass, and missed being in on the big Round Rock shootout by just a few hours. Shortly afterwards, the rangers underwent a shakeup in order to better streamline the command, and the now Sergeant Gillett headed out toward El Paso with Lieutenant George W. Baylor and Company C.

Governor Roberts dispatched the rangers as a direct result of the El Paso Salt War. Although the killings were largely over, further trouble might still break out due to an overabundant supply of hard feelings. The Governor ordered Baylor to reconcile the various factions if possible, and not to direct a punitive expedition against the Mexicans.

The tiny detachment left San Antonio on August 2, 1879, and arrived forty-two days later. Mrs. Baylor, her sister, and two Baylor children, Helen and Mary, traveled with the party. The ranger force set up camp in a clump of cottonwoods at Ysleta, then the county seat.

That October, a party of Indians attacked a stage station at Fabens, and fled into Mexico. Within hours Gillett and a small force galloped out in pursuit, teaming up in the process with a larger Mexican force. The small army plunged nearly a hundred miles south of the border, fought an inconclusive day-long mountainside battle, and returned to Ysleta. The rangers lost one good horse; Gillett killed one Apache.

A month later Victorio and his Apaches swept through Carbajal, Mexico, looting and killing. Mexican fighters charged after them, and sent a message to the rangers, inviting them along. The rangers went, and did the best they could, even though they missed the heavy action. For the most part they were a burial detail, arriving at a fight just in time to help shovel under the losers.

By September of 1880, Victorio had broken out of the reservation and was shooting his way through northern Mexico. Once again the Mexican Army took to the field, and once again Baylor's rangers were invited to participate. Baylor, Gillett and eleven rangers responded to the call. However, when the Apache chieftan and his war party were finally brought to bay, the Mexicans wanted to handle the fighting themselves. General Terrazas ordered the rangers and other American units out of the area, and on the following day he led an attack at

Tres Castillos which killed Victorio, and for the time being, ended Apache depredations in Mexico.

Several of the Indians managed to escape back into the United States where in early 1881, they ambushed a company of soldiers near Van Horn, waylaid an emigrant train, and then wiped out a squad of black troopers near Fort Quitman.

The army and the Texas Rangers were now frantically trying to round up the Apache strays, with the honors finally going to the rangers in what has been called the last Indian fight in Texas. On a bitterly cold January 29, Baylor and his men ambushed the Apaches at daybreak. In the wild shooting and resultant confusion, the rangers found it impossible to tell the difference between the squaws and the braves. Three women and two children were killed. A dozen or so warriors were slain and scalped.

Meanwhile, events were taking place in Socorro, New Mexico that would have far reaching consequences for Sergeant Gillett. A. M. Conklin, owner and editor of the Socorro *Sun* was brutally murdered while at church on Christmas Eve, 1880.

Intense excitement prevailed. Most Anglos believed the Mexicans planned a general uprising, to murder them in their beds. Pleas for assistance were wired to the Governor, as well as to other communities. At San Marcial, New Mexico, Anglos armed themselves to the teeth, forcibly took over a train and nearly ran it off the tracks getting to Socorro. Fortunately, considerable bloodshed was averted when the U. S. Army moved in, took over and kept the peace.

Abran and Enofrio Baca, the two murderers, escaped in the confusion and fled south to El Paso and beyond. The Territory offered a reward of $500 ($250 apiece) for the brothers, an amount of interest to the rangers, especially Gillett. He kept a close watch on the home of El Paso County Judge Baca in Ysleta, an uncle of the fugitives. One day he noticed a couple of strangers sitting on the judge's front porch, placed them under arrest, ironed their wrists and ankles, and took them to Socorro. One was innocent; the other Abran Baca. Gillett took his $250, and went to look for Enofrio.

An informant told him that Baca clerked in a Zaragosa, Mexico store, the little village being right across the river from Ysleta. Gillett double checked the information, was convinced of its accuracy, and called upon Corporal George Lloyd to assist in the arrest. Both men splashed across the Rio Grande and reined in at the store front. Lloyd held the horses while Gillett went inside.

As Baca stood bending over the counter measuring dry goods for a woman customer, Gillett grabbed him by the collar, poked a six-shooter alongside the ear, and told him to step lively toward the front door. The female patron fainted.

Gillett dragged Baca outside and forced him on a horse as the town began to organize against them. Then began a wild dash for the river. However, the rangers had too big a start, and the distance back to Ysleta too short, for any reasonable Mexican expectations of catching them.

With Baca chained to a tree, Gillett sent telegrams to the New Mexico governor asking what disposition he wanted with the prisoner. The Governor, knowing the mood of the Socorro townspeople, ordered Baca delivered in Santa Fe. However, Gillett had to go through Socorro to reach the capital, and upon his arrival, a group of Socorro residents invaded the train, paid Gillett the $250 reward, removed Baca, and hanged him to a gate post.

By now Gillett's unauthorized entry into Mexico had created an international uproar. Telegrams zipped back and forth between Austin, Mexico City and Washington, D. C. Baylor severely chastised Gillett, angrily saying he was lucky the Mexicans hadn't shot him to dollrags in Zaragosa. In the end, nothing came of the incident except for reprimands. Never again did rangers cross over into Old Mexico to make unauthorized arrests.

The incident cost Gillett his job. He went to work as captain of the Santa Fe railroad guards at $150 a month, worked there only a few months, and then he hired out as deputy marshal to Dallas Stoudenmire in El Paso. When the marshal resigned in 1882, Gillett moved into the top position, and only once was he obliged to discipline his former boss.

Billy Bell and Bill Page, two El Paso toughs and former deputy marshals, got into an altercation in the Acme Saloon as Dallas happened upon the scene. In an effort to separate his two friends, he grabbed Page about the body and half-carried, half-pushed him to Doyle's Concert Hall (another saloon) where both men drank until midnight, at which time they returned to the Acme and started quarreling. Stoudenmire jerked one of his pistols and fired, as Page, sobering fast, knocked the weapon up in the air.

Stoudenmire now might have killed Page except for a very distinct and identifiable cocking noise behind him. Dallas turned and saw himself looking down the gaping holes of a double-barreled shotgun held in Gillett's firm hands. Stoudenmire and Page each paid a $25 fine in court the next morning for disturbing the peace.

Prior to all this, Gillett had married the sixteen-year-old Helen Baylor, daughter of the ranger commander. They tied the knot on February 10, 1881 in Ysleta and for several months lived with her father. When Jim became town marshal they moved to El Paso where an already shaky marriage rapidly began falling apart. Helen was a sentimental romantic teenager; church going, party loving and culture conscious. According to some tales she neglected her housework, and was prone to stay in bed reading love stories while Gillett fixed his own breakfast.

She bore him two children, Baylor and Harper Gillett. Baylor died at the age of three, whereas Harper took the name of Harper Lee and became the first American bullfighter in Mexico. He and his father became estranged over the years and rarely saw each other.

As family pressures mounted on Gillett, he argued with Mayor protem Paul Keating. A rumor, supposedly traced to Gillett, accused Keating of oftentimes being too drunk to attend to city business. Keating promptly insinuated that Gillett had not properly accounted for fines and other monies.

The two antagonists met in the street where Gillett struck the alderman several times with his fist and threatened to shoot him.

Keating swore out a warrant for Gillett's arrest, charging "assault and battery and threats of shooting." Although in serious trouble, Captain Gillett, as his friends called him, had the town's support and possibly could have survived. Still, it seemed like a good time to quit. He had been considering for a long time entering the ranching business around Marfa, so he resigned.

Unfortunately, it was the worst possible moment to become a rancher. Within weeks his cattle died of the fever. Hat in hand, he reapproached the El Paso City Council for a job, and they put him back on the payroll as a common deputy. He served from 1883 to 1885 when he resigned again, once more to enter the cattle business.

The marital situation between him and Helen worsened. In 1889 she filed for divorce, charging he spent too much time with prostitutes. In 1892 she met and married Captain Frank Jones. Not too long afterwards he died heroically in a skirmish near Fabens.

Gillett married again, and settled down once more to ranching in the Marfa area. He wrote his memoirs entitled *Six Years With the Texas Rangers,* a classic which has since undergone many reprints. Over the years he got religion, and became a leading organizer, as well as one of the most popular speakers, at the Marfa Cowboy Camp Meetings. He died in June, 1937.

27

PEARL HART, JOHN RINGO & JACK SLADE

WOMEN'S LIB never flourished in the Old West. The average female lived an unbelievably hard life, aging quickly and dying young. Ninety-five out of every hundred women left practically no records of their lives other than the usual faded photographs, birth and death dates, and the number of children, a figure always including several stillborn. On God's tally sheet their rewards must now be great; for few ever found any happiness, or comfort, or ease or freedom from privation and pain on this earth.

Of the prostitutes we know about, theirs was perhaps the greater tragedy. Most were used and abused, herded around and treated like cattle, rejected by family, friends and church, then abandoned or shot when their charms faded.

Of several examples, Etta Place is a starting point. Like most females who consorted with outlaws and gunfighters, she received her early training in a brothel. She was an attractive woman by any standards, as tough as she was good looking, and she became the sweetheart of the Sundance Kid. She assisted with train robberies, went with the Wild Bunch to South America, and dropped out of sight about 1907.

*Pearl Hart . . . stagecoach hold-up artist . . . the only
convict ever known to become pregnant
in the Yuma Territorial Prison.*

The legendary Calamity Jane who had the face and figure only a grizzly bear could love, became well known over the years because of her association with Wild Bill Hickok. The fast gunman tried to avoid her as much as possible, but she got her revenge after his death by telling all sorts of wild and windy tales regarding their relationship. When Jane passed away in 1903, the most logical place to plant her was right beside Hickok. One old-timer at the funeral sadly shook his head and remarked, "It's a good thing Bill is dead. He'd never 'a stood for this."

Another wild and woolly one was Belle Starr. She could spit tobacco juice farther than any man, and in fact looked like she might have swallowed a great deal of it. She took up early with Cole Younger, a side-kick of Jesse James, and a couple of months after Cole rode away, she had a child. Over the years Belle stole horses, rustled cattle, is said to have robbed stagecoaches, and in general did all right for a working girl in her time and place. It all ended in February of 1889 when someone mysteriously shot her in the back.

A couple of female hard-cases were Jennie Stevens and Annie McDoulet, members of the Doolin gang in Oklahoma. The former became known as "Little Britches," and the latter as "Cattle Annie." Federals arrested both for stealing livestock and selling whiskey to the Indians, and each served two years in the Federal prison at Framingham, Massachusetts. After their release, Little Britches settled down whereas Cattle Annie moved to New York and died of consumption.

Rose Dunn, better known as the "Rose of Cimarron," also hung out with the Doolin bunch, and she loved George "Bitter Creek" Newcomb. During a couple of wild shootouts with law officers, she kept the guns loaded while George banged away. After he was seriously wounded, she nursed him back to health. Finally, however, old Bitter Creek's luck ran all the way out when some marshals shot him out of the saddle for the last time. Rose mourned him for a few weeks, then married a blacksmith and became an honest woman.

And then we have Pearl Hart, the last of the Western road agents. She was born in Ontario, Canada, about 1871, and by seventeen had left home, becoming a woman of doubtful, if interesting, virtue.

About 1889 in Arizona she took up with Joe Boot, a young miner with scruples against work. Between the two of them, Pearl would lure unwary lovers into her room, where Joe would crack their skulls and relieve them of any cash. However, since most western characters were notorious for being short of money, the take for this was not particularly impressive. So they turned to stage robbing, and were inept in that too.

Pearl cut her hair and put on men's clothing, but did not fool anyone when she and Joe showed up in the middle of the road and pointed revolvers at the driver. Altogether they picked up over $400 from the Globe stage, and then tried to escape by fleeing across country. Both became lost, and when they finally cut the dirt road again, they were only a mile or so away from the holdup site. A sheriff and posse found them sleeping under a clump of salt cedars.

Pearl told such a sad tale at the trial of how her mother needed money, that the jury set her free. A furious judge had her rearrested for carrying a gun, and this time she went to the Yuma Territorial Prison, the only female ever to be incarcerated there. She might have stayed for much longer had she not convinced the warden of her pregnancy. Since the only two men known to have been alone with her were a leading clergyman and the Arizona governor, she received a discreet pardon and a bit of advice to leave Arizona.

For years she bummed around the country, occasionally getting arrested for picking pockets or prostitution. For awhile she rode with the Buffalo Bill Wild West Show. The story of her demise is unclear, but the facts seem to be that she returned to Globe, married a rancher, and lived to near ninety. She died in the early 1960's.

Most gunfighters were ladies' men, when they could find these females, and one of the best known was John Ringo, a mysterious individual probably born in Missouri sometime during the 1850's. He epitomized raw courage and fearlessness, and yet the string of dead men haunting his back trail is practically nil.

Ringo showed up in Texas during the 1870's and participated in the Sutton-Taylor feud. After being in and out of jail a few times, he wandered to Shakespeare, New Mexico, and then drifted on into Tombstone, Arizona. He gave the appearance of a good education, and is said to have quoted freely by memory from the bards of yore.

But if John kept a little poetry in his soul, he kept rot whiskey by the gallon in his stomach. He alternated between drunkenness and deep depression, and more than once rode up into the hills to be by himself for days.

His trigger temper kept him constantly in trouble, one such incident coming when a saloon drunk made an unkind remark about a lady currently plying her trade in the street. The sullen Ringo bashed the drunk over the head with a six-shooter, and then shot him through the throat. A funeral took place on the following day at Row 8 on Boot Hill.

Ringo openly sided with the Clantons against the Earps. In particular he despised Doc Holliday, and on several occasions the two men just barely avoided a shootout.

After the OK Corral gunfight, which Ringo missed, his hatred for the Earps cranked up several more notches. Undoubtedly he was one of the ambushers of Virgil Earp on the night of December 28, 1881, a bushwhacking that left Virgil alive but crippled for life.

Six months later Ringo himself met one of the most puzzling deaths ever recorded in western history. He, Buckskin Frank Leslie and Billy Claiborne, all notorious Tombstone gunmen, left town in the aftermath of a wild drinking spree. The next day they split up, and on July 14 a fellow came into town with the strange story of a body found sitting beneath a tree in Turkey Creek Canyon in the San Simon Valley.

Ringo lay there with a pistol in one hand, a single shot fired. His newly purchased boots, too small for his feet, were tied to the saddle of his horse. The swollen feet were bound with torn strips of undershirt; otherwise Ringo was fully clothed. In his head between the right eye and the ear was a gaping hole large enough to place two fingers. In his pockets was $2.60 in change, a pocket comb, a watch and a few other items.

The jury agreed that John Ringo committed suicide, primarily on the basis of a fired gun lying nearby, plus the fact of Ringo's often expressed threat of suicide. Unexplained however, was a cartridge belt that was on upside down, plus the fact that someone appeared to have tried to scalp him.

A strange gunman similar to John Ringo was Jack Slade. He grew up in Carlyle, Illinois, and after serving in the Mexican War, which whetted his taste for blood and thunder, he hired on as a trouble-shooter for the Overland Stage. The short, roly-poly, oftentimes schizophrenic Slade, also married one of the prettiest girls in the area, a young lady named Virginia who weighed in at about 160 pounds.

Slade was a working fool, a fighting fool and a drinking fool and he could do any of the three with equal vigor and joy. The company sent him to Julesburg as a division manager. All he needed to do was clean up the trouble there.

A Frenchman, Jules Beni, had stolen many of the company horses, and according to local rumors had killed and disposed of several emigrants. Jules would be no pushover for the mighty Slade.

The two men met in the street, and Jack Slade realized right away that he should have stayed with the main office. Beni started shooting immediately. His first two shots knocked Slade down. Three more bullets struck the writhing man. Not yet satisfied, Beni found a shotgun and emptied a barrel of that into Slade. In all, Slade absorbed thirteen slugs, and he still survived. Several employees carried his blood-soaked body off to a bunkhouse, and after a long period of convalescence, he recovered.

Slade offered $500 for anyone who would bring Beni into town, and naturally that kind of money produced results. Four cowboys caught the unfortunate man, dragged him in, and Slade tied him to a post. Swigging deeply from a whiskey flask, Slade methodically began to shoot Beni in the arms and legs. When the victim had nearly passed out from pain, Jack jammed his revolver into the wounded man's mouth and pulled the trigger. As an afterthought he sliced off the dead man's ears, and carried them for years on his watch fob.

Drinking became a serious problem, and the management fired Slade. He and his wife moved to Wyoming where Jack killed a man in a drunken brawl. So it was on to Virginia City (not named after his wife as has been claimed) where they started ranching. He and Virginia had an agreement: she would stay at the ranch and run things; he would remain mostly in town and see that the saloons stayed solvent.

Slade never killed anyone in Virginia City, and the worst that could be said about him was that he was a bully as well as a drunk and a nuisance. He stormed through the town breaking windows, overturning bars, smashing doors. The final straw came when he and some sodden buddies cut the milk wagon loose from the horses, and laughed in glee as the Virginia City milk supply went clanging and banging end-over-end down a steep hill.

That was too much. The famous Virginia City vigilantes had already captured and hanged the Henry Plummer gang, and so picking up their shotguns and rifles they went after Slade. Jack blustered as they led him to the cross bar of a corral gate, and all of a sudden he realized these men were serious.

Pleading for his life, he managed to get someone to go for his wife Virginia, eight miles away. If she could get there in time, she could scatter those vigilantes and cowboys with either a cuss word or a right cross, and everybody there knew it.

Still, they hung him anyway, and when Virginia rode in an hour later, they had just cut the victim down. Throwing herself across the body, she shrieked, "Why didn't you shoot him, and not make him endure the shame of being hanged."

Ironically, since Slade liked booze so well, his wife dipped him in raw alcohol and shipped the remains to Salt Lake City. On July 20, 1864, the Mormons furnished a grave site.

Virginia sold the ranch, married and then divorced. No one is quite sure what happened to her after that. It is said she died in Omaha or Chicago while running a brothel.

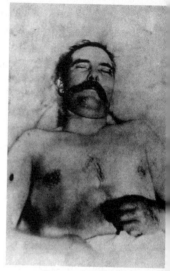

Coroner's photo

Concordia Cemetery, El Paso

John Wesley Hardin . . . died quickly, and must have crashed to the floor thinking he was only going to sleep with another monumental hangover.

28

JOHN WESLEY HARDIN

JOHN WESLEY HARDIN may well have been the West's greatest gunfighter, although this statement is a matter of opinion, judgment and
interpretation. Certainly he was the most dangerous man ever to walk
the wide and dusty streets of El Paso, and that community has known
such manslayers as Dallas Stoudenmire, Pat Garrett, Wyatt Earp,
John Selman, George Scarborough, Jeff Milton, Mannen Clements
and Jim Miller.

His father, the Rev. J. G. Hardin, named him John Wesley Hardin
in honor of the founder of Methodism. Wes was born May 26, 1853,
in Bonham, Texas, quit school at the age of fifteen (typical of his
time), and got his start as a gunfighter by shooting Reconstruction soldiers and Negroes. In those days such acts were not considered much
of a crime, which explains why Hardin remained free as long as he
did.

According to Hardin's own statement, the killings started in November of 1868 when an ex-slave refused to move off of a public road
so that Hardin could take all of it. John Wesley pumped three .44
slugs in him, and that settled the issue. He later wrote that all the white
folks thought he did a good thing.

Carpetbaggers ran Texas in those days, as they did throughout the South, and with soldiers enforcing the law, they picked up Hardin's trail near Sumpter. Unfortunately for them, Hardin saw three Blue Coats coming and he ambushed them at a creek crossing. He killed two with a shotgun, and a third with a revolver. Sympathetic civilians hid the bodies while John Wesley Hardin fled the vicinity.

For the next five years Hardin's career is simply one killing after another, all in self-defense he said. He killed a bully named Bradly, and followed it by fatally punching the ticket of a circus worker who tried to "push him around."

Near Kosse, Texas, the eighteen-year-old lad fell for the charms of a young lady who lured him into a barn where her boyfriend waited with a gun. In a shakedown racket as old as the Big Thicket, the crooks learned their lessons early. The man poked a shotgun at Hardin and demanded his money. John Wesley took it from his pocket, dropped some on the floor. When the greedy holdup man reached to scoop it up, Hardin pulled a pistol and shot him between the eyes. After retrieving his cash he left town in the usual manner, on the run.

Fleeing for the Louisiana line, Hardin made it to Marshall, Texas where the law caught up with him for the first time. As they returned toward the interior of the state, Wes killed one of the guards and escaped. Since he was now near his parents, he paused for a few days and his father advised him to flee to Mexico.

Hardin had journeyed only a short distance from home when three state policemen took him into custody. As they camped that night, the guard carelessly dozed off. Hardin got hold of his shotgun, and the sleepy officer never woke up.

The Clements', shirt-tail relatives of the Hardin family, took him in near Gonzales, Texas and discouraged him from heading for Mexico. Instead they encouraged his participation in a Kansas cattle drive. It would get him out of the state, and provide enough time to allow his troubles to die down.

As they drove the cattle across Indian Territory, Hardin killed two Indians who tried to tax the herd ten cents a head. A few miles further at a bend in the Arkansas River, much more serious trouble came up. A following trail herd came on too fast, which meant that the cattle mixed with one another, and the cowboys had a tough time sorting them out and separating them.

Hardin and the oncoming trail boss argued, and each side agreed to meet on the prairie and shoot it out. Hardin and his cousin Jim Clements met the other party which consisted of six, and with a wild yell the two factions charged each other on horseback. When the shooting stopped a few minutes later, the six challengers lay dead. Witnesses said Hardin killed five, and Clements one.

From that moment on, Hardin would have a nick-name. Friends and enemies called him "Little Arkansas," a reference to the river where the battle took place.

There is a story that in Abilene, Kansas, Hardin next tangled with Wild Bill Hickok, a new marshal just now reaching the height of his powers. Since the law forbade wearing guns in town, and since Hardin carried his in plain sight, Hickok approached John Wesley in a saloon and asked for his weapons. Hardin extended the butt forward, then executed the so-called "Road Agent's Spin" where the revolver twirls on the finger and slips back into the hand ready to fire.

The only substance for this story is Hardin's word, which may or may not have been an exaggeration. Most historians now tend to scoff at the tale. Such a wise old pro as Hickok would not likely have been fooled by such a stunt.

According to his story, Hardin did not linger around Abilene. He killed a man in a card game, shot a prowler to pieces whom he caught going through his clothes one night and figured he had pushed his luck as far as practicable in Kansas.

Back in Texas, between shooting encounters, he married Jane Bowen, and over the years they had three children, two daughters and a son. Wes told himself he planned to settle down and become a horse trader.

His peacefulness did not last long. In the summer of 1872 he and fellow gambler Phil Sublet argued over ten pins, and Sublet reacted first. He emptied a shotgun into Hardin. The Clements just managed to get John Wesley out of town before the police arrived. However, the law did not easily give up. Lawmen tracked the bleeding Hardin from one hideout to another, and finally pinned him down in a shed. As the siege wore on, Hardin agreed to surrender to Sheriff Dick Reagan of Cherokee County. Reagan and his deputies entered the building rather nervously, none being sure but what Hardin might change his mind and start shooting again. They were so relieved when Hardin tossed his gun aside that one deputy accidentally discharged his own weapon and wounded the already shot-up Hardin when the bullet struck him near the knee.

The posse took him to jail in Gonzales, and after Hardin had healed well enough to walk, a friend slipped him a saw and he cut his way out. Hardin fled to DeWitt County in East Texas, scene of the bloody Sutton-Taylor feud.

Over the years several men had already died in the violence, and Hardin's presence ran the total up even higher. He chose the Taylor side (they were relatives too), and initially killed J. B. Morgan, a deputy sheriff supporting the Suttons. A few days later Hardin added the sheriff to his list of dead bodies, justifying it later by referring to the lawman as "a horror to all law-abiding citizens."

Altogether Hardin had now slain about thirty men, plus or minus a body here and there. But on his twenty-first birthday, May 26, 1874, he notched another victim, and that proved his undoing. Ironically, it may have been the only time in his bloody career that he actually reacted in self-defense, and for that he went to prison.

Charlie Webb, the Brown County deputy sheriff, left his own jurisdiction to visit Comanche. Hardin claimed Webb planned to kill him. Maybe so; maybe not. Perhaps Webb simply reacted to the opportunity. At any rate, the two met in a saloon, spoke and shook hands. When Hardin turned toward the bar, Webb supposedly reached for his gun.

Someone screamed a warning, Hardin drew, turned and fired. Webb shot Hardin in the side; Hardin shot Webb in the head. As Webb hit the wall and slid toward the floor, the Clements, who were with Hardin, pumped several more bullets into him.

Hardin took off running for the east coast, leaving some of his relatives to take the consequences. An angry mob lynched his older brother Joe, a sort of early day confidence man who never harmed anyone except in the pocketbook.

The state put a $4,000 reward on Hardin's dark curly head, and that sort of cash drew the attention of the Texas Rangers, in particular Lieutenant John B. Armstrong. Hardin hid out in Florida, Georgia and Alabama, and went under the alias of J. H. Swain.

Armstrong learned of Hardin's whereabouts, and trapped him on board a train in Pensacola, Florida. A young companion of Hardin's drew a gun, and the rangers instantly killed him. In the meantime Hardin jumped into the aisle screaming "Robbers! Protect me!" He jerked his own pistol, but couldn't get it free because the hammer caught in his suspenders. One ranger later chuckled that Hardin practically pulled his pants over his head trying to get his gun loose.

Armstrong cracked Hardin over the head with a cane and then followed it with a gun barrel. When John Wesley woke up two hours later, the handcuffs were on tight. Turning to Armstrong he asked if any papers existed for his arrest. Armstrong said no, but he'd get some.

A jury found Hardin guilty of second degree murder in the death of Charles Webb, and sentenced him to twenty-five years in the state penitentiary at Huntsville. Before long Hardin underwent a remarkable change of character as unexpected aspects of his nature began to appear. He read voraciously. The Bible especially interested him, and he gave it a scholar's attention. He became superintendent of the Sunday School class, and head of the debating team.

For awhile he planned to become a minister, then changed his mind in favor of the law. He penned long and affectionate letters to his wife and children. Most of the letters were saved and are in the hands of the Hardin descendants today. Every letter begged his children to follow in the path of righteousness, to trust in God. "If you wish to be successful in life," he wrote, "be temperate and control your passions; if you don't, ruin and death is the inevitable result." Old John Wesley knew what he was talking about.

According to his correspondence, he planned upon release to take his family to a small town where he could practice law. All of his dreams came unraveled, however, on November 6, 1892, when his wife died at the age of thirty-six. Had it not been for her untimely death, it is possible that the future life and career of John Wesley Hardin might have had a more respectable ending.

After fifteen years in prison, the state released him in February of 1894. A month later the Governor granted a full pardon. He walked out of prison a free man, the coals of violence banked, but still burning.

He moved to Gonzales, passed his legal examination, and involved himself in politics. The man he backed for sheriff lost the election, and in frustration he moved to Junction, Texas, where on January 8, 1895, he married fourteen-year-old Callie Lewis after winning her in a poker game. The father, who lost, forced the daughter to go through with the ceremony, but naturally such an arrangement did not work out. Hardin, drunk at the time, realized the unworkable situation, so he left for El Paso.

He hung out his shingle which said "John W. Hardin, Attorney at Law." Unfortunately, he spent most of his time in the bars, and soon the El Paso scene braced itself for some of the most remarkable and violent scenes in its history.

John Wesley Hardin left prison and reached El Paso in 1895 with the announced intention of practicing law. But an honest intention was one thing, and circumstances something else. For in El Paso there lived another gunfighter.

Old John Selman was half-blind, crippled, and scarred from the effects of Mexican Black Smallpox. Like Hardin, he had been a terror in his day. Both men were similar in the respect that their bloody careers had pinched out long ago. Yet, each had waiting for him one final convulsion before that last long sleep in Concordia Cemetery. Their final meeting would become a most controversial affair.

To the north near Carlsbad, New Mexico, a good-looking ex-prostitute and her cattle rustling husband Martin Morose were fleeing the authorities and heading for Juarez, Mexico. No one pursued Beulah, so she took a train. Martin, just a few strides ahead of a lynch mob, understandably moved in more of a hurry. He jumped on a horse and, with his partner Vic Queen, never paused until splashing across the Rio Grande.

Meanwhile, Hardin's law office was about as busy as a church on Saturday night. Instead of folks coming in and discussing legal technicalities, they invited him to the bars where the topic invariably turned toward his fast gun and the number of dead men buried along his back trail.

One morning the bosomy Helen Beulah Morose appeared in his office and asked him to represent her husband. Wes accepted the case. His retainer fee, paid in part by Beulah's charms, set the wheels in motion to clear the honest name of Martin Morose. In the process, Hardin almost irrevocably turned his back on any likelihood of a

260

decent life. If it was any comfort, Beulah's smile made the slide much easier.

As Hardin became more familiar with his female client, his interest in seeing Morose a free man grew faint indeed. Beulah spent most of her time in the arms of her attorney, and from across the river Martin raged with jealousy.

The cuckolded husband called Tom Finnessy and a gunman known only as Lightfoot, two of his old friends, down from Eddy County (Carlsbad). Instead of slipping into El Paso and shooting Hardin, they wrote personal letters daring the middle-aged gunfighter to show his face in Juarez. So on Sunday, April 11, 1895, John Wesley stuck a revolver in his belt, ran a comb through his thinning dark hair, and headed across the river. On a Juarez street he met Jeff Milton, the El Paso chief of police, and George Scarborough, a United States deputy marshal.

As it seemed a good day for a drink, the trio strolled into the back room of a saloon, and by coincidence came face-to-face with Lightfoot and Finnessy, Martin Morose being absent. Everybody settled down for a talk since it was obviously a little late to be backing out. Lightfoot promptly set the pace by calling unfavorable attention to Hardin's relationship with Beulah, and pointing out that John Wesley did not appear to have the rustler husband's best interests at heart.

"That's a lie," Hardin snapped, and both men jumped to their feet. Hardin struck Lightfoot a crack across the face, knocked him against the wall and shoved a six-gun into his belly. Milton intervened and forcibly removed Hardin's gun. John Wesley then turned and smacked Tom Finnessy a whistling wallop in the jaw, the sound echoing clear out into the street. Hardin challenged both Finnessy and Lightfoot to a shootout, but the two men, still reeling under the weight of his hand, declined the invitation. Wes and the two police officers turned and left.

In retrospect, the scene could have been Hardin's finest hour in El Paso. He showed fire and spirit, a wellhead of dangerous aggressiveness. As a gunfighter it was his last hurrah.

The old Hardin would have looked up Morose and killed him. The new Hardin decided to have him assassinated. Although the facts are vague and incomplete, it appears that Hardin hired Police Chief Milton, George Scarborough, John Selman and Texas Ranger

Frank Mahon (a brother-in-law of Scarborough) to handle the killing. Those involved would split the New Mexico reward (reportedly $1,000), plus a share of any cash found in his pockets.

Scarborough crossed the river several times and spoke with Morose, trying to convince him that he was actually on Martin's side. Using Beulah as bait, he talked the rustler into a midnight rendezvous with her on the El Paso side of the river.

On June 29, Scarborough and Morose met in the middle of the Mexican Central Railroad bridge near the foot of El Paso Street. Morose hesitated, uncertain, suspicious. "Come on! Beulah's waiting," George urged.

The two men reached the end of the trestle and jumped off into a sunflower patch about where the United States bridge immigration building is now. As they took the trail toward town, Milton and the others rose from the bushes and commenced firing with shotguns, rifles and pistols. Scarborough turned and shot directly into the chest of Morose. The rustler pulled his pistol, fired once into the ground, stumbled and fell twice while in the process of receiving over half-a-dozen wounds. As he struggled to rise a second time, Milton placed a boot squarely in the middle of his chest and held him down until he died.

On the following day an undertaker went into the street and found four strangers to help him lay the outlaw to rest. At Concordia Cemetery only two mourners showed up: the tearful widow, Mrs. Helen Beulah Morose and her attorney.

The brutal slaying shocked El Paso. While the community had no use for Morose, everyone agreed the wanted man deserved a better fate than that. The district attorney swore out murder warrants for Milton, Scarborough and McMahon. All were acquitted, and Hardin and Selman were not even indicted.

Something unexpected now happened to John Wesley Hardin. For the first time in his life a killing seemed to unravel him. He doubled his liquor intake, and spent more time at the gambling tables. Soon he owed money to every saloon in town, and became a well-known poor loser. Enraged at losses in the Acme Saloon, he scooped up the pot and walked off. Nobody said a word, and he did not even have to draw a gun.

On the next day, at another saloon (the Gem), a card dealer

made a jesting remark about Hardin's playing. Instantly he was staring into the business end of a revolver. Hardin demanded $95. "This is all I want," he said, "only what I lost and no more."

When leaving, he overheard an unflattering remark about his lack of sportsmanship. Hardin dashed back upstairs (in the old days of El Paso, the saloon bars were downstairs and the gambling tables were upstairs) and shouted, "Those who don't like the play, trot out and show your manhood." At his trial a month later, one witness wryly remarked: "Since no one trotted out, I guess they liked the play."

Sheriff Simmons placed Hardin under arrest, and charged him not with robbery, but with carrying a weapon. A jury found him guilty and imposed a fine of $25.

A month later Hardin went to Carlsbad on business, and during his absence Helen Beulah Morose, usually referred to in the local papers as Mrs. Hardin, went on a drunken toot and challenged the twenty-one-year old police officer John Selman, Jr. to a shooting match. Young Selman tossed her in jail, and she paid a $50 fine the next morning in Recorder's (Corporation) Court.

Her relationship with Hardin had already been taking a sour turn. Both drank like the liquor stores were down to their last fifty barrels, and they brawled repeatedly. He once threatened to kill her after making her write a note saying she was committing suicide. Before she had it written, he passed out on the bed and began snoring. So she and the landlady went to see a justice of the peace. When Hardin woke up and stumbled outside, the police arrested him and dragged him before the judge who placed him under a $100 peace bond.

Beulah made up her mind to leave for Arizona, and she went as far as Deming, New Mexico, where she experienced a premonition of his death. "I feel you are in trouble and I'm coming back," she wired.

She returned, but the situation between them did not improve. A few days later she left again, this time for good.

Hardin sank lower into degradation, and his trips to the gin-mills became almost hourly affairs. When the liquor effects began to wear off, he sat on the edge of his bed waiting for the gunfire in his head to cease.

The Morose affair bothered him, and in a drunken stupor he

made some unwise remarks about hiring George Scarborough and Jeff Milton to do the killing. He hinted about making a confession and clearing his conscience.

Neither Scarborough nor Milton could afford this. Scarborough found him first, and grabbing him by the arm led him to the El Paso *Times* where Wes dictated the following statement:

". . . .while under the influence of liquor, I made a talk against George Scarborough, stating that I had hired George Scarborough to kill Martin Morose. I do not recollect making any such statement and if I did, the statement was absolutely false and superinduced by drink and frenzy."

Between drinking and gambling and lying in the gutter, Hardin managed to finish his memoirs, an autobiography no doubt begun in prison.

For reasons still not quite understood, Old John Selman planned to kill Hardin. Afterwards Selman would be tried for murder, and be defended by A. B. Fall. A hung jury caused a mistrial, and while waiting to go to court again Selman was shot down by George Scarborough in the alley beside the present-day State Theatre, then the Wigwam Saloon. Four years later to the day, Scarborough would be wounded by New Mexico train robbers and would die, like Selman, on the operating table.

But that's ahead of the story. On August 19, 1895, history has recorded that Selman and Hardin argued over the arrest of Beulah Morose by Young John Selman. There is another equally plausible tale that considerable cash was removed from the clothes of Morose, and Hardin did not split any of it with Selman.

Whatever the truth, Hardin walked into the Acme Saloon that evening (where Lerner's Dress Shop in downtown El Paso is now), and commenced gambling with grocer Brown. Picking up the dice, Hardin gave them a shake and said, "Brown, you have four sixes to beat."

Those were his last words. Old John Selman came storming through the bat-wing doors, and with a blazing .45 shot Hardin once in the head, once in the chest and once in the arm.

Historians argue over whether the first bullet struck Hardin in the front or the back of the head. Evidence exists for both points of view. Either way, to Hardin it really did not make any difference. He never had a chance.

Hardin lay sprawled on the wooden floor with his brains oozing through the cracks for over two hours while the whole town paraded by for a look. Then the undertakers removed the body, cleaned it up, and made it ready for the photographers. A newspaper remarked that except for being dead, Hardin appeared to be in fine shape.

All things considered, Hardin couldn't have asked for a more fitting way to go. Life had already drained from him like whiskey from one of his bottles. All that remained were memories of the past, to a greatness that was no more, and perhaps these thoughts were more haunting than they were pleasant. He died quickly, and must have crashed to the floor thinking he was only going to sleep with another monumental hangover.

Kustom Quality

Doc Holliday

Rose Collection

Wyatt Earp

*. . . the famous
gunfight at the OK
Corral merely
punctuated two
already tumultuous
careers.*

29

DOC HOLLIDAY & WYATT EARP

JOHN HENRY HOLLIDAY, historically better known as Doc Holliday, was one of the most dangerous and fearless killers to ever tote a shotgun. Born at Griffin, Georgia in 1851, he won his fame with Wyatt Earp during the OK Corral shootout in Tombstone, Arizona. Yet the OK Corral merely punctuated an already tumultuous career.

Doc spent a lifetime just one cough away from the cemetery. Tuberculosis struck him at an early age, and gained ground on almost a day-by-day basis. Because of the pain he drank heavily, sometimes consuming as much as two and three quarts of whiskey a day. He told a friend that liquor couldn't cure him, but it made dying a whole lot more pleasurable.

The nickname of "Doc" came from the practice of dentistry. No one could save an unhealthy tooth in those days. If it hurt, out it came. Barbers and itinerant medicine show men did most of the pulling. They lined sufferers up in the town square, and jerked their teeth for the benefit of paying crowds. After the fun, "dentists" sold bottles of elixir to the onlookers, guaranteeing their colored water to not only prevent further tooth-decay, but to slow down the advent of appendicitis, shingles, and moon-madness.

Some written accounts go to great length proving that Doc graduated from an eastern dental school, usually in Baltimore. The facts are that he did not graduate from anywhere. He learned the trade by observing other dentists (a standard apprenticeship at the time; after that one purchased a pair of pliers and hung out a shingle).

While he practiced dentistry off and on during his lifetime, it never became a primary source of income. Perhaps he frightened his patients with that chronic, consumptive cough constantly erupting in their faces. Another reason for Doc's failure to take the business seriously was his compulsive gambling. In spite of occasional streaks of bad luck common to all card sharps, Doc made more money in poker than he ever did in extracting teeth.

He left Georgia in the early 1870's and headed for Dallas. Behind him he left one, and possibly three, dead Negroes. Holliday caught the blacks splashing around in what he regarded as his private swimming hole on the Withlacoochee River. His pistol banged and the water ran red. Authorities declined to prosecute.

Over the years that nasty temper of Doc's continued to develop. He and Charles Austin, a saloon owner, exchanged shots on New Year's Day, 1875, in one of the few occasions where Doc missed his mark. The police arrested and fined them for disturbing the peace.

During the next few years Doc drifted to Fort Davis and Fort Griffin, Texas. In Jacksboro he tangled with a Fort Richardson soldier who accused Doc of holding too many aces. A fight started and the soldier came out second best. After the funeral, Doc prudently left town.

Back in Fort Griffin (near Abilene, Texas), Holliday met Wyatt Earp and Katherine Elder, the latter better known around the saloons and brothels as "Big Nose Kate Fisher." Occasionally she used the alias of Kate Earp, a sure indication that during her past she and Wyatt had shared more than just a glass of beer. As a career prostitute, she possessed the traditional heart of gold even though some of her other qualities were not quite sterling. Kate was flamboyant in her actions, strong in her beliefs, and salty in her language. Those who knew her said she could hit harder than any man and was burly enough to wrestle bears.

The relationship between her and Holliday paid off just as Doc's expectations of dying by tuberculosis appeared somewhat premature.

As usual he and a card player had a falling out. As the opponent reached for his gun, Holliday stuck him with a knife. Several friends of the deceased thought Doc should be measured for a hemp necktie, and they gathered in front of the jail to express their thoughts. The deputies showed no real interest in protecting the prisoner, and nervously marked time until they could turn him over and still claim they had done their best to protect him.

Doc would have choked on more than his faulty lungs if Kate had not acted. She set fire to a barn, successfully distracted the citizens, and while they fought the blaze, she released the prisoner. Together they fled to Dodge City.

Their relationship sputtered in Kansas. Dr. and Mrs. John H. Holliday (they never married) took rooms in a boarding house, and for awhile Doc hung out his shingle and managed to avoid trouble. But as a professional woman, Kate saw a lot of money going to waste with all those Texas cowpokes in town. She and Doc argued over her returning to the brothels on a part-time basis, but Kate would not be denied. She stormed out of the hotel to circulate her charms up and down Front Street. Thus began the first of Kate and Doc's many love-hate wars and separations.

Holliday confided his woes to Earp, himself a man of many women, very few of them respectable. Wyatt merely grinned and shook his head. Long experience had taught him that he did not understand females either.

A few evenings later, Texas ranchers Tobe Driskill and Ed Morrison brought their trail hands into Dodge for a celebration. Killing Earp headed their list of important things to do, and all they needed was an opportunity. Since Earp packed only a six-gun, he tried to keep a respectable distance between himself and the cowboys as he eased toward the Long Branch Saloon and the shotgun there. However, within a few feet of the door and possible safety, Driskill's waddies caught him. Twenty-five of the bunch backed him against the wall, and it looked for an anxious moment that the career of Wyatt Earp might end before he had time to tell some tall lies to his biographer.

At that instant the Long Branch door swung open and out stepped Doc Holliday with Earp's shotgun. Doc cowed the toughs while Earp cracked Driskill across the head with a long-barreled revolver. The cowboys spent the night in jail.

Holliday gradually tired of Dodge and sold his services to the Colorado railroad war brewing between the Santa Fe and the Denver and Rio Grande during the spring of 1879. As the conflict alternated between hot lead and United States Supreme Court decisions the two sides finally worked out a compromise which freed a lot of hired guns to wander the state. Holliday drifted south toward Las Vegas, New Mexico, and somewhere near Trinidad, Colorado, he allegedly killed two men and wounded a gambler named Kid Colton.

In Las Vegas he purchased part interest in a saloon, and hired as a waitress (among her other duties) the mistress of Mike Gordon, an ex-army scout. In the afternoon of July 19, 1879, Mike fired a shot into the saloon from the center of the street.

The patrons good-naturedly forgave the first round, and even Holliday did not react too belligerently. However, when Mike sent another ball crashing through the walls, Doc decided enough was enough. With a shotgun he blew more holes in Mike than a doctor could cork. Gordon died the next day, and some of the townspeople suggested that Las Vegas would become a more decent community if Doc moved on.

As it turned out, he was ready to leave. His old nemesis Kate had caught up with him, and much to his own disgust he took her back. Both had a neurotic need for each other, and while each found the other's presence depressing, they were nevertheless prisoners of their own emotional hangups. Not long afterwards they headed for Tombstone, Arizona, already the scene of big trouble.

Wyatt Earp

Thanks largely to television, few gunfighters in history have been as publicized or as fictionalized as Wyatt Earp. As portrayed by Hugh O'Brien, the Wild West's answer to Mr. Clean, he punished bad guys and made Kansas safe for settlement. In truth, historians are not certain if Earp was a bonafide frontier Paladin, or a scoundrel with a clever biographer. Right now the evidence leans toward the latter assessment.

He was born Wyatt Berry Stapp Earp in Monmouth, Illinois, on March 19, 1848. For awhile the family lived in Iowa, then Missouri, then California and then back to Missouri. As a farmer during his early years, Earp grew to about six-foot-two inches of bone and muscle, a lean and wiry individual who weighed about 185 pounds. A bushy and thick mustache drooped under the blue eyes and straight nose.

Folks around Iowa and Missouri knew the family as the "Fighting Earps" since most of the sons fought for the Union during the Civil War. (Wyatt was too young to be involved.) All of the brothers were scrappers, and although they had their disputes and falling-outs, they hung together through much of their violent lives.

Wyatt married a Miss Sutherland when he was twenty-one but she died a few months later, possibly of typhoid. Not long afterwards, he tried his hand for the first time at law enforcement, a calling that would exert a strong pull on him for a lifetime. Like many men in those days, he operated close to the line between outlawry and honest employment. The difference was that wearing a badge allowed him (and most other frontier lawmen) to live a life of excitement without running the risk of going to jail. So in 1870 Earp campaigned for constable of Lamar County, Missouri, and was elected. Things were so dull for him there that his biggest case was when he arrested two brothers for being drunk and disorderly.

He left Missouri and drifted south into the Cherokee Nation (Oklahoma) where in 1871 he and two companions (one with the interesting name of Edward Kennedy) became horse thieves. Although they rode day and night to avoid pursuit, federal lawmen finally tracked the fugitives down and jailed them. Earp paid his $500 bond and fled the territory. For the next three years he settled in Kansas and kept a low profile.

Gambling, booze and girls were his way of life as he moved from Hays City to Ellsworth, and then on to Wichita in 1874. These communities owed their existence to the railroads and the Texas trail herds. From 1867 to 1885, millions of Longhorns trailed north from the Lone Star State in one of the truly magnificent spectacles of all time. Cowboys loyal to their brand fought Indians, blizzards, drought and each other, but were defeated by an insect they did not even know existed. A tick clung to the rangy Longhorns, causing it no ill effects. As the steers crossed the Kansas grasslands, many of these insects fell off, later attaching themselves to northern animals which had no built-in immunity. Nobody could cure this dreaded Texas

Fever as it came to be called. Animal deaths followed everywhere the Longhorn went, and in self-defense farmers fenced in their lands, denying their property to the trail herds. In less than twenty years the great cattle drives were over, stopped completely by a tiny bug and a few strands of barbed wire.

Until the end, hundreds of lonesome Texas cowpokes were loose in Kansas, anxious to spend their money and "see the elephant." West Wichita in particular became an "everything goes" town, and Wyatt saw an opportunity for all sorts of business enterprises. He wired his brothers Jim and Morgan to come on the run, and to bring their mistresses. Within a short time the Earps had girls working in many of the better known brothels. Several of the ladies used the Earp name as their own.

Earp gambled for his living, and on a lark joined forces with a Wichita policeman to track down a fellow who left town with a wagon he neglected to pay for. Seventy-five miles away the officers overtook their quarry, and at the point of a gun extracted $146 for payment, fees and expenses. Obviously Earp could see some very real possibilities and opportunities in law enforcement, so on April 21, 1875, he joined the Wichita force as an ordinary policeman.

The police department was modeled after its eastern counterparts. The men were called policemen and not deputies, although their chief generally took the title of Town Marshal. Tradition has it that cattle town law enforcement was generally handed over to fast-drawing marshals, each operating virtually single-handedly, motivated and guided by a personal commitment against lawlessness.

Such images make great legends, but never touch reality. Kansas police departments were composed of up to five men, and with the exception of the marshal who was sometimes elected, the officers were appointed by the mayor and city council. Politics played a heavy role in the selections. The law had to be enforced, and yet it couldn't be enforced too rigidly or else the trailherds might boycott the town and go somewhere else.

As a $60 a month policeman, Earp's abilities attracted little notice. Only rarely did the newspapers mention his name, the Wichita *Weekly Beacon* describing him as an excellent officer whose "conduct has been unexceptionable."

Wichita's streets at night were filled with teamsters, railroad workers, army scouts, soldiers and the usual disreputable assortment of drifters such as buffalo hunters, itinerant liquor dealers and way-ward husbands two jumps and three drinks ahead of the eastern sheriffs. Through this mass of humanity, with its definite paucity of soap and water, strode the Wichita police force making its usual arrests, most of the charges being for drunk and disorderly conduct. There is no record that Wyatt ever shot anyone in Wichita.

When a homicide did occur, the citizens and newspapers were apt to dismiss it as the foolishness of "high spirited boys." Many of the editors were very sentimental, capable of devoting reams of space to a poor lad whose mother "we understand is widowed, without means of support, and wishes to see her wayward son before she departs this earth as she is suffering from an incurable disease." The youngsters always "planned to catch the next train to their mother's bedside after being released."

Nevertheless, living on $60 a month wasn't too easy even in pre-inflation days, so Earp always earned extra cash either by gambling or shaking down prostitutes, acts common to most policemen and politicians in those days. No one ever thought of the girls as having rights or feelings; they were two-legged, female cattle, a commodity to be bought and sold.

The most exciting event in Earp's Wichita career was when his six-shooter slipped from his holster and hit the saloon floor. When fully loaded, a revolver carried six rounds of live cartridges in the cylinder, but most gun-toters stuck in only five, preferring to have the hammer resting on an empty chamber in order to prevent an accidental discharge. Earp violated the basic maxim about five bullets, and when his pistol struck the ground, it gave a thunderous roar. A bullet narrowly missed adding another button hole to Wyatt's shirt.

As the time went on, Earp became politically involved in the city marshal election. Mike Meagher won the position in 1875, and a year later came up for reelection against Billy Smith. Earp naturally supported his boss, and in doing so became the focus of the campaign. Smith accused Meagher of plotting to place the entire Earp clan on the city police force.

Though the charge was probably correct, Earp wouldn't admit it. He went looking for Smith, and found him in conference with Meagher. Wyatt battered Smith with his fists, and left him lying sprawled on the floor.

Earp was arrested, charged with disturbing the peace and fined

$30 plus $2 in court costs. The city council further ordered his dismissal just as soon as a replacement could be named.

In the meantime Meagher won the election, and he argued to retain Earp. The council considered the suggestion, and then voted six to two against reinstatement. Following additional debate, the second vote was a four to four tie, after which the matter was tabled.

The official dismissal came on April 20, 1876. Two weeks later the city fathers recommended that the marshal arrest Wyatt and his brother Morgan on vagrancy charges. The two men took the hint and left town.

Wyatt Earp in Dodge City

Dodge City, Kansas, is perhaps best known as the scene for the *Gunsmoke* series on television. The format changed over the years, but you may recall Matt Dillon standing in the center of Boot Hill and reciting homilies to the effect that "crime does not pay, and here lies the proof." It is therefore ironic to learn that while Dodge was wild and wicked and full of violence in its heyday, the total number of gunfights never equaled those that took place in El Paso.

Another intriguing fact is that Dodge City is today fully capitalizing on its legendary past, while El Paso is just beginning to tap the possibilities. For instance, thousands of tourists flock into Dodge each week, handing over untold amounts of money to see Boot Hill. Yet the Boot Hill these visitors walk through is as phony as Kitty's eyelashes or Doc's medical bag. The real Boot Hill lies under a schoolhouse.

On the other hand, El Paso has a bonafide Boot Hill in Concordia Cemetery, although some of the gunmen lying there (such as John Selman) are, I suspect, looking up at concrete foundations in nearby housing developments. As a unique and authentic part of El Paso's heritage, Concordia should be earning tourist dollars. Instead it is an eyesore, a source of dismay rather than civic pride.

When Wyatt Earp first made his appearance in Dodge City, the town was just beginning to shed its reputation as a headquarters for buffalo hunters. Buffalo hides by the thousands were being shipped east each year. The streets were caked with drying blood, and the stench and flies would have driven anyone but a buffalo hunter out of his senses.

Everyone knew that the day of the buffalo was about over, and plans were laid for Dodge City to accommodate the Texas cattle drovers. Naturally this would swell the regular population of about 1000 to several times that amount in season. With the cowboys would come the criminals, gamblers, gunmen and prostitutes who habitually existed on the fringes of society.

Wyatt Earp and his brother Morgan hit Dodge City in May of 1876, where Wyatt hired on as a $75-a-month deputy city marshal. (A $2 bonus was paid for each court conviction of persons he arrested.) For the next year Earp and city marshal Lawrence E. "Larry" Deger constituted the entire force. Some reports say Earp actually ran the department, that Deger was marshal in name only. Such judgments might have been true as Deger weighed over 300 pounds, a factor hampering his mobility.

Folks called the main thoroughfare Front Street, a road divided by the Atchison, Topeka and Santa Fe Railroad. Most of the saloons and brothels lay south of the tracks, or "across the deadline" as it was referred to. In his off hours Wyatt gambled in James "Dog" Kelly's Alhambra Saloon, while his brother Morgan worked as a part-time deputy sheriff and occasional faro dealer in the Long Branch.

There is not much of a record regarding Earp's initial tenure as a deputy marshal in Dodge. He and Bat Masterson, later a sheriff, became friends, and Wyatt renewed old acquaintances with Doc Holliday. One of Earp's better known adventures concerned the time he tangled with Patrick "Red" Sweeney, a six-foot-six, 245-pound mauler. They argued over the affections of a Long Branch Saloon "hostess," and finally came to blows when the girl chose Sweeney.

Earp took a severe beating in the brawl, but Sweeney and the girl left town before they could be arrested. Back in Texas, Sweeney vowed he would return to Dodge next year and kill Earp. However, on the way back his number came up during a cattle stampede.

A year after signing on the Dodge police force, Earp resigned to visit the Black Hills of South Dakota, returning to Dodge in July of 1877 where he collided on Front Street with saloon girl Frankie Bell. Since Frankie thought Earp should have been more careful about where he was walking, she made some unkind references to his ancestors. Earp slapped her, and both were arrested. He paid a $1 fine. The newspapers said Frankie "received a night's lodging in the dog house and a reception at the police court next morning, the expense of which was about $20." (Women's lib didn't have a prayer in old Dodge City.)

Earp left town again and when he returned in May of 1878, he had a young lady named Matilda "Mattie" Blaylock in tow. Some authorities think she and Earp were married. At any rate, Earp signed on as assistant marshal once again, this time being appointed by "Dog" Kelly who had been elected mayor on the "Saloon Ticket."

All things taken into consideration, it is difficult to properly assess Earp's effectiveness as a lawman. That he shookdown saloon owners for protection money, that he occasionally worked girls in the brothels, that he himself was a gambler and card sharp, no one denies. It is a fact that practically all police officers came from the hard-case saloon crowds. Out of their aimless, often tragic lives, emerged a truth that they too were human, products of the forces that shaped them. Communities wanted tough policemen, officers who could crack heads when necessary, who would kill and who expected to be killed. Small and even moderate amounts of corruption were to be expected.

Some of Earp's contemporaries called him a fighting pimp, a blow-hard, a liar. Other people just as outspoken, plus the newspapers, respected his abilities. The Dodge City *Times* said Earp "had a quiet way of taking the most desperate characters into custody." Some folks called him "a square, courageous and likeable man" who "on a great many occasions, at the risk of his life, rendered valuable service in upholding the law."

Perhaps the most interesting (and the most difficult praise to swallow) came from a Dodge City law firm which presented Earp with a Bible following his acceptance as a church deacon. An inscription on the flyleaf read: "To Wyatt S. Earp, as a slight recognition of his many Christian virtues and steady following in the footsteps of the meek and lowly Jesus."

Those records that are available do not show Earp as an especially hard-working policeman, but they do show him as exerting more effort than any other law officer in Dodge. Yet in a year's time he arrested a total of thirty-two persons, less than three a month. Nevertheless, he still locked up more people than anyone else on the force, which numbered a half-dozen men.

On July 26, 1878, George R. Hoyt and a cowboy friend shot up the Comique Theater after an argument with the manager. Assistant marshals Earp and Jim Masterson fired as the mounted cowboys fled for the toll bridge across the Arkansas River. Several citizens joined in the fun too, and during the fusillade a bullet struck Hoyt in the arm. He tumbled off his horse, breaking the same arm in another place during the fall. A Fort Dodge surgeon amputated the limb, but Hoyt died immediately afterwards. Earp took credit for the shot which brought Hoyt down, and during Wyatt's career on the Dodge police force, this is his only recorded slaying.

In August some trail hands shot up the Comique again, only to be clubbed into submission. Shortly afterwards, Earp and a posse shot and wounded Jim Kennedy, wanted for the murder of "actress" Fannie Keenan, better known as Dora Hand.

In May of 1879, three drifters attempted to "take the town" as the newspapers worded it. Earp collared them, and pinching one tightly on the ear, headed them all in the direction of the jail. Along the way, the other two started getting rebellious, and things might have gotten out of hand had not Sheriff Masterson assisted. He clubbed both lawbreakers with his revolver, and the trip to the cell became much more quiet.

Earp and several peace officers also shot it out with a group of Texas cowboys who refused to check their weapons as required by law. One of the cowhands stopped a slug with his leg, and the others fled. The wounded man was patched up and released; no arrests were made.

As Dodge City grew tranquil, Wyatt sought new excitement, new places to see. This restless urge seems to have been a mark of the entire Earp clan, an uncontrollable desire to stay on the move.

He resigned from the force in September of 1879, and with his mistress (considered an intelligent, pretty, likeable girl) he left for Texas. In Mobeetie, he and Mysterious Dave Mather sold gold bricks, but were run out of town by the sheriff. Afterwards Wyatt and Mattie visited Fort Worth, parts of West Texas, and then moved on to Las Vegas, New Mexico.

Hearing of big mining strikes in Tombstone, Arizona, Wyatt

talked his brothers Jim, Morgan and Virgil into joining him there. Thus the Earps moved to the scene of what would become their greatest and most controversial accomplishment, a thunderclap of violence that still echoes to this day.

Tombstone

Western towns never sprung up without a reason, and Tombstone, Arizona was no exception. Practically all communities west of the Mississippi owe their existence to at least one of four basic ingredients: cattle, mines, railroads, or military.

Tombstone, Arizona had silver for a midwife. Itinerant miners struck the mother lode in 1877, and the boom was on. In 1879 Tombstone had 1000 residents, and by 1881 nearly 10,000 folks called it home.

With the mines running full blast, and lots of money being available, Tombstone attracted more than its share of troublemakers. Yet in spite of its wicked reputation as the "town too tough to die" (a reputation now worth millions of tourist dollars), only a small minority of its citizens ever got into trouble outside of the usual Saturday night binge. Most men spent sixty hours a week, ten hours a day, underground in the mines. They were burly laborers, uneducated, exploited, many of foreign extraction and speaking little English, with little time or inclination for big-time gambling or shootouts. Fights were settled with fists or clubs. Miners rarely carried side-arms.

In addition there were the merchants, the cowboys and the gunmen. Altogether it was a strange conglomeration of humanity, one more common in the Old West than generally thought. While a few non-fiction books have tried to explain towns like Tombstone, it remained for a fictional piece entitled *Warlock*, by Oakley Hall, to do the best job.

Living outside of town, but causing trouble on the inside, were the Cowboys, a group of rustlers and gunmen operating south of Tombstone near the Sonora line. They harassed Mexican ranchers with swift and devastating raids, rounding up herds of cattle for sale in Arizona.

Old Man Clanton led the Cowboys. As a tough, roguish outlaw, he left Texas for the California gold rush, and later drifted south to Arizona, bringing with him his three sons, Ike, Phineas and William. Ten or fifteen miles southwest of Tombstone, he established a ranch headquarters. Outside of the army at Fort Huachuca, these Cowboys were probably the strongest power in the region.

In August of 1881, the Cowboys waylaid a pack train of Mexican smugglers, killing several and escaping with coins, silver bullion, cattle, horses and liquor. Less than ten days later as Old Man Clanton drove a herd of stolen stock out of Mexico, he too was ambushed. Five Cowboys, including Old Man Clanton, were shot dead and went to join the Ghost Riders in the Sky, for if ever a song was written for a specific group of individuals, it had to be the Clanton Cowboys.

Curly Bill Brocius, a rip-snorting, fun-loving, deadly killer took over Cowboy leadership. All of the gang stuck with him, including the Clanton sons, the two McLowery (or McLaury) brothers, Frank and Tom, plus the strangest and most dangerous gunman who ever strapped on a six-shooter, John Ringo.

Meanwhile, back in Tombstone, Wyatt Earp and his brothers organized the "Law and Order League," a faction stoutly supported by John P. Clum, former Indian agent and then editor of the Tombstone *Epitaph*. Depending upon whom one believes, Clum was a staunch defender of law and liberty, or he was a vain, egocentric man who ran a newspaper because he liked to see his name in print. Maybe he was both. At any rate, he considered the Earps as "tall, gaunt, intrepid men," and it was largely through his editorials that the Earp reputation in Tombstone emerged with as much respectability as it did.

The political power struggle revolved around the position of sheriff, always a very lucrative job in the Old West. The sheriff collected taxes under the Arizona territorial charter, and by law he kept ten percent of everything. Historians estimate the position of sheriff in Tombstone to have been worth between thirty and forty thousand dollars a year.

However, the Earps initially had trouble finding suitable law enforcement work. Wyatt hired on as a deputy to Sheriff Charles Shibell, an arrangement that did not work out. Shibell dismissed Earp, and placed John Behan, a tall, balding, former Missourian on the payroll. A very angry Wyatt Earp went to work as a shotgun guard for Wells Fargo.

One afternoon town marshal Fred White asked Virgil Earp for

assistance in quelling a Cowboy disturbance. A scuffle broke out, and the pistol of Curly Bill discharged while pointed at White. The marshal lived long enough to gasp that he did not think Bill intentionally shot him. Curly was arrested and stood trial, but the jury did not fault his actions since what happened seemed understandable. White shouldn't have gotten in the way.

Virgil became marshal, and then lost the next election to a fellow named Ben Sippy.

Events were now outrunning the people. Republican John Clum ran for mayor, and much to his surprise, he made it. Over in the statehouse, the legislators were slicing up Pima County, one chunk being called Cochise. Tombstone became the county seat. Since Republican Governor John Charles Fremont (the old Pathfinder) had the honor of appointing county officials prior to regular elections, everyone expected Wyatt Earp to become sheriff. He was a Republican, and he had the backing of Mayor Clum. Nobody knows why things went wrong, but Fremont appointed John Behan, a Democrat. The Earps got the Governor's best wishes.

Other troubles stunned the Earps. The Benson stage underwent an attempted holdup on March 15, 1881, several miles out of Tombstone. Three masked men tried to stop it as the stage lumbered across a deep arroyo, and although the outlaws killed the driver and a passenger, the shotgun guard whipped the horses past the inept bandits and finally outdistanced a fusillade of bullets.

Several posses searched for the outlaws, turning up nobody but identifying the suspects as Jim Crane, Harry Head (a name like that simply had to be an alias or a father's bad joke), and Bill Leonard, all Cowboys. Doc Holliday took his licks as a possible participant, since it just so happened that he was out of town on the day of the holdup. According to the rumors, Holliday shot and killed the stage driver, a charge which may or may not have been correct, but it did put some heat on the Earps as he and they were close friends and associates.

Other bits of gossip accused Wyatt Earp of planning the robbery. His sister-in-law (Virgil's wife) later wrote that he cached masks and various other disguises in his home. And according to a tale told by Ike Clanton (hardly an unbiased witness), Earp offered him the $2,000 Wells Fargo reward money if Clanton would kill Crane, Head and Leonard—evidently so they wouldn't talk.

Clanton said he turned the deal down, but it did not matter at this late date. Leonard and Harry Head tried their holdup skills on a store in Eureka, New Mexico, and were killed. Crane was slain soon afterwards. With the exception of Doc Holliday, all of the alleged holdup men were now dead.

Doc might have outlasted the rumors, but he could not outlast his mistress Kate. She and Doc were still fighting and feuding, and on one occasion he blacked her eye and split her lip. Kate retaliated by drinking with Sheriff Behan, who sympathetically agreed that Doc was an ingrate.

When their bottle session ended, the blind-drunk Kate Elder signed a document accusing Holliday of attempting to rob the stage and of murdering the driver. Holliday was arrested and released on $5,000 bond.

The Earps now jailed Kate in order to keep her away from liquor. As a result she showed up sober at the trial and repudiated her original statement, testifying that she was too drunk to realize what she was signing.

Doc went free, immediately swearing out a warrant for Kate's arrest, charging her with threatening his life. After her release, Virgil Earp picked her up again for being drunk and disorderly. The judge assessed a fine of $12.50.

Big Nose Kate Elder left Tombstone, her affair with Doc thoroughly burned out. To the end of her misspent and tragic life, she tried to pass herself off as Mrs. John H. Holliday, wife of a man to whom she meant so much and so little.

As for the Earps, in their opinion Sheriff Behan and the Cowboy faction were not only trying to get rid of Doc Holliday, but the Earps as well. Tempers rose, and soon the dirt streets of Tombstone would run red with blood.

Prelude to a showdown

No one is absolutely certain just when the various Tombstone elements split into factions, since it took awhile for the Earp presence to create any hard feelings. No doubt there was some curiosity, even consternation, among local lawmen as Wyatt Earp stepped in and became deputy sheriff right away. But the position slipped through his fingers like warm beer in the Oriental Saloon as John Behan edged him aside.

Behan became the first duly appointed sheriff of Cochise County, a definite set-back to Wyatt's aspirations. Earp now had two reasons to dislike Behan; a woman would provide the reason for Behan to dislike Earp.

Over in Prescott, Arizona, a Miss Josephine Sarah Marcus (her friends called her Sadie) was winding down a theatrical engagement which had been barnstorming its way across the Southwest. Those who knew Sadie described her as an attractive, full-bodied young lady who liked the bright lights as well as exciting men. Along the way someone introduced her to Sheriff Behan, a quiet, modest, retiring man, according to one source, and a conceited, spineless wastrel according to another. He brought Sadie to Tombstone and set her up in housekeeping. After several weeks of living with Behan, Sadie met Wyatt Earp, a much more charming spender than Behan.

As for Mattie, she reacted with both dismay and anger. She tore up several of Earp's white shirts, telling her sister-in-law that it was too much to do the washing, starching and ironing and then have them stained with another woman's lip rouge. However, this flurry ended her anger and rebellion. She continued shining his dusty boots, and sometimes cleaning and oiling his gun, the latter being a risk that a wiser man might have avoided.

With Behan and Earp now at odds, Cochise County began choosing up sides. Throwing in with the Earps were such stalwarts as Buckskin Frank Leslie, Bat Masterson, Luke Short and Doc Holliday. (Masterson and Short skipped out before the final showdown.) Also favoring the Earps was Mayor John Clum and his Tombstone *Epitaph*. The other faction was composed of Behan, the Clanton Cowboys and a competing newspaper called the Tombstone *Nugget*. Oddly, the *Nugget* has been substantially ignored as historians have sought to piece together the events that took place in Tombstone. Apparently its point of view does not always support various preconceived notions about what actually happened.

A big break came for the Earps on June 6, 1881, when city marshal Ben Sippy mysteriously left town and did not return. John Clum exercised his authority as mayor and appointed Virgil Earp to the post.

Virgil in turn appointed his brothers and Doc Holliday as deputies. Cochise County now had two very distinct and very antagonistic law enforcement groups. The Earps dominated the town of Tombstone while Behan, said to be in cahoots with the Cowboys, controlled the county.

The two factions spent so much time making threats that genuine law enforcement lagged. Bandits held up the stagecoaches with monotonous regularity. A fire gutted an entire block of downtown Tombstone. The Tombstone *Epitaph* and the *Nugget* railed against each other and their supporters, each accusing the other of crimes. Looking back on the situation from the vantage point of nearly a century of hindsight, it seems obvious that two different bands of thieves were fighting for control.

On September 8 the Bisbee stage rolled out of Tombstone with four passengers on board, and several thousand dollars in the strongbox. Outside of town, outlaws forced it into an unscheduled stop, removed the cash box and shook down the passengers. When it was over, one of the highwaymen stated, "Looks like we got all the sugar."

The expressing of "sugar," meaning loot, happened to be a favorite word of Frank Stilwell, a deputy sheriff. Within hours a posse had Frank and his partner Pete Spence under arrest and charged with robbing the mails, a federal offense. Wyatt Earp spread word around that Stilwell and Spence were not only sheriff deputies, but Clanton Cowboys as well.

Charges and countercharges flew as both sides armed for trouble. On October 25, Ike Clanton and Doc Holliday met in a restaurant. Doc called him some hard names, and told him to go for his gun. Clanton prudently declined, taking due note of Virgil Earp sitting near the lunch counter, a hand inside his coat.

Clanton eased his way outside as Doc continued to curse and threaten. Out on the sidewalk, other Earps joined in the taunts, snarling at Clanton to prove himself a man. Ike walked away, asking Morgan not to shoot him in the back.

On the following morning Ike appeared on the Tombstone streets fully armed, the handle of a revolver plainly showing as he went about his business. Virgil and Morgan Earp walked up behind him and said he was under arrest for violating the city ordinance against carrying firearms. Virgil removed the weapon, all the while mocking Ike who protested that he needed the gun to keep the deputies and the other Earps from murdering him. Obviously Ike should not have said that, even if it were true. An infuriated Virgil bashed Clanton across the head, and dragged him off to the courthouse where Judge Wallace assessed a $25 fine for carrying a gun and disturbing the peace.

Less than an hour later, Wyatt Earp approached Tom McLowery. As they talked, Tom stuck his hands in his pockets, giving Earp an opportunity to strike him in the face. "Are you armed?" Wyatt snarled.

"No, I'm not," McLowery replied, and he removed his hands to reveal empty pockets. Earp jerked his revolver and pistol-whipped McLowery, dropping the youngster bleeding and semi-conscious into a gutter. A friend passed by and assisted Tom as he staggered away.

Still spoiling for a fight, the Earps found Frank McLowery's horse tied half way up on the sidewalk. Wyatt grabbed the bridle and was jerking the animal backwards when Frank and Billy Clanton stepped outside a saloon and took the horse to the OK Corral. At this point, neither Frank nor Billy were aware of the brewing trouble, both having just arrived that day in Tombstone, each dressed in overalls, looking more like farmers than ranchers.

Soon all of the Clantons and McLowerys were gathered in a vacant lot behind the OK Corral, obviously discussing strategy. Should they attack the Earps, try to avoid additional confrontations, or simply leave town?

Whatever their thoughts, word soon reached the Earps that the Cowboys were talking of a fight. So the Earps rounded up old reliable Doc Holliday, and headed for the corral at about 1:30 in the afternoon. Within minutes they would be involved in the most famous and controversial blood-letting in Western history.

Gunfight at the OK Corral

Trying to understand exactly what happened at the OK Corral gunfight is like writing obituaries on soap bubbles.

There are as many stories as there were participants. The Clantons and the Earps naturally pushed their own points of view. Those who witnessed the affair, or were privy to various bits and pieces of private information, or who favored one faction at the expense of the other, saw things differently from others. The only facts we can be sure of are that when the acrid smoke cleared, three men were dead, three were wounded and a legend had been created that would live forever.

The afternoon's events began as Sheriff Behan sat in a barber chair getting his customary shave. Someone rushed in to say that the Clantons and Earps were about to kill each other, so Behan dashed down the street where a crowd had gathered. In a vacant lot behind the OK Corral he found Ike and Billy Clanton, Frank and Tom McLowery, and Billy Claiborne.

Behan ordered them to surrender their arms. According to his story later, Ike Clanton and Tom McLowery were unarmed. Claiborne also had no weapon, and claimed to be there in the capacity of a friend who was trying to talk everybody into leaving town.

Only Frank McLowery and Billy Clanton had six-shooters, and they refused to give them up, stating they would be returning to the ranch in just a few minutes. Supporting this statement were saddled horses standing beside them, each man holding on to the reins of his particular mount. Ike Clanton, whose head still throbbed from the pistol-whipping, said they were waiting on a wagon to be brought from around the corner. He did not feel like riding a jolting horse all the way home.

At this moment, Behan saw the Earps and Doc Holliday marching down Fremont Street. Cautioning the Cowboys to remain where they were, the sheriff hurried to meet the lawmen, telling them that the Clantons and McLowerys were unarmed. The Earps brushed him aside and walked grimly on, not pausing until a distance of about five feet separated the two parties.

If one believes the Earp story, they called upon their antagonists to surrender and were rebuffed. If one believes the Clantons, the Earps opened fire without warning. Whatever the truth, hardly a second went by before the vacant lot alongside Fremont Street (not the OK Corral) erupted with noise and flame and smoke and blood.

According to Wyatt Earp, this is how it began. "They—Billy Clanton and Frank McLowery—commenced to draw their pistols; at the same time Tom McLowery threw his hand to his hip and jumped behind a horse. I had my pistol in my overcoat pocket where I had put it when Behan told me he had disarmed the other party. When I saw

Billy and Frank draw their pistols, I drew my pistol. Billy Clanton leveled his pistol at me, but I did not aim at him. I knew that Frank McLowery had the reputation of being a good shot and a dangerous man and I aimed at him. The first two shots which were fired were fired by Billy Clanton and myself; he shot at me and I shot at Frank McLowery. The fight then became general."

Both Billy Claiborne and Ike Clanton broke and ran for cover, escaping in the melee. Earp said later that Ike grabbed him by the left arm and began pleading for his life, and that Wyatt brushed him aside, telling him to either fight or get out of the way. Ike scrambled away.

Frank McLowery took an Earp bullet in the stomach, a slug that inflicted an ugly and fatal wound. Desperately he staggered around, struggling to wrench a Winchester from his rearing horse. When he couldn't get it free, he snapped off several shots from a six-shooter. One of his bullets ricocheted off Doc Holliday's holster, and skinned a streak off Doc's back. McLowery's plunging mount now dragged him completely out into the intersection of Fremont and Third, fifty or sixty feet from the vacant lot. Here, Frank toppled over on his head and died.

Holliday kept the action brisk and moving along. After firing a nickel-plated revolver several times, he pulled a shotgun from beneath his coat and it began to boom.

Several witnesses claimed Tom McLowery had his arms raised when Doc fired. Who knows? The shotgun blast caught him squarely under the right arm and he died instantly. He was unarmed.

Nineteen-year-old Billy Clanton held out the longest, if twenty or thirty seconds can be considered a long time. Someone's bullet hit him in the chest; another struck him in the right wrist. Slumping against a building, he kept his revolver banging. Billy shot Virgil in the right leg and wounded Morgan Earp near the base of the neck, the slug chipping off a piece of vertebra as it passed through. Morgan dropped to the ground, stunned, groaning and effectively out of the fight. As Billy dragged himself out onto Fremont Street, desperately trying to cock his pistol for one more shot, a bystander reached down and took the weapon. Billy looked up at him and gasped, "Give me more cartridges."

Clanton survived but a few minutes, and tales are told of how he asked someone to remove his shoes because he had promised his mother not to die with his boots on. Actually it's a good story, and although old-time cowboys were very sentimental about their mothers, Billy was in no shape now to philosophize about this. One does not necessarily die nobly or even quietly after being shot. In most instances it is an excruciating experience, and it was especially so for Billy Clanton. He screamed in agony before dying, and was finally quieted by two injections of morphine.

Following the battle which lasted less than a minute, citizens loaded the dead into wagons and hauled them to the undertaker. The wounded went home to recuperate, uncertain of what might happen next. On October 29, three days after the battle, the Territory of Arizona lodged charges of premeditated murder against the Earps and Doc Holliday. All of the Earps were dismissed as town marshals, and released from jail under $10,000 bond each. A week later on the basis of "new evidence," Wyatt Earp and Doc Holliday were jailed until November 20, at which time they were rereleased under the same bond.

Justice of the Peace Wells Spicer conducted the initial hearings, and the testimony lasted until November 30 when the judge freed the Earps and Holliday on the grounds that "the defendants were fully justified in committing these homicides," that Billy Clanton and Frank McLowery drew their weapons when called upon to surrender, and the question of whether or not Tom McLowery even had a gun was "of no controlling importance." The judge pointed out that Tom had been involved in the dispute all along, and there was a Winchester rifle on his horse when the shooting started.

As for Ike Clanton, the judge commented that it was he the Earps hated the most. Ike could have been slain if the Earps had so desired, but he saved his life because he was unarmed. This ended the hearing, as the grand jury did not return any indictments.

However, many citizens of Tombstone expressed anger at the decision. Most folks believed the Earps and Doc Holliday were little more than stagecoach robbers, and the killings had merely eliminated the opposition.

As for the slain Cowboys, Billy Clanton and the two McLowery brothers became semi-martyrs to a lost cause. Undertakers dressed out the youthful bodies in the finest clothes available, and placed the dead on display in a hardware store window. On funeral day theirs became the largest and longest procession ever seen in town. Burial came on a wind-swept hillside, the inscription of their headstones reading "Murdered on the streets of Tombstone."

Wyatt Earp: end of a shooter

When word of the OK Corral shootings reached the mines, a series of shrill, ear-piercing whistles blew, and miners poured out of those dark holes like ants after a piece of candy. Into town they streamed, arming themselves with guns and clubs, preparing to meet violence with more violence. However, the mob lacked strong leadership. It wanted to crack heads, but no one agreed on which heads to crack. So the miners angrily milled about, muttering, drinking and threatening vengeance until finally they wearied of cussing and discussing and went home.

The Earps could see that they were not going to be attacked, so they removed mattresses from the windows, and stepped outside their home to take charge of Tombstone's law enforcement bodies.

Tombstone *Epitaph* editor John Clum wrote a blazing series of articles praising the Earps and denouncing the so-called lawless element, the latter represented by Cowboys. Yet, even Clum feared for his life, and when the excuse came to leave town legitimately and visit relatives in Washington, D. C., he did so. On December 15, 1881, he hopped aboard the nighttime Tucson stage, which was ambushed three miles outside of town. Highwaymen shot "Whistling Dick," the driver, through the leg, inflicting a painful but not a disabling wound. He cursed and whipped the horses on through the gunfire, and had no sooner reached safety when the lead animal collapsed and died. Dick and a couple of passengers cut the dead horse loose, and kept the stage traveling to the next town.

No one knew for sure if the attack represented an attempt to assassinate Clum, or if it was a bungling effort to hold up the stage. Clum believed the former, and when the first shots started, he opened the stage door and bailed out. After spending a night wandering around in the desert (the stage did not even miss him for several hours), he found transportation the next day and continued on to his destination.

During the next few years he wrote, "It All Happened in Tombstone," an account of his career (all carefully doctored and guaranteed to present himself in the most favorable light), and a justification for the Earp participation in the famous OK Corral gunfight. Fifty years after that shootout, Clum once again returned to Tombstone. By this time bygones were bygones, and the Chamber of Commerce was seeing the possibilities of turning that blood-letting into a tourist bonanza. Therefore Clum's welcome was a most joyous one, a fact that warmed his heart. He died on May 2, 1932, in Los Angeles.

Two weeks after Clum left Tombstone, assassins tried to kill Virgil Earp. As a deputy United States marshal (the only law enforcement power any of the Earps possessed), Virgil left the Oriental Saloon and headed for his room in the Cosmopolitan Hotel. When halfway across Allen Street, three men fired five shotgun blasts at him and escaped by fleeing down Tough Nut Road. Somehow Virgil survived. The slugs meant for his life, shattered his left arm and crippled him permanently.

On March 18, 1882, Morgan Earp played a difficult billiards shot, and as he straightened up over the pool table a bullet broke his spine and lodged in the thigh of George Berry, a bystander. Berry keeled over with a heart attack and died even though his wound was not serious. Across the room another slug buried itself a couple feet above the head of Wyatt Earp who was leaning back in a straight chair and watching the game.

As the murderers fled, Wyatt and several men carried Morgan to a couch where doctors pronounced the wound fatal. The injured gunman did not live long, his final words being, "That's the last game of pool I'll ever play."

A woman identified Morgan's slayers. Because her husband had beaten her, Mrs. Pete Spence accused him, Frank Stilwell (a Bisbee stage robber) and Indian Charley Cruz, the latter being a loafer around town, as the assassins.

The Earps loaded Morgan on a train for burial in California.

When it chugged into Tucson, the entire Earp party, with the exception of Virgil, jumped off and began looking for Frank Stilwell who supposedly worked in the yards. An hour later they cornered their prey, broke both his legs with shotgun blasts, and put four rifle slugs and two loads of buckshot in his body. Instead of burying Stilwell, some say the county should have sold him for scrap metal.

The Territory swore out charges of murder against the Earps, but the authorities were understandably hesitant about serving the warrants. While law officers vacillated between doing their duty and running for office, the Earps nosed around for Pete Spence. They did not find Pete, but they did find Indian Charley and blew five holes in him. Now there were two murder charges against the former Tombstone officers.

As for Spence, with both his partners dead, he surrendered to Sheriff Behan and asked for protection. Behan locked him up and put plenty of deputies on guard. The Earps never did get an opportunity to put Spence in the ground.

Meanwhile, Wyatt Earp allegedly shot and killed Curly Bill Brocius. This particular slaying is hotly disputed among historians, as many do not believe Earp actually did it. (Among his many other accomplishments, Wyatt was a teller of tall tales.) What adds credence to Earp's story is the fact that Curly Bill seems to have dropped off the earth at about the same time, and no one has seen him since.

The Earp gang split up and fled Arizona to avoid being arrested for murder. Wyatt and Doc Holliday headed for Colorado where Sadie awaited. Back in Arizona the loyal Mattie Blaylock (who may also have been married to Wyatt, but the record has never been found) drifted from one place to another until committing suicide on July 3, 1888, from an overdose of laudanum (a pain killing derivative of opium).

Holliday and Earp split up in Colorado, still friends but going their separate ways. In May of 1882 the Arizona authorities tried to extradite Doc from Denver, and make him face charges for the murder of Frank Stilwell. The Governor refused to sign the necessary papers, however, so Doc escaped the rope even though he went on to suffer a much more cruel and prolonged death. By now his lungs resembled shredded wheat with the milk soaked up. He checked into the Glenwood Springs, Colorado, sanitarium, and died on November 3, 1887, at the age of thirty-six. "This is funny," he said as he lapsed into unconsciousness.

Wyatt Earp became a wanderer. While never returning to Arizona where murder charges hung over his head, he, Sadie and his brother Jim traveled all over the western United States supporting themselves by gambling and working confidence games. He and Jim were found guilty on two counts of claim jumping in Idaho, typical of the many charges and accusations leveled against Wyatt during the coming years.

Then on December 2, 1896, he made national headlines on sporting pages across the country.

Somehow he talked San Francisco authorities into naming him as a referee for the heavyweight fight between Bob Fitzsimmons and Tom Sharkey. The fight lasted for eight rounds, and most ringside experts believed Fitzsimmons to be ahead at that point, weathering nicely the many fouls that Sharkey threw. Then Fitzsimmons fouled Sharkey, or at least Earp said he did. (A lot of people did not see the blow, and some went so far as to state that the "foul" was actually a hard right to the chin.) Nevertheless, the fight was over and Sharkey had the decision, no matter how controversial.

The uproar was heard for weeks. Investigations followed investigations. There were charges (never proven) that Earp stopped the fight in order to win gambling bets. The San Francisco *Chronicle* of December 9 denounced Earp as "filled with joy over the notoriety that has come upon him in the last few days. He enjoys hugely the curiosity of the people whenever he appears in a public place and gratifies himself by parading in localities where the biggest crowds congregate."

Nevertheless, the investigations proved nothing. The fighters took their purse, Earp took his fee, and all went their way. For awhile Wyatt and Sadie lived in Alaska and Nevada. At the age of sixty-three, in 1911, Los Angeles authorities placed him under arrest for vagrancy and attempting to fleece a tourist out of $25,000 in a bunco game.

He met William S. Hart of cowboy movie fame, and tried to get Hart to portray his life. When that flopped, Earp began writing notes on his life, and seeking a biographer. He found one in journalist Stuart N. Lake, and out of their relationship, fraught with misunderstandings, controversies and troubles (Sadie had more to say about the final version than her husband), emerged *Wyatt Earp: Frontier Marshal,* one of the most blatantly false and fictitious books ever published. It made Earp famous, a hero to the white-hat crowd. The rest is movie and television history.

Wyatt Earp died of prostate cancer on January 3, 1929, and his remains were cremated.

And so this trail has ended. If you have read these accounts and see no reference to your favorite shooter, please consider that it is virtually impossible to research everybody in less than several life-times. This manuscript contains accurate facts insofar as they are humanly possible to come by. All persons described here did, for certain, exist and I am grateful to them all for having left their reportable impressions on history — and myself.

BIBLIOGRAPHY

Gunfighter books are controversial and there is disagreement regarding the most reliable sources. Although a few books are bound to have been overlooked in compiling this bibliography, these titles nevertheless represent what I regard as the best in gunfighter facts and literature. These volumes include the most up-to-date scholarship (May, 1976). A few of these will be out of print and available only through libraries and rare book dealers. The reader is advised that there are numerous reliable gunfighter accounts in historical journals, magazines, diaries, court records, government documents and newspapers. However, for bibliographical purposes, these sources are not listed because of their relative inaccessibility.

LCM

Chapter 1

SHOOTERS

Guard, Wayne, *Frontier Justice* (U. of Okla. 1949)
Jordan, Philip D., *Frontier Law and Order* (U. of Neb., 1970)
Prassel, Frank Richard, *The Western Peace Officer* (U. of Okla., 1972)
Rosa, Joseph G., *The Gunfighter: Man or Myth* (U. of Okla., 1969)
Steckmesser, Kent L. *The Western Hero in History and Legend* (U. of Okla., 1965)

Chapter 2

BILLY:
THE ENDURING LEGEND

Adams, Roman, *A Fitting Death for Billy the Kid* (U. of Okla., 1960)
Ball, Eve, *Ma'am Jones of the Pecos* (U. of Ariz., 1969)
Coe, George W., *Frontier Fighter* (U. of N.M., 1951)

Dykes, Jeff C., *Billy the Kid: Bibliography of A Legend* (U. of N.M., 1952)
Fulton, Maurice G. (Ed. by R. N. Mullin) *History of the Lincoln County War* (U. of Ariz., 1968)
Garrett, Jarvis (intro.), *The Authentic Life of Billy the Kid* (Horn and Wallace, 1964)
Garrett, Pat F., *The Authentic Life of Billy the Kid* (U. of Okla., 1965)
Hunt, Frazier, *Tragic Days of Billy the Kid* (Hastings House, 1956)
Keleher, William H., *Violence in Lincoln County* (U. of N.M., 1957)
Koop, W. A., *Billy the Kid: Trail of a Kansas Legend* (Kansas City Westerners, Kansas City, Mo., 1964)
Metz, Leon C., *Pat Garrett: The Story of a Western Lawman* (U. of Okla., 1974)
Mullin, R. N., *A Chronology of the Lincoln County War* (Press of the Territorian, Santa Fe, 1966)
Mullin, R. N., *The Boyhood of Billy the Kid* (Texas Western Press, 1967)

293

Nolan, Frederick W., *The Life and Death of John Henry Tunstall* (U. of N.M., 1965)

Poe, John, *The Death of Billy the Kid* (Houghton Mifflin, 1933)

Chapter 3

SAM BASS:
A SQUARE SHOOTER

Gard, Wayne, *Sam Bass* (Houghton Mifflin, 1936)

Martin, Charles L., *A Sketch of Sam Bass* (U. of Okla., 1956)

Chapter 4

BLACK JACK KETCHUM:
A TRUE LOSER

Bartholomew, Ed., *Black Jack Ketchum: Last of the Holdup Kings* (Frontier Press, 1955)

Burton, Jeff, *Dynamite and Six-Shooter* (Palomino Press, Santa Fe, 1970)

Stanley, F., *No Tears for Blackjack Ketchum* (World Press, 1950)

Chapter 5

TOM SMITH:
HE BROUGHT THEM
IN ALIVE

Drago, Harry Sinclair, *Wild, Woolly and Wicked* (Clarkson N. Potter, 1960)

Miller, Nyle H. and Joseph W. Snell, *Why the West Was Wild* (Kansas State Hist. Soc., 1963)

Raine, William MacLeod, *Guns of the Frontier* (Houghton Mifflin, 1940)

Schaefer, Jack, *Heroes Without Glory: Some Goodmen of the Old West* (Houghton Mifflin, 1965)

Chapter 6

THE JAMES BOYS

Croy, Homer, *Jesse James Was My Neighbor* (Duell, Sloan and Pearce, 1949)

Love, Robertus, *The Rise and Fall of Jesse James* (G. P. Putnam's Sons, 1926)

Settle, William A., *Jesse James Was His Name* (U. of Mo., 1966)

Wellman, Paul, *A Dynasty of Western Outlaws* (Doubleday, 1961)

Younger, Cole, *The Story of Cole Younger by Himself* (Henneberry Co., 1903)

Chapter 7

THE DALTONS:
BROTHERS ON THE PROWL

Preece, Harold, *The Dalton Gang* (Hastings House, 1963)

Shirley, Glen, *Six Gun and Silver Star* (U. of N.M., 1955)

Wellman, Paul, *A Dynasty of Western Outlaws* (Doubleday, 1961)

Chapter 8

ELFEGO BACA: LAST OF
THE OLD-TIME SHOOTERS

Beckett, V. B., *Baca's Battle* (Stagecoach Press, 1962)

Cook, James, *Fifty Years on the Old Frontier* (Yale, 1923)

Crichton, Kyle S., *Law and Order, Ltd.* (N.M. Pub. Corp., 1928)

Chapter 9

PRINT OLIVE: JUST PLAIN MEAN AS HELL

Chrisman, Harry E., *The Story of I.P. (Print) Olive* (Sage, 1962)
Crabb, Richard, *Empire on the Platte* (World Pub. Co., 1967)

Chapter 10

STOUDENMIRE: EL PASO MARSHAL

Metz, Leon C., *Dallas Stoudenmire: El Paso Marshal* (Pemberton, 1969)

Chapter 11

KING FISHER: FRONTIER DANDY

Fisher, O.C., *King Fisher: His Life and Times* (U. of Okla., 1966)
Streeter, Floyd B., *Ben Thompson, Man with a Gun* (Frederick Fell, 1957)
Walton, W.N., *Life and Adventures of Ben Thompson* (Steck, 1956)

Chapter 12

BUTCH CASSIDY AND THE SUNDANCE KID

Baker, Pearl, *The Wild Bunch at Robber's Roost* (Abelard Schuman, 1971)
Betenson, Lula Parker (as told to Dora Flack), *Butch Cassidy: My Brother* (Brigham Young U., 1975)
Horan, James E., *Desperate Men* (Doubleday, 1962)
Kelly, Charles, *The Outlaw Trail* (Devin-Adair, 1959)
Swallow, Alan, (ed.), *The Wild Bunch* (Sage, 1966)

Chapter 13

DAVE MATHER: A DEADLY SHOOTER

Miller, Nyle H. and Joseph W. Snell, *Why the West Was Wild* (Kansas State Hist. Soc., 1963)
Rickards, Colin, *Mysterious Dave Mather* (Press of the Territorian, Santa Fe, 1968)

Chapter 14

PAT GARRETT

Dykes, Jeff, *Law on a Wild Frontier: Four Sheriffs of Lincoln County* (Potomac Corral of the Westerners, 1969)
Gibson, A.M., *The Life and Death of Colonel Albert Jennings Fountain* (U. of Okla., 1965)
Metz, Leon C., *Pat Garrett: The Story of a Western Lawman* (U. of Okla., 1974)
Mullin, R.N., *The Strange Story of Wayne Brazel* (Panhandle Plains Historical Society)

Chapter 15

JIM MILLER: BUSHWHACKER

James, Bill C., *Mysterious Killer, James Brown Miller 1861-1909* (Privately printed, 1976)

Shirley, Glen, *Shotgun for Hire* (U. of Okla., 1969)

Sonnichsen, C.L., *Ten Texas Feuds* (U. of N.M., 1957)

Chapter 16

CHISUM: CATTLE BARON

Keleher, William H., *The Fabulous Frontier* (Rydal, 1945)

Klasner, Lily (ed. by Eve Ball) *My Girlhood Among Outlaws* (U. of Ariz., 1972)

Chapter 17

LUKE SHORT & JIM COURTRIGHT: A CLASSIC CONFRONTATION

Cox, William, *Luke Short and His Era* (Doubleday, 1961)

Schoenberger, Dale T., *The Gunfighters* (Caxton Printers, 1971)

Stanley, F., *Longhair Jim Courtright* (World Press, 1957)

Chapter 18

JOHNSON COUNTY WAR

Mercer, A. S., *Banditti of the Plains* (U. of Okla., 1954)

Smith, Helena Huntington, *The War on Powder River* (McGraw-Hill, 1966)

Chapter 19

BUFFALO BILL: THE REMARKABLE SHOWMAN

Burke, John, *Buffalo Bill: The Noblest Whiteskin* (G. P. Putnam's Sons, 1973)

Russel, Don., *The Lives and Legends of Buffalo Bill* (U. of Okla., 1960)

Chapter 20

WILD BILL HICKOK

Rosa, Joseph G., *They Called Him Wild Bill* (U. of Okla., 1974)

Chapter 21

CLAY ALLISON: WILD WOLF OF THE WASHITA

Clark, O.S., *Clay Allison of the Washita* (Frontier Press, 1954)

Schoenberger, Dale T., *The Gunfighters* (Caxton Printers, 1971)

Stanley, F., *Clay Allison* (World Press, 1956)

Chapter 22

TEXAS RANGERS

Adams, Verdon, *Tom White: The Life of A Lawman* (Texas Western Press, 1972)

Frost, H. Gordon and John H. Jenkins, *I'm Frank Hamer: The Life of a Texas Peace Officer* (Pemberton, 1968)

Garst, Shannon, *Big Foot Wallace of the Texas Rangers* (Messner, 1951)

Gillett, James, *Six Years with the Texas Rangers* (Yale, 1963)

Hughes, W. J., *Rebellious Ranger: Rip Ford and the Old Southwest* (U. of Texas, 1964)

Kilgore, D. E., *A Ranger Legacy* (Madrona, 1973)

Preece, Harold, *Lone Star Man: Ira Aten* (Hastings House, 1960)

Stephens, Robert W., *Walter Durbin: Texas Ranger and Sheriff* (Clarendon, 1970)

Stephens, Robert W., *Texas Ranger Sketches* (Robert W. Stephens, 1972)

Sterling, William Warren, *Trails and Trials of a Texas Ranger* (U. of Okla., 1959)

Wantland, Clyde (as told to by George Durham), *Taming the Nueces Strip* (U. of Texas, 1962)

Webb, Walter Prescott, *The Texas Rangers: A Century of Frontier Defense* (Houghton Mifflin, 1935)

Chapter 23

BLOOD AND SALT

Sonnichsen, C. L., *The El Paso Salt War* (Texas Western Press, 1973)

Webb, Walter, *The Texas Rangers* (Houghton Mifflin, 1935)

Chapter 24

JOHN LARN: TEXAS KILLER

Metz, Leon Claire, *John Selman: Texas Gunfighter* (Hastings House, 1966)

Chapter 25

BASS OUTLAW

Metz, Leon Claire, *John Selman: Texas Gunfighter* (Hastings House, 1966)

Chapter 26

JAMES GILLETT: TEXAS RANGER

Gillett, James, *Six Years with the Texas Rangers* (Yale, 1963)

Chapter 27

PEARL HEART, JOHN RINGO AND JACK SLADE

Aikman, Duncan, *Calamity Jane and the Lady Wildcats* (Henry Holt & Co., 1927)

Dinsdale, Thomas J., *The Vigilantes of Montana* (U. of Okla., 1953)

Erwin, Allan A., *The Southwest of John H. Slaughter* (Arthur H. Clark, 1965)

Towle, Virginia Rowe, *Vigilante Women* (A.S. Barnes & Co., 1966)

Chapter 28

JOHN WESLEY HARDIN

Haley, J. Evetts, *Jeff Milton: A Good Man with a Gun* (U. of Okla., 1953)

Hardin, John Wesley, (intro. written by Robert G. McCubbin), *The Life of John Wesley Hardin* (U. of Okla., 1961)

Metz, Leon Claire, *John Selman: Texas Gunfighter* (Hastings House, 1966)

Nordike, Lewis, *John Wesley Hardin: Texas Gunman* (Morrow, 1957)

Chapter 29

DOC HOLLIDAY &
WYATT EARP

Bartholomew, Ed., *Wyatt Earp* (2 vols.) (Frontier Book Co., 1964)

Faulk, Odie B., *Tombstone* (Oxford, 1972)

Jahns, Pat, *Frontier World of Doc Holliday* (Hastings House, 1957)

Lake, Stuart, *Wyatt Earp: Frontier Marshal* (Houghton Mifflin, 1931)

Miller, Nyle H. and Joseph W. Snell, *Why the West Was Wild* (Kansas State Hist. Soc., 1963)

Myers, John, *Doc Holliday* (Little Brown, 1955)

Pendleton, Albert S. and Susan McKay Thomas, *In Search of the Hollidays* (Little River Press, Valdosta, Ga., 1973)

Schoenberger, Dale T., *The Gunfighters* (Caxton Printers, 1971)

Waters, Frank, *The Earp Brothers of Tombstone* (Clarkson Potter, 1960)

ACKNOWLEDGEMENTS

I wish to thank my editors and publishers, Frank and Judy Mangan, for their confidence and patience; Bob McCubbin for his shared knowledge regarding books and shooters; Bill Latham for risking such a series in The El Paso *Times;* Ambrosio Sarmiento of *The Times* who did the newspaper editing; the proof-readers (God bless 'em) without whom this book would never have emerged in readable form: William Schilling, Cheryl Metz, Frank and Judy Mangan, Martha Peterson, Bob McCubbin, Jonell Haley, Kathy Edwards, Millard McKinney; and artists Mike Taylor and Alabama's Michael Schreck.

I would especially like to thank "Blue Eyes" for mumbling only occasionally and very softly: "We are always at home in the evening, we never go anywhere" —while I typed through the nights with the aid of a reasonably trusty fluorescent bulb.

LCM